ROGUE

ROGUE

The Inside Story of SARS's
Elite Crime-busting Unit

JOHANN VAN LOGGERENBERG
WITH ADRIAN LACKAY

JONATHAN BALL PUBLISHERS
Johannesburg & Cape Town

Originally published in South Africa in 2016 by
JONATHAN BALL PUBLISHERS
A division of Media24 (Pty) Ltd
PO Box 33977
Jeppestown
2043

ISBN 978-1-86842-740-6
ebook ISBN 978-1-86842-741-3

*Every effort has been made to trace the copyright holders and
to obtain their permission for the use of copyright material. The
publishers apologise for any errors or omissions and would be grateful
to be notified of any corrections that should be incorporated in future
editions of this book.*

Twitter: www.twitter.com/JonathanBallPub
Facebook: www.facebook.com/JonathanBallPublishers
Blog: http://jonathanball.bookslive.co.za/

Cover by publicide
Design and typesetting by Triple M Design
Editing by Mark Ronan
Proofreading by Kathleen Sutton
Indexing by Sanet le Roux
Printed and bound by CTP Printers, Cape Town
Set in 11/16 pt Minion Pro

I would like to dedicate this book firstly to my wife, Nicole, and her family for standing by me and believing in me no matter what. Secondly, to all the former and current SARS officials and their families who have been affected by these events. Lastly, to all civil servants in our country who continue to strive to make our country a better place.
JOHANN VAN LOGGERENBERG

For Mia Beulah and Ava Christina. In the face of injustice, let your voices not lie silent.
ADRIAN LACKAY

Contents

Authors' note

This book tells the story of an investigative unit that operated in the South African Revenue Service (SARS) between 2007 and 2014. This unit, at its height, comprised just 26 people. By 2010 only seven remained. To the general public, this was a fairly unremarkable section within SARS and it didn't attract much attention. That is, until October 2014.

Then, suddenly, it falsely became branded as a SARS 'rogue unit' that had supposedly been involved in several serious criminal activities. In more than 30 articles spanning two years, the *Sunday Times* claimed the officials associated with this unit were corrupt and accused them, among other things, of using secret funds to the tune of hundreds of millions of rands, planting listening devices, spying on President Jacob Zuma, other politicians and top cops, running a brothel and entering into illegal tax settlements.

Many SARS officials, who had had long and distinguished track records as civil servants, lost their jobs and their livelihood as a result. Their reputations were tarnished and their families suffered and continue to do so.

The contrived allegations concerning this 'rogue unit' were used to discredit and dismiss nearly the entire top management tier at SARS. Some of those affected are former anti-apartheid stalwarts.

At least four internal SARS panels, an investigation by the Inspector

General of Intelligence, a number of investigations by the Directorate for Priority Crime Investigation (the Hawks) and national intelligence probed this unit – at a cost of millions of rands to the state and, by implication, the taxpayer.

You will come to discover why these investigations were flawed, and how those who were affected by them were never even given the chance to be heard. Yet the findings and reports of these panels were leaked, mainly to the *Sunday Times*. None of those affected were afforded a right of reply.

Eventually, the 'rogue-unit' narrative became so firmly embedded in the public mind that whatever information to the contrary that surfaced over time in other media had little effect in countering it. SARS, a once proud state institution that was hailed worldwide as an example to all, suffered tremendous reputational harm.

Nearly two years after it had published the first reports about me, Johann van Loggerenberg, and the 'rogue unit', the *Sunday Times* – under a new editor – publicly apologised and attempted to set the record straight. The newspaper admitted there had been fundamental flaws in its processes and effectively repudiated the content of a number of previous news articles.

Bongani Siqoko, who took over as *Sunday Times* editor in January 2016, and some of his colleagues, must be commended for this.

During the two years that this 'rogue-unit' story was being punted by the *Sunday Times* and others, nobody paused to ask a basic question, what exactly does this unit do? The aim of this book, therefore, is, firstly, to tell the story of those who have not had their voices heard. It is intended to clarify what this unit actually did for SARS and for South Africa.

Secondly, we are motivated to tell this story in the interest of South Africa's public institutions, in the interest of justice and in the public interest. These interests, in our view, are espoused by the values of our Constitution. The public has a right to know; the truth must out.

But telling this story is tricky. Like other revenue and customs agencies around the world, SARS has legal provisions to ensure that taxpayer information stays confidential. Chapter 6 of the Tax Administration Act, which was promulgated in 2011, places certain restrictions on what is defined as 'SARS confidential information' and 'taxpayer information'.[1]

These clauses mean that no SARS official, past or present, may disclose information concerning a taxpayer or reveal information that is considered confidential to SARS unless certain circumstances apply. Luckily, some of these circumstances do apply for us and, fortunately, there are also other exclusions to these rules. One big advantage is that the legal prohibition does not apply to information already in the public domain, which we have heavily relied on in telling this story.

This category of information includes publicly available records contained in court cases, news articles, labour dispute cases, independent oversight bodies and tribunals; criminal complaints registered or reported to the police; matters before the Commission for Conciliation, Mediation and Arbitration; complaints to the Press Ombudsman and the Broadcast Complaints Commission of South Africa; and various cases of litigation and their related correspondence, court files, affidavits, submissions to various statutory entities and legal letters.

In any event, the unit that is the subject of this book was never involved in SARS audits, customs inspections or tax and customs settlements and its investigations were conducted in a manner no different from how other law-enforcement agencies and private investigators conduct theirs. So, in writing this book, we reveal no trade secrets or information pertaining to investigations or prosecutions that may be regarded as classified under Section 39 of the Promotion of Access to Information Act 2 of 2000.[2]

Nevertheless, we had to choose our words carefully. In the past, there have been threats of and, in some instances, actual legal proceedings instituted against people who have sought to reveal the truth. We had to be mindful of the risk of frivolous and vexatious litigation intended to quash the truth being told. What we state in these pages is authentic and supported by facts.

We had to approach the issues from the outside in, and not vice versa. This meant we had to scour documents and records that are already in the public domain and obtain details from sources outside of SARS who were therefore not restricted by legislation, and thread these various different narratives together into a story that we had lived through, as insiders, but cannot openly talk about unless certain conditions apply. Certain information and records had to be sought *post facto*, even though we knew about them during our tenure at SARS. In other words, we had to corroborate these facts anew as private citizens, retrospectively.

There is some precedence for publishing information about SARS and its investigations. Since 2012, SARS has used the services of external authors to study real cases, interview SARS officials and then write them up for public dissemination as case studies. SARS has also collaborated with academic institutions over the years and allowed them to publish studies and books about SARS and its inner workings.

Some of the information we relied upon to write this book was made available to SARS, the Sikhakhane Panel, the Kroon Advisory Board and audit firm KPMG, as well as to the Ministry of Finance and law-enforcement agencies after we had left SARS. This information is therefore also publicly available.

As SARS never objected to any of the numerous leaks from the reports produced by these panels and organisations, particularly as published in the *Sunday Times*, they lent approval to us to use the information that had been reported on.

On 28 April 2015, SARS published the so-called Sikhakhane report, citing 'public interest' as justification to publish a report that indiscriminately refers to 'taxpayer information', confidential SARS employee information and 'confidential SARS information'. This report refers to a range of annexures and submissions that it relied upon or disregarded.

If SARS and the Kroon Board believed the report was in the public interest, it stands to reason that the same goes for the annexures and submissions it relied on or disregarded, even if they weren't made public – an anomaly that has never been explained by SARS or questioned by the media.

In addition to the constitutional imperative to serve justice and to act in the public interest, at least two other laws offered us the scope to navigate around the legal limitations placed upon us. Section 34 of the Prevention and Combating of Corrupt Activities Act 12 of 2004[3] provides for the public reporting of offences to law-enforcement agencies, as does the Prevention of Organised Crime Act 121 of 1998 to any law-enforcement agency,[4] while both override the Tax Administration Act.

Importantly, Chapter 6 of the Tax Administration Act[5] states that 'the disclosure of taxpayer information by a person who is a current or former SARS official to the South African Police Service or the National Prosecuting Authority' is *not* prohibited 'if the information is public information. Furthermore, if it relates to, and constitutes material information for the proving of a tax offence, as a witness in civil or criminal proceedings under a tax Act or under any other Act which expressly provides for the disclosure of the information despite the provisions in this Chapter'.[6]

I reported incidents to the Hawks, the police and other statutory bodies of alleged corruption, money laundering, fraud, the concealment of these offences, and manipulation and misuse of state agencies and powers by a handful of individuals. The information was placed in their records and is therefore publicly accessible.

I compiled a formal complaint when events started unfolding at SARS, and updated this after I had left the institution. In early 2015 I presented an affidavit to the Hawks and later provided more facts and evidence to the police. This effectively placed me in the position of a whistle-blower, a complainant, a witness, and a victim of certain crimes, and this helped place critical information in the public realm. Why these claims haven't been investigated or acted upon by the authorities is a matter for another day.

Moreover, in early 2015 former SARS spokesperson and co-author of this book, Adrian Lackay, did a very brave thing, something for which I came to respect him even more than ever. He wrote a formal letter to two committees of Parliament in which he made a lengthy submission of certain facts that dealt with the events at SARS from 2014 onwards and pointed them to substantiating evidence. A Member of Parliament took it upon himself to publish this document without consulting Lackay. To date, SARS has never disputed the contents of this now public document but has instituted civil proceedings against Lackay for defamation. I think it significant that none of the South African websites, nor any local newspaper that reported on the content, or even the MP who originally publicised and released the document, were sued by SARS.

In 2016, another complaint concerning these matters was once again formally registered with the Hawks.

At certain points, we had to limit our narration to specific aspects to avoid causing harm to SARS or the 14 000 or more SARS employees who serve the South African public with dedication. We also had to make some changes to ensure we stay within the ambit of the law. Where necessary, names of places, officials and taxpayers have been changed.

In some instances, we also made up composites of certain characters because documenting the work of everyone involved in the so-called rogue unit would require at least three volumes. Some narrations have been fictionalised to a certain extent. In some cases, we have also created dialogue and in so doing allowed ourselves a little poetic licence. We know the individuals and the cases well enough and wanted to convey something of the drama that often came with the work that they did. Where required, permission was sought and obtained from the people involved or referred to.

Given these limitations, there may invariably be some gaps. But from a material and substantive point of view, nothing meaningful was overlooked or avoided. In the end the reader will have to make up his or her own mind about who acted in good or bad faith, or no faith at all.

JOHANN VAN LOGGERENBERG AND ADRIAN LACKAY

Foreword

When I was invited to write a foreword for this book, I accepted with unseemly alacrity. After all, a judge – even a retired one – is supposed to take time to consider matters, even attractive invitations, and, in any event, should avoid controversy.

But there was good reason for my reaction. Indeed, a whole succession of compelling reasons, the first of which was that I felt honoured to be given an opportunity to associate myself with a band of remarkable public servants for whose efforts I have gained profound admiration. In common with millions of fascinated readers, I had, Sunday after Sunday, been scandalised by a succession of sensational front-page reports about the outrageous actions of the so-called SARS 'rogue unit'.

I was therefore intrigued when I then came to meet some of the rogues in person and learn a little of what they had achieved in honing and polishing our country's vital revenue-collection capacity. I appreciated the helpless frustration they felt in the face of a vicious media campaign, one that clearly fed on inside knowledge and was shrewdly designed to besmirch their reputations, destroy their careers and ruin the fine-tuned agency they had built.

More importantly, I could understand their incomprehension at the unjust treatment meted out to them by supposedly independent investigators and professional analysts who should have known better. Besides sharing their incomprehension, I was disgusted that professional consultants, ostensibly professional investigators, could presume to make adverse findings of fact and draw condemnatory inferences without bothering to give those targeted – and condemned – the elementary benefit of being heard in their defence. This, to my mind, flew in the face of the ancient principles of fairness and made nonsense of our Constitution. It also contributed to the one-sided and potentially misleading picture that was presented to the public.

Ultimately, though, I was motivated by a personal sense of outrage at what these dirty tricks said about the rule of law in our country. For, however opaque and perverted this Kafkaesque tale, there was a discernible pattern – discernible across a number of public institutions – where key individuals, experienced, reputable and independent-minded public servants, have been cynically shunted aside, or out. Typically, the process starts with some or other alleged transgression, relatively trivial and/or outdated. That then triggers well-publicised suspension and disciplinary proceedings with concomitant humiliation, harassment and, ultimately, dismissal, constructive or actual. Then, with breathtaking speed, a hand-picked acting successor steps in and cleans out senior management; and when you look again there's a brand-new crop of compliant and grateful faces.

In the process, honourable women and men have been ground down, ignominiously kicked out, their reputations ruined and their life savings exhausted. Often even the most feisty individual has been driven to exhaustion, physical, emotional and, of course, financial. Examples of broadly the same pattern of administrative abuse are to be found in a whole range of parastatals: think, for instance, of South African Airways, Denel, Eskom and the SABC. And of numerous senior public servants – Vusi Pikoli, Mxolisi Nxasana, Glynnis Breytenbach, Anwa Dramat, Shadrack Sibiya, Johan Booysen and Robert McBride, to speak only of the criminal-justice sector – who've been hounded out of office.

This book records what has been done in similar fashion to some others at SARS: Ivan Pillay, Johann van Loggerenberg and Adrian Lackay, and their teams of loyal colleagues. Their case is even more disturbing, however. Here we are dealing not merely with a law-enforcement agency, but with an elite specialist unit, created and functioning at the very heart of our new public service to fill the state's coffers, to provide the very life-blood on which our transformational society is to survive. By all informed accounts, this unit was highly efficient, professional, independent of political control and squeaky clean.

More pertinently, the investigative unit's track record was formidable, and every one of the allegations made against it and its former officers has been withdrawn or seems insupportable. The skill and know-how it acquired, the team it built, the increasing sums of revenue it raised (running into literally billions), the legal and forensic victories it achieved, the serious tax criminals it nailed – these are acknowledged even by its critics and are the envy of many a taxman, not only in Africa but wider afield. Impairing SARS's capacity by blunting its investigative edge has therefore been tantamount to sabotage.

Fittingly, the attack on this prime target and its leadership was a little different. Here it was more Le Carré than Kafka. While the individuals were officially pursued in the customary manner, there was also a cunningly orchestrated accompaniment of disinformation by top journalists in a national newspaper. The word 'rogue' was used so often and so dramatically in reports of such lurid activities that many of us came to associate the word subliminally with SARS.

Meanwhile, a cadre with no evident experience was deployed from the prison service to take over from Pillay to head SARS, elements of the state's clandestine agencies skulked around the investigative unit and Finance Minister Nhlanhla Nene was summarily dismissed and briefly replaced with an unknown backbencher. When Minister Pravin Gordhan was reappointed in the wake of the consequent outcry in December 2015, he was subjected to a crude attempt at bullying at the hands of the newly appointed (and controversial) head of the Hawks. Predictably, this was accompanied by wide publicity and dark threats of prosecution.

What lies behind these events, I don't know. What I do know is that the full story should be told. Our Constitution demands and guarantees a 'system of democratic government to ensure accountability, responsiveness and openness'.

It is for the people of South Africa to decide for themselves where the truth lies: they're entitled to no less.

JOHANN KRIEGLER
Johannesburg

Acronyms and abbreviations

ACAS	Anti-Corruption and Security Division
ACTT	Anti-Corruption Task Team
AFU	Asset Forfeiture Unit
BAT	British American Tobacco
CATS	Crimes Against the State Unit
CCMA	Commission for Conciliation, Mediation and Arbitration
DSO	Directorate of Special Operations
FATF	Financial Action Task Force
FITA	Fair-Trade Independent Tobacco Association
GDP	gross domestic product
HRIU	High-Risk Investigations Unit
IPID	Independent Police Investigative Directorate
MCM	Marine Coastal Management
NEU	National Enforcement Unit
NIA	National Intelligence Agency
NPA	National Prosecuting Authority
NRG	National Research Group
OECD	Organisation for Economic Co-operation and Development
SANDF	South African National Defence Force
SANParks	South African National Parks

SAPA   South African Press Agency
SAPS   South African Police Service
SARS   South African Revenue Service
SCOF   Standing Committee on Finance
SPU   Special Projects Unit
SSA   State Security Agency
TISA   Tobacco Institute of Southern Africa
TRC   Truth and Reconciliation Commission
UDF   United Democratic Front

1

The exodus

In March 2016 Pravin Gordhan, the Minister of Finance, in response to a written question in Parliament, documented that 55 senior officials had left SARS over the previous 19 months. The number and the level of seniority of those who had left were unprecedented in the history of any public or private institution in post-democratic South Africa. The group included senior managers, executives, group executives and chief officers who served on the SARS Executive Committee, the chief operating officer and the Deputy Commissioner, Ivan Pillay.

Virtually all these resignations were in one way or another connected to events that had unfolded after the *Sunday Times* started reporting on the existence of a so-called rogue unit at SARS and its supposed illegal activities. These reports were the publicly stated reasons by the SARS Commissioner, Tom Moyane, for suspending a number of high-ranking officials within six weeks after his appointment on 1 October 2014.[1]

However, by then SARS, and specifically the division within which I worked, had been threatened by outside forces with malevolent intent for a number of years. I believe the high-risk investigations we were doing into certain industries and individuals lay at the root of it.

By then, SARS had been inundated with media enquiries, usually sparked by anonymous 'dossiers' that were leaked to the press and which made outlandish claims against our top investigators and the SARS senior management. These so-called dossiers all contained small aspects of the truth but the few facts were mixed with a host of falsehoods.

Threats to the institution had been escalating for some time. We had managed to withstand most of these attacks, but barely. A number of us had sensed that something bad was on the way, but we had no idea yet as to the what, when, who or how.

I remember how, one day early in 2014, a few of us managers had stayed behind in the boardroom at the SARS head office building, in Pretoria, after our weekly management meeting. Ivan, Deputy Commissioner and acting commissioner at the time, sat in his usual spot at the end of the large boardroom table. He looked concerned.

Ivan never normally looks as worried as he did. In fact, he is usually a difficult person to read, as he seldom shows his emotions. The look on his face made me worry too.

'A storm's brewing,' he said. 'We better batten down the hatches.'

'Yes, sir. I guess so,' I responded.

I didn't know exactly what was weighing on his mind, but I'd also had an uneasy feeling for some time that something was impending. In February 2014, for instance, I had received a tip-off from an attorney who told me that he had been approached by, among others, a member of the police Crime Intelligence Division, Lieutenant Colonel Hennie Niemann, who was assigned to the Illicit-Tobacco Task Team (a unit I'll return to later in the book), looking for 'dirt on JvL'.[2] This information was recorded in a SARS letter that was forwarded to the former head of the Hawks, General Anwa Dramat, that same month.

Some of the officials who worked under me also reported instances where they believed they were under surveillance and in one case we managed to trace a vehicle's registration number to the Crime Intelligence Division. Early in 2014 Ivan had also been told that he was under 'surveillance' and some of our homes were burgled under strange circumstances.

In February 2015 I walked through the gates of the SARS head office for the last time in my life on official business. I'd gone to hand-deliver my letter of resignation to a bodyguard of Moyane. I had served the institution with an unblemished record for over 16 years as one of its lead investigators.

The building is called Lehae La SARS, which in Sotho means the home of SARS. For many years it was my home, too, as I practically lived there, working mostly six to seven days a week, sometimes sleeping on a stretcher in my office. In the months before my resignation, I had lost over 10 kilograms and the red rings around my eyes accentuated the desperate look of someone perpetually deprived of sleep. The suit I wore that day, in the event that I might have had to meet the new commissioner, hung on me like a sack.

I felt tired. Depressed. Beleaguered. Sporadically, a deep-seated feeling of sadness would boil over into tears. I was quitting when everything inside shouted for me to keep fighting.

As I walked out of the premises with my head down, I bumped into two colleagues with whom I'd worked for many years. I stopped to greet them and saw the look of shock on their faces. 'Jesus, Johann, look at you!'

'This can't go on. Walk away,' one advised me. 'You're just skin and bones. You're greyer than ever. This thing is going to kill you.'

I nodded. I didn't have the courage or the time to explain that I had just resigned.

An uncomfortable silence descended. There was not much left to say. We all knew what had happened to me – and to the institution – since August 2014, when the first reports about me had appeared in the *Sunday Times*. I feigned haste. 'Hang in there, guys,' I said.

'Be strong, JvL.'

I gave them a thumbs up as I walked off.

My birth name is Johannes Hendrikus van Loggerenberg; at SARS, I was mostly referred to as JvL. At the time of my resignation in early 2015, I was the group executive for SARS's Tax and Customs Enforcement Investigations, a position in which I oversaw five units: Centralised Projects was a fairly small, centrally based unit focusing on significant projects and cases. National Projects had regional offices countrywide and its members used various skills, combining tax, and customs-and-excise expertise with civil and criminal investigations to combat revenue-related offences.

The Tactical Intervention Unit, which also had bases in most of the provinces, focused on customs-and-excise enforcement activities. Evidence Management and Technical Support centrally housed experts who liaised with other law-enforcement and state agencies, as well as with tax, customs, excise, legal and other experts.

And, finally, there was the High-Risk Investigations Unit (HRIU) – a tiny division of six people who worked on matters that presented a risk to our other investigators. This unit was established in 2007 and consisted of 26 members at the time. It had started off as the Special Projects Unit (SPU), but was renamed the National Research Group (NRG) before it became the HRIU. This is the unit that became known in the *Sunday Times* reports as the 'rogue unit'.

The day after my resignation, the news headlines carried two media statements – mine and that of SARS. Both statements basically said that SARS and I had parted ways amicably and that I had left with immediate effect.[3] In my statement I said it was an honour to have worked for SARS and that I wished the revenue service well in its future endeavours.[4] SARS thanked me for my service of over 16 years and for 'a degree of loyalty which SARS appreciates' – whatever that is supposed to mean.

A month later Adrian Lackay, the public face and voice of SARS, who for more than a decade had headed the service's media-communications team in the commissioner's office and was the organisation's official spokesperson, also left SARS. During his tenure, he received a number of accolades and awards as the best government spokesperson. However, since November 2014, he had featured much less in the media on SARS matters.

As Adrian became increasingly sidelined, Luther Lebelo, an executive in the human-resources department, effectively became the de facto SARS spokesperson. Lebelo had joined SARS from Telkom on the ticket of Oupa Magashula, the former SARS commissioner.[5]

When the Presidency announced Moyane's appointment as commissioner in September 2014, no one at SARS had been prepared for, or had even received any formal notice of, the new appointment. The SARS executive was informed of the appointment two hours before it was announced to the media. In May 2014, Pravin Gordhan had been removed as Finance Minister in the reconstituted Cabinet after the general elections. What exactly informed President Zuma's appointment of Moyane in this manner remains the subject of much speculation, especially considering the events that were to follow almost immediately.

In his capacity as HR official, Lebelo executed the high-level suspensions that would soon follow and which ended with the ultimate departure of virtually the entire SARS senior executive.

On 9 April 2015, *Business Day* reported the following events:

> At least two more senior staffers at the South African Revenue Service (SARS) are understood to have quit, bringing to 10 the number who have left in the past six months ... The revenue service has since November lost enforcement head Johann van Loggerenberg, anti-corruption head Clifford Collings, [group] executive for strategy and planning Peter Richer [suspended] and chief operations officer Barry Hore. They had held critical posts.[6]

Four months before this report, Collings, head of the service's Anti-Corruption and Security Division (ACAS), had agreed with SARS to go on medical pension.

The mass exodus from SARS continued. By April 2015 Yolisa Pikie, an adviser to Deputy Commissioner Ivan Pillay, and Gene Ravele, the Chief Officer for SARS Enforcement and Customs Investigations, to whom I reported by the time I resigned, had also left. Both had seemingly thrown in the towel to avoid persecution. In Ravele's case, it was claimed that he had refused to accede to an 'instruction'.[7] Marika Muller, SARS's Deputy Spokesperson, departed shortly thereafter.

The following month, Ivan and Peter Richer, Group Executive for Strategy, Planning and Risk, also resigned with immediate effect. Both had been suspended twice during the preceding five months and had little choice but to resign.

The institution was haemorrhaging.

Within less than six months after Moyane's appointment, the storm we had anticipated in March 2014 turned out to be a howling hurricane. It was going to hurt, but by then at least we knew the 'what', 'when' and 'who' – and a little bit about the 'how'.

The storm hit the institution on 10 August 2014 when the *Sunday Times* published a number of articles. The front-page lead was a story under the headline 'Love affair rocks SARS'.[8] The accompanying editorial stated: 'In the interest of all South Africans we tell this story.'[9] Both articles were about a brief relationship I was involved in with attorney Belinda Walter from November 2013 to May 2014 and made certain claims about the impact this supposedly had on the work I did at SARS.

Despite having been aware of this relationship from as early as 1 February 2014, the then editor of the *Sunday Times*, Phylicia Oppelt, was at pains to justify why the story was suddenly now of public interest in August 2014, and emphasised that the *Sunday Times* wasn't being 'played' by its sources.[10]

The same edition of the newspaper carried a shorter article that questioned the legality of Pillay's appointment as acting SARS commissioner. This was based on a totally flawed legal interpretation of the SARS Act. But the die had been cast.

Two months later the storm intensified after the *Sunday Times* ran another front-page article, on 12 October 2014: 'SARS bugged Zuma'.[11] This report stated, as if fact, that a top-secret 'rogue unit' existed at SARS, that its members had broken into Zuma's private residence before he became president and planted listening devices. It also claimed that Ivan had paid the former head of 'the unit' a bribe of over R3 million to keep quiet about these activities after he purportedly 'blackmailed SARS'.[12]

About four weeks later, early in the morning on Sunday 9 November 2014, I received a call from Johnny,[13] an exemplary investigator who had been my colleague at SARS for many years. He had started out at the Special Projects Unit. Johnny sounded so upset that I struggled to understand what he was saying.

'JvL, you have to come,' he said. Then, with more urgency, 'You need to help me. Now!'

I asked him what was going on. 'Get the *Sunday Times* on your way over. My wife doesn't believe me. Please help me.'

I sped off and when I got to his place I was met with a scene I never thought I'd see in that household. To me, Johnny's had always been the quintessentially happy family. Both parents were dedicated civil servants who cared for each other and for their son.

But, on this day Johnny's wife, Sandy,[14] stood fuming on one side of the room, with her husband at the opposite end. Their small son was cowering in the corner. The expression on the little boy's face was one of complete and utter panic. Everybody was crying.

On the coffee table lay a copy of the *Sunday Times*. It carried the big, bold headline: 'Taxman's rogue unit ran brothel.'[15]

'What were you guys doing with prostitutes?' Sandy yelled at me. I told her the report wasn't true and that we were up against forces we didn't fully understand. 'Why would a big newspaper like the *Sunday Times* publish such a story if it wasn't true?' she cried.

I tried to reason with her; Johnny tried to reason with her. In between all this, our mobile phones were ringing incessantly. I received calls and messages from my family, friends and colleagues at SARS with the same question: 'Have you seen the *Sunday Times*?'

Eventually we all sat down. Sandy, holding her son in her lap and wiping the tears from her face, wanted to know why SARS had not refuted the story. In part, I was able to convince her that the unit never operated a brothel, but I was unable to explain why SARS had not denied the claims made by the newspaper.

At that point, all my efforts to meet with Moyane after the first *Sunday Times* articles appeared had been stonewalled. I had no idea why he wasn't doing anything to protect the integrity of SARS. I told Sandy that I had been forbidden by my employer to speak to the media – not that the *Sunday Times* had asked me for my comment on the story, in any event.

The whole time, Johnny was pacing up and down, interjecting now and then. He was angry. 'This is starting to affect our families. Something is wrong here, JvL, very wrong.'

I nodded in agreement. I had realised for a while that something like this was coming but there was nothing I could do about it.

Later, when I drove off, the picture of the sheer horror on their little boy's face remained stuck in my mind and it still haunts me to this day.

For many months the narrative of a SARS 'rogue unit' had been presented as fact and in bold, harrowing headlines by one of the largest-circulation newspapers in South Africa. It claimed that an illegal, covert and previously unheard-of 'rogue unit' at SARS had been operating in the shadows for years, spying on taxpayers and politicians, and plotting to remove SARS officials. Members of the unit allegedly received new cars and homes, spied on Zuma, had fake identities and sophisticated spyware; operated with secret funds; ran brothels; 'tracked' high-ranking police officers; and posed as bodyguards for politicians to eavesdrop on their conversations.

Week after week, front page after front page, exposé after exposé, the *Sunday Times* published these stories, claiming them as fact. Those implicated in the articles were painted as dishonest SARS officials – all corrupt and untrustworthy.

During this period, numerous reports, documents and leaks – as they were termed – were distributed to the *Sunday Times* from within SARS, by 'former SARS officials' and 'intelligence officials', as one of the journalists involved ultimately acknowledged.[16] Many of these were internal SARS documents, confidential human-resource files with employee information, uncorroborated reports and narrations, and confidential taxpayer information.

In response to these articles, Lebelo, on behalf of SARS, would claim that the tax authority was 'deeply shocked'[17] and then decline to comment until investigations into the 'rogue unit' were completed.[18]

Meanwhile, as these events played out in the public domain, none of the affected persons were allowed by SARS to publicly defend themselves. Despite repeated formal complaints and requests by me and others to SARS to ascertain where the leaks came from within the tax authority, and to hold the *Sunday Times* to account for the salacious content of its news articles, as far as I am aware, none of these written requests were attended to. In fact, SARS never even responded to them.

So the *Sunday Times*' claims about me had to be true, right? Well, actually, no.

On 10 November 2014, the day after the 'brothel' article was published, Moyane suspended the entire executive committee of SARS. The following Sunday, the *Sunday Times* ran a story under the headline 'SARS chief acts on brothel claim'.[19] 'The commissioner gave them a dressing-down,' the report read. 'He did not take questions. He said it was disgusting that SARS was now running brothels …'[20]

In the following pages I'm going to take you into the heart of this 'rogue unit'. You will learn more about some of the key players at SARS, about me and about the 'rogues'. As much as this is my story, it is theirs too.

In the end, it will be up to you, the reader, to conclude why these things were allowed to happen and who the real rogues are.

2

The rise of SARS

In the early days of our new-found democracy, very little was publicly known about SARS. It came into being in 1997 when the Customs and Excise Department, and the Department of Inland Revenue merged. Then, SARS was a low-profile organ of state and people only really took note of it when they received notices by mail for tax assessments or refunds, or when traders imported and exported goods through ports of entry.

However, within a decade the tax authority grew into probably the most respected state institution in the country. Its efficiency and excellent service delivery instilled awe in most South Africans, and fear in some. The rise of SARS from a fairly nondescript institution to one of the most trusted state organisations can be ascribed to the strong leadership and vision of individuals such as former Minister of Finance Trevor Manuel and Pravin Gordhan, Commissioner of SARS from 1999 to 2009.[1]

Under Gordhan, the emphasis was on appointing highly skilled, extremely capable and dedicated people. His and Manuel's vision was informed by their long history in the liberation struggle.

'It is noteworthy that the first [sic] Commissioner of SARS (Pravin Gordhan) as well as the long-serving former Minister of Finance (Trevor Manuel) are longstanding ANC stalwarts – who believe that tax collection is key in the shared political project of economic growth with redistribution,' wrote renowned experts in the field of revenue authorities and their functions in modern democracies, Odd-Helge Fjeldstad and Mick Moore.[2]

Manuel was an executive member of anti-apartheid organisation the United Democratic Front (UDF). In 1985 he was detained several times by the notorious Security Branch and later declared a banned person. The ban was lifted in 1986 after he challenged it in court but he was detained again from 1986 to 1988. He was then released under severe restrictions, only to be detained again in 1988 until 1989. Manuel's release came with stringent restriction orders.

In those days, when the Security Branch 'detained' you, it wasn't just a matter of being locked up in a cell. They terrorised you, tortured you, isolated you from your loved ones and effectively did anything possible to break your spirit. That Manuel survived such police brutality several times and continued in his role as a leading UDF figure speaks volumes for the man's character. He went on to become the longest-serving minister of finance in the world (1996 to 2009).

I had little opportunity to interact with Manuel, but the few times I did, he left a lasting impression. Three aspects about him will always stand out for me: he has one of the sharpest minds in the business. He understood everything we as tax collectors were about. And he worked relentless hours, and expected everybody else to do the same.

More importantly, his constant refrain was that the struggle for a free, liberated South Africa was not yet over. Political freedom was but a part of the struggle. Economic freedom had to be attained, and SARS would be one of the instruments to take that struggle forward, believed Manuel.

Gordhan graduated from the University of Durban-Westville with a degree in pharmacy. He completed his internship at the King Edward Hospital, in Durban, but was later dismissed by the Natal provincial administration because of his political activities as a member of the Natal Indian Congress. He was detained by the apartheid regime in 1981 and released from jail in 1982. He was immediately served with banning orders that were effective until 1983.

At the start of the transition era in 1991, Gordhan attended the preparatory meeting for the Convention for a Democratic South Africa (Codesa) and was later appointed as a delegate to the steering committee responsible for organising the convention. In 1993 Gordhan was appointed to the panel of chairpersons on the planning committee of the multiparty negotiation process.

I had the privilege of interacting with Gordhan almost from the beginning of SARS's formative years after I joined the institution late in 1998. For an accurate description of Gordhan as a leader, I turn to a letter written by Manuel that was published in a SARS book on Gordhan's career as commissioner: 'It is not a leadership that emanates from being elected into positions of authority, rather it is a leadership strength that is a rare combination of an incredibly fine and organised mind, a deep passion to effect change in the lives of all and a determination to see every project to its conclusion. This is the story of his entire adult life.'[3]

Gordhan is one of the most inspiring people I have ever met. From 1999, his doctrine of 'serving the higher purpose' became the mantra for all SARS employees. This ethic entailed the service acting as a mechanism to help the state to deliver on its social contract by collecting the revenue that would help fund government programmes that provide services to the citizenry.

Vuso Shabalala, who worked at SARS from 1999 to 2008 in various senior positions, and currently an adviser to the Zuma Presidency, once wrote, 'The most positive impact is that under Pravin SARS has developed an organisational performance management system probably unequalled in the public sector.'[4] Shabalala, a former ANC underground operative, is a man of absolute integrity, a deep thinker and philosopher, and one who follows his own mind. He was never afraid to disagree and often steered discussions and plans towards a more deeply thought-out solution in his own, almost silent manner.

Then there's Judy Parfitt, a former journalist who went into exile and later became a founding member of South Africa's Commission for

Conciliation, Mediation and Arbitration (CCMA). She joined SARS to overhaul its entire human-resources management system. Her efforts and SARS's achievements in this project were documented in a Princeton University case study.[5]

Another individual who deserves credit for the development of SARS and tax compliance in South Africa is Ivan Pillay. Ivan was part of the ANC unit that smuggled Mac Maharaj, another ANC stalwart, out of South Africa in 1977. Soon thereafter Ivan left for Swaziland, joining Umkhonto we Sizwe, the armed military wing of the ANC. He became a member of the Internal Political Reconstruction Committee, and from 1980 to 1985 he was the commander of an underground unit of the ANC known as MJK (Mandla Judson Kuzwayo). He was also a member of the Central Committee of the South African Communist Party.

In the 1980s Pillay was based in Lusaka and Swaziland. He was intricately involved in the armed struggle and sent people and weapons into South Africa from these bases while in exile. In the early 1990s he would be unmasked as a key member of Operation Vula, a secret mission of the ANC that would have been actioned if the apartheid regime were found to have negotiated in bad faith during Codesa. He joined SARS in 1999 and features prominently in the 'rogue-unit' saga.

I knew Ivan before we both worked at SARS, but that's a story for another day. During my years at SARS he was one of the colleagues I worked with most closely. He was a mentor and to a large extent a father figure to me for many years. He resigned – or rather, was obligated to resign – from SARS in May 2015.

All these individuals share certain characteristics: they have all sacrificed much for the freedom of our country; they don't suffer fools; they work like machines; and they're absolutely clear that much is still to be done in South Africa to give democracy its full meaning. They are also serious and incorruptible individuals, who have remained willing to sacrifice anything for a free South Africa and they are steadfast in the belief that legitimate government agencies must abide by their civil contract with citizens.

There is perhaps another common thread to be found among these individuals. Despite the hardships they endured under apartheid – being detained, tortured and exiled, losing friends and family to the struggle, and giving up a significant part of their adult lives to help attain political freedom – not a single one of them conveyed hate or aggression towards their former oppressors.

In fact, remarkably, they all appeared to have that mature ability to look at the former enemy and those who benefited from the apartheid system, and distinguish between friend and foe. They realised that the forces of balance had changed, and they were able and willing to seek out from the old guard people with the necessary skills and experience to help take SARS forward.

At the inception of SARS as we know the organisation today, they shared a common vision: SARS would advance the struggle for freedom by ensuring that it collected the revenue needed for government to deliver on its promises to citizens. And they had a plan for how to achieve this.

Of course, many others were also involved in the development of the institution over the years. Various people from the old guard joined hands with the new leaders because they shared the same vision. One example is Kosie Louw, who is considered a world-expert in fiscal policy and tax and customs legislation, and, at the time of writing, is chair of the Global Forum on Transparency and Exchange of Information for Tax Purposes.[6]

Between 1999 and 2014, many others came, left their mark at SARS and moved on. Such instrumental 'newcomers' include Intikhab Shaik,[7] a former Customs and Excise official who was a key role player in modernising the customs systems at SARS; Jerome Frey, a world-class information-technology expert; and Barry Hore, previously executive director of Technology and Operations at Nedcor. Hore was selected as one of the World Economic Forum's 100 Global Leaders for Tomorrow in 1999.[8]

Nathaniel Mabetwa,[9] who headed operations at hundreds of SARS branch offices that are the primary point of contact with millions of taxpayers across the country, was a Harvard graduate who later moved to

Barclays/ABSA as a senior executive. Mfundo Nkuhlu[10] was in charge of strategy, operations and IT at SARS, and later became chief operating officer at Nedbank. Another mentor of mine was the enigmatic Shirish Soni, a former freedom fighter, who was brutally tortured to within an inch of his life by the Security Branch in the 1980s. He joined SARS at the helm of Customs and left an indelible impression on everyone he met. He went on to become South Africa's ambassador to Kazakhstan in later years.[11]

With their sharp minds and strong work ethic, these were the people who, together with their teams, delivered the first SARS service centres and tax practitioner unit centres, and established electronic filing for taxes and customs, to name but a few of their achievements.

It would be remiss of me not to mention Oupa Magashula, the first black SARS Commissioner, who was appointed in 2009 when Gordhan became Minister of Finance. Magashula is an affable, larger-than-life personality who has the ability to disarm most people and make you want to work with him instantly.

At an African Tax Administration Forum gala dinner in Uganda in 2009, Magashula made several insightful remarks about the significance and role of revenue authorities in Africa. Taxation, he said, is without a doubt a formidable potential source of development finance. 'Therefore, it is important for African countries to mobilise resources, in a sustainable manner, which are essential to finance development agendas.'[12]

This statement clearly demonstrated why revenue authorities formed a key pillar for fiscal sustainability in any democracy, especially in developing nations. Revenue authorities served a higher purpose and it was this notion that underpinned the SARS success story from 1999 to 2014.

Magashula resigned in July 2013 following a media report of an intercepted telephone conversation recorded under extremely suspicious circumstances. Magashula was recorded when he offered a young female chartered accountant a job at SARS and this was leaked to the media. An inquiry instituted by Gordhan as Minister of Finance and chaired by a retired Constitutional Court judge investigated this incident. Ultimately, however, it seems it was Magashula's own decision to resign from SARS – something that I respect immensely and admire him for.[13] In a sense, I would follow his lead a couple of years later when I decided to leave SARS in February 2015.

The incident with Magashula should perhaps have set off warning signals for all of us. We should have realised that there were unseen forces at play, powers that had access to intercept our communications and spy on us. By then, SARS was under threat from powerful and sinister outside forces.

The purpose of that intercepted telephone conversation between Magashula and the young accountant is yet to be revealed. Only a small portion of what was clearly an incomplete recording was leaked to the media. Subsequent attempts by Ivan, who acted as commissioner after Magashula's resignation, to ascertain from the various intelligence agencies how and why the phone conversation was recorded, and Ivan's requests to have the matter investigated, fell on deaf ears.[14]

Over the years SARS was guided by a number of grounding principles, which also helped to ensure its success. Firstly, as mentioned, there was the organisation's vision of always serving a higher purpose. Secondly, SARS based its operating model on three components: service, education and enforcement.[15] The underlying philosophy of this model was that most taxpayers and traders want to do the right thing. Our approach was that those who participate in economic activities in our country want to conduct their affairs legitimately, and will pay their fair share of taxes and duties to the fiscus if they can be persuaded that this obligation is a part that they play in our democratic project.

Finally, those who were economically active, to the extent that they had to comply with tax and customs laws, had to be offered easy access to efficient services, so SARS sought to reduce the administrative burden that came with having to comply with the law. With this service offering, SARS would over time reduce the paperwork and the number of tax returns to be completed, improve services at branch offices and, later, through eFiling, introduce some of the best technology to enable electronic submissions and transactions.

It was equally important that taxpayers and traders were sufficiently educated, not only about how to comply and when to do so, but also to be reassured that their financial contributions to the state went towards government programmes aimed at developing society as a whole. For those who deliberately choose not to comply, there needed to be a credible enforcement capability that demonstrated the negative consequences of disregarding the law.

SARS's enforcement strategy also had three legs. The first aimed to demonstrate that SARS's enforcement units had the ability to reach all tax types and all taxpayer types in all the corners of the country. This was commonly referred to as the 'width' part of the strategy. The second leg, called the 'depth' part, projected the ability and capacity to deal with the most complex of tax crimes for as long as they may take and regardless of delaying tactics or procrastination. The last leg was called 'leverage'. Here, by combining the width and depth legs, SARS would join hands with other law-enforcement agencies and state departments to seek capacity that could effectively be leveraged to 'punch above our weight', as Ivan used to say.

My story focuses on the enforcement capability of SARS during the years 1999 to 2014.

It was understood from early on that SARS differed from conventional law-enforcement agencies, such as the police and the National Prosecuting Authority (NPA), in that it fulfilled more roles. SARS is primarily an administrator of tax and customs laws, regulating millions of tax transactions, taxpayers and traders. But the organisation simultaneously fulfils the role of a law-enforcement agency, a function that applies to offences related to tax, unpaid taxes, prohibited goods moving through ports of entry, goods in transit or in warehouses, and illicit or controlled goods of any kind. These dynamics necessitated an approach not found in conventional law-enforcement agencies such as the police.

The relationship between SARS and taxpayers, customs traders and those acting as their intermediaries (i.e. tax practitioners and clearing agents) was also identified as a constant interaction that imposed continuous obligations on both sides. This also differentiates SARS from conventional law-enforcement agencies, which only engage with the citizenry when a crime has been committed or is suspected. A citizen would then become a complainant, a witness, a suspect or an accused.[16]

SARS, like any other state department, faces challenges in respect of the size of its workforce, and its capacity and skills. The size of the SARS workforce, compared with that of other law-enforcement agencies, is negligible and the investigative components of SARS are actually very small in proportion to the primary SARS functions, which deal with day-to-day tax and customs operations.

The total staff complement throughout the period under discussion here was around 14 500, of whom fewer than 1 500 were actually involved in investigations into tax and customs offences. For the vast majority of SARS officials, their core function never involved conducting investigations.

SARS also differs from conventional law-enforcement agencies, in that the punitive measures that typically follow non-compliant behaviour are not limited to instituting criminal proceedings. SARS has powers of investigation that allow it to apply the most appropriate punitive measures, which may range from civil sanctions, such as fines, to instituting criminal proceedings, which may result in prosecution.[17]

Given the constant constraints on resources and backlogs in the criminal courts, SARS understood from very early on that the merits of each case should determine the most appropriate punitive consequence for a defaulting taxpayer or trader.

This approach was developed by SARS from 1999 onwards and by around 2002 came to be known as the 'tax-gap strategy'.[18] Internationally, it is accepted that, to varying degrees, each country has a phenomenon called the tax gap. This is defined as 'the difference between total taxes owed and taxes paid on time',[19] and serves as an indicator of potential revenue loss in a particular tax year. Because the tax gap is born from evasive actions, it is difficult to quantify accurately, however.

SARS had to contend with the reality that in South Africa, this strategy is highly complex because the formal, regulated side of our economy (think financial services, mining or manufacturing) exists alongside an ever-expanding informal economy, which, to a large extent, is cash-based – for instance, the taxi industry, informal traders and the cash-and-carry retail sector that support the latter. These two tiers of South Africa's economic landscape are typical of many emerging-market economies. A significant portion of the tax-gap strategy included predicate offences in the illicit economy that led to non-payment of taxes or duties.

This strategy ultimately morphed into SARS's 'illicit economy strategy', which was approved by Gordhan and implemented in 2007.[20] Earlier versions of this strategy document had been presented to various parliamentary committees, which had continually asked SARS to help curb rising crime levels in South Africa. I remember the day when this document was signed off. At a meeting with the enforcement division, Gordhan, in his usual stern manner, cautioned: 'Crime is a scourge and we as SARS must do what we can to help the state. We are at war with criminals.'

From then on, this strategy informed business planning for SARS's enforcement units.[21]

From 2000 onwards, as Manuel and Gordhan's vision began to play itself out, SARS's profile grew and accolades for the new SARS followed from all over the world. Many revenue authorities and international academic institutions came to South Africa to engage with SARS and to study the success of the institution. Numerous case studies of SARS were compiled and published, and some even form part of the academic curricula of universities worldwide today.

Aspects of SARS's journey have also been the topic of several master's dissertations and doctoral theses. By 2013 SARS also had a number of master's and doctoral graduates within its ranks. More than 8 000 of its employees were also, in some way or another, involved in social-upliftment causes, charities and activities. Continued studying and involvement in such projects were openly encouraged.

In the end, what made SARS so successful was the entire team of over 14 000 people. They may have spoken different languages, had different backgrounds and cultures, and come from all walks of life, but they were all moving in the same direction – and serving the higher purpose. These people are the real heroes of SARS's success story – true activists who continued to take the struggle for complete freedom in our country forward.

This dream team made SARS a feather in the cap of the South African Government, something most South Africans seemed very proud of.

That is, until late in 2014, when disaster struck.

3

SARS declares war on organised crime

I joined SARS in November 1998 shortly after I had been withdrawn from the field as a long-term, deep-cover agent for the South African Police,[1] where I had served for many years. I had received two offers of employment in October 1998, one from what was then known as the South African Secret Service, the foreign civilian intelligence arm of government. The other was an offer from SARS.

The revenue service proposed appointing me at the level of General Manager: Special Investigations and that I should serve on its executive committee. I was instinctively attracted to the Secret Service offer, though, primarily because I could continue working in a field I was familiar with.

I sought counsel from various people and ultimately decided to go against my grain and accept the offer from SARS. But with one condition: I asked for the post grading and the remuneration offer to be lowered because I did not consider myself capable of functioning at the level of the position that they had offered. I was just 29, going on 30 and, truth be told, I was intimidated by such a high-level position and the prospect of serving on SARS's executive committee.

There has been much speculation about my past. Some people with nefarious motives even advanced that I was an 'apartheid spy'. Nothing can be further from the truth. In April 1991, the detective service in the police launched an organised-crime project with a specific focus to deal with the ever-rising incidence of organised crime. Consequently, the first government structure to deal directly with organised crime was established – known as the Organised Crime Intelligence Unit, which functioned until 1998.

I worked in this new unit, and my job was to infiltrate suspected criminal syndicates and guide investigations into their illegal activities. As a deep-cover agent, I effectively had to cut all ties with family and friends, and function as someone entirely different. I had to assume a completely new identity and live it out in all aspects of 'normal' life.

Although I received two Commissioner Commendations for my work, with the benefit of hindsight I would never do it again. Perhaps one day I will tell that story but, for now, I can only say that the price I paid for offering up the biggest part of my 20s – important years in any person's social growth – was just too high.

At SARS, I was placed in the Special Investigations Department. This had three basic and separate functions. First, several so-called inspectorates conducted tax audits throughout the country. Secondly, a Customs Special Investigations Division fulfilled a similar function for customs activities. Lastly, two small hubs, one in Cape Town and one in Pretoria, had teams comprising former commercial-crime police detectives and the sum total of two former NPA prosecutors.

I found it quite shocking that these units were allowed to indiscriminately investigate anybody. There was no real logic or intelligent mechanism to inform our decisions on who to investigate or why. (According to an urban myth I once heard at SARS, a certain tax inspector was unhappy with the taste or cut of his meat at a weekend braai, so the following Monday he promptly launched an audit into the affairs of his local butchery.)

My first few months were spent mostly trying to understand SARS as an institution and its enforcement activities, and studying reports of cases and audits. At night, I read and studied tax law, case law and revenue-authority models. I wasn't really given particular tasks and was largely dependent on myself to generate work and outputs to justify my position.

I worked closely with two other administrative staff members and started building a database of all the incoming progress reports of investigations that were being conducted and reported on at the time. I had the idea that by analysing these, both from a geographical and tax-type perspective, certain trends would appear, which would help inform how SARS should best focus its limited enforcement capacity at that time.

At the time two former 'old hands' made it known to me that a new head for the Special Investigations Department was about to be appointed. These colleagues were both white Afrikaans-speakers, and, in my view, embodied the typical conservative Afrikaner caricature of the old order. Perhaps emboldened by the assumption that, as a fellow Afrikaner, I would be one of them, one unashamedly referred to the new appointee as a 'little coolie'[2] who thought that he was so clever and that he would understand how things work. 'We will show him how we work,' he said.

And so, Ivan Pillay arrived at SARS in 1999. He was appointed as General Manager: Special Investigations. Ivan was soft-spoken, never judgemental and always willing to learn. I already knew him as a man with integrity and a sharp mind who was also always prepared to listen and hear anybody out.

Special Investigations was later converted and renamed Criminal Investigations. This unit had always been the backbone of SARS's enforcement capacity. The team members were mostly retired detectives from the Commercial Crimes Division of the South African Police Service (SAPS) who had joined SARS, and officials from the former Inspectorates and Customs Special Investigations units.

Adrian joined SARS in September 2003 as a research analyst in the Communications Division. His priorities were to get a grasp on the institution by talking to employees and by studying the interim reports of the Katz Commission, and various SARS annual reports.

Adrian summarised his research in a document that was used by SARS in various external publications and briefings to Parliament. His findings identified that in the South African context, customs was arguably the area most affected by non-compliance with the law. As the Commission of Inquiry headed by Professor Michael Katz noted, this was a direct result of the impact that the apartheid system had had on local trade. The increasing restrictions and sanctions on South Africa during its isolation years led the former government to resort to unlawful tactics to stimulate foreign trade. Customs controls were circumvented and opportunities to defraud the Customs Department led to growth in certain irregular trends in various sectors of the economy. Criminal elements were becoming more powerful.

By 1999, with Gordhan at the SARS helm, customs reform was in full progress. 'A new work culture is emerging – a work culture characterised by more innovation, greater boldness, better service and which is far more risk-focused. Customs, although historically neglected, is now receiving the support and resources needed to perform its difficult mandate,' Gordhan reported.[3]

That year, South Africa also negotiated mutual assistance treaties with several countries. Customs was faced with implementing the protocols and standards of an increasing number of international trade agreements – including trade requirements of the World Customs Organization.

As the new SARS commissioner, Gordhan told Parliament in 2000 that organisational changes at SARS had to be implemented without losing track of the organisation's responsibility to protect the economy by collecting billions of rands to meet a formidable revenue target that the Minister of Finance had set for 2000/01.

In addition to obvious measurables in the transformation journey, such as the initiatives to ensure better operational effectiveness, SARS had also embraced the Katz Commission's recommendations on transparency in reporting mechanisms. For the 2000/01 financial year, SARS presented to Parliament a more detailed and comprehensive annual report than it had in previous years and, from then on, this standard of reporting became a hallmark of the SARS annual reports, which served as contracts of accountability to Parliament and the South African public at large. In observing its statutory duty to the legislature, SARS demonstrated a new boldness by publicly declaring its future objectives with clearly defined timelines for their implementation. This was all part of the new business culture that now imbued SARS. The revenue service quickly realised that specific areas of concern where it could make a meaningful impact were the clothing and textile industry, the tobacco industry and even the figures for national priority crime that featured on the threat assessments of the country's various law-enforcement agencies.[4] A list of individuals who were considered to be national crime threats was drawn up collectively by the law-enforcement agencies and this list was provided to SARS.

Adrian's research also described how in 1994 the new democratic dispensation had inherited a budget deficit of 7.4% of GDP – a debt trap created by unacceptably high government borrowing. SARS never had an audit policy or audit plans in its early years. Rather, cases were selected on a reactive and random basis, with a focus on perceived rather than actual risk. Consequently, the auditing was very fragmented and focused only on some types of taxes while ignoring others. This resulted in significant losses for the fiscus.

New auditing techniques necessitated special training for SARS officials. During the second half of 2000, SARS trainers, with the assistance of the US Internal Revenue Service, drafted a new audit training course.

In addition, SARS undertook to establish a central intelligence unit (which I was to join), to be staffed by skilled investigators who would analyse taxpayer, market and industry data for use in risk profiling. The idea, which was presented to Parliament, was that this unit would focus on revenue- and customs-related offences, leading to prosecutions, while the audit function concentrated on civil procedures to optimise revenue yield. The merging of these functions resulted in sharpened enforcement skills, which led to cross-functional synergy in administering revenue laws. Soon after Ivan had joined SARS, the Tax and Customs Intelligence Unit was formed.[5] At its birth, it comprised two administrative staff members, another former policeman, a person who had joined us from the Department of Water Affairs and me. Together we formed a manual system for collecting investigations reports, complaints by the public and reports by SARS staff, which we used to analyse and identify trends. This approach would inform future investigations. The manual system we had developed was later automated and incorporated into the highly regarded SARS risk engine, which selects cases for audit and investigations.[6]

Later in 2000 I left this unit to start an experimental outfit called the Special Compliance Unit.[7]

With SARS's new mandate to get its teeth into big corporate commercial crime, a number of landmark cases in the early 2000s were formative in defining the organisation's enforcement operations.

One of the first big cases I worked on was the so-called Metcash case. This case arose from a dispute with the company over its exports, mainly to Lesotho. In essence, the case concerned a dispute over VAT claims and their income-tax implications. Metcash Trading Ltd, a JSE-listed company, was described in court as a wholesaler and retailer of fast-moving consumer goods. In the court case it came to light that SARS had found in certain instances that no goods were sold or delivered and, accordingly, no input tax on the transactions in question could have been claimed. The total amount of the claim by SARS for input-tax irregularities in respect of these transactions came to over R77 million with penalties amounting to over R265 million in total.[8]

After Gordhan's appointment as SARS Commissioner, the institution was beginning to take on big players in the retail sector – and Metcash Trading Ltd was one it had in its sights. This had never been done before, at least not to this extent. This legal dispute with one of the big guns in the retail industry also played itself out rather publicly. Commenting on the landmark legal decision, in November 2000 the media reported: 'Metro Cash and Carry will pay the SARS R128m in a settlement over a long-standing VAT dispute which led to a raid on Metcash's offices last year.'[9]

The *Metcash Trading Ltd v Commissioner for the South African Revenue Service* case went all the way to the highest court in the land. In 2000 the Constitutional Court established the important new rule of 'pay now, argue later' in the administration of tax law. Effectively, this decision allowed SARS to collect taxes due even when the parties had declared a dispute to challenge the tax debt. Previously, wealthy, errant taxpayers, who could afford the best lawyers, used the dispute mechanisms and the tax courts as ways to delay having to pay tax that, in SARS's view, was legitimately due to the fiscus. It could take many years for such disputes to be resolved legally before the courts. The Constitutional Court judgment was a lesson to big business in South Africa, showing that SARS had teeth.[10]

The context in which a case such as Metcash, and others, came about was that, as Ivan put it, 'large parts of big business were in bed with the old government, and were selective on compliance. Others, who were previously unwilling to support the tax system, had to be persuaded.' Ivan explained this reasoning some years later to David Hausman, a research fellow from Princeton University.[11]

According to Hausman's research paper, under the apartheid government tax evasion had become a form of protest and this of course cut into the collection of revenue: 'At the same time, customs officials worked from inside the organization to circumvent international sanctions against the apartheid government ... The legitimacy of the [new] revenue service was a prerequisite for the operation of the rest of the government.'[12]

Furthermore, according to Hausman, government wanted to keep tax rates low enough 'to prevent international investors from pulling their money out of the country. The solution was to persuade more citizens to pay their taxes.'[13]

The evolution of SARS's enforcement capabilities should be viewed in the context of a changing compliance climate in South Africa and the efficacy (or lack thereof) of the criminal-justice system. Forms of tax evasion locally and abroad were changing and becoming more complex, and legislative reforms influenced the development of SARS's operating model.

Over the years SARS refined and improved its capacity to analyse enormous amounts of economic data and understand taxpayer behaviour, and it developed the ability to act on this information in a manner that encouraged taxpayers to abide by the law voluntarily. Those who intentionally transgressed tax laws became the focus of enforcement actions.

Yet SARS was never intrinsically considered to be a law-enforcement agency. During the service's early years, from 1999 to about 2001, the public and the law-enforcement agencies had limited expectations that SARS would address crime. After all, SARS was just another government department, a nuisance at best.

From around 2002 onwards, however, numerous changes occurred within South Africa's broader law-enforcement community and the state developed new capabilities for combating crime. Some examples are the establishment of the Asset Forfeiture Unit (AFU), the Directorate of Special Operations (DSO, or the Scorpions) and the Special Investigations Unit. When these departments began their investigations, they expected SARS to participate and help them in their efforts to fight crime.[14]

This onus of enforcement that had been placed on SARS grew over time and became more pronounced as new laws were enacted to contend with the emergence of new forms of criminality. New legislation placed more statutory obligations on SARS to act, for example, against drug-related offences, corruption and organised crime, and to gather financial intelligence. There were also a number of developments in case law in South Africa as SARS began to grow into its new role as a powerful crime-combating force.

During this period, the domestic statutory requirements imposed on SARS were compounded by the provisions of international mutual-assistance agreements and double-taxation agreements with other tax jurisdictions. Various international bodies also placed increasing obligation on SARS to participate in the exchange of information and to assist with cases concerning international crime.

From 2009 the South African Police Service Amendment Act 57 of 2008 allowed various government agencies to address crime using a multidisciplinary approach. This legislation specifically provided for the secondment of SARS staff to the Directorate of Priority Crimes Investigations, or the Hawks (which replaced the Scorpions), which has happened on a number of occasions since then.

As SARS's enforcement capability began to flex its muscles, the organisation's enforcement components tried and tested various models, which were informed mainly by international benchmarking studies. This required pooling complementary skill sets – for example, those of a lawyer, a criminal investigator and an auditor – in a joint team. Often we would work closely with the then National Intelligence Agency (NIA), the police, the NPA and the South African National Defence Force (SANDF) on a number of crime-fighting projects, as well as with administrative committees.

In the early years, SARS entered into various agreements with other law-enforcement agencies, including the NIA and NPA. There was also an operational agreement, for example, with the Commercial Crimes Division of the SAPS, which guided criminal investigations conducted by SARS, bolstered somewhat by case law.[15]

It is within this context that SARS and the NPA agreed that a dedicated team of prosecutors would be allowed to work on cases of tax-specific offences, and people were delegated for this purpose. This relationship grew to a point where there was an agreement that SARS would provide funding to the NPA for the creation of Special Tax Units for one year.[16]

This model of recruiting, funding and setting up a dedicated capacity in other state agencies to cooperate with SARS in tax or customs investigations later informed the concept and the creation of what ultimately became known in the media as the 'rogue unit'.

All the while, however, the workforce capacity at SARS that was dedicated to these efforts did not grow at the same rate as the demands increasingly imposed on SARS. Often, other law-enforcement agencies expected more than SARS was capable of delivering.

Provisions in legislation prohibited SARS from exchanging taxpayer information and we found this was often interpreted by officials in other agencies as a reluctance on our part to cooperate with their efforts in combating crime. Some officials in law enforcement expected us to bend the rules and pass information on to them, even though, by law, such information was held by SARS in confidential files.

We refused to comply with such requests, and this, unfortunately, caused acrimony among individuals from certain agencies. Their failure to understand these dynamics, combined with the complexities that come with tax and customs investigations, perpetuated this sentiment.[17]

SARS began to experiment with various models and tactical and strategic approaches on how best to use the scarce resources available to give maximum effect to its enforcement strategy and have an impact on crime in the most meaningful manner possible.

There is a particular case that epitomises this approach. One day in 2000, a SARS official by the name of Charles Christopher Chipps came to visit us in our tiny broom closet of an office, which was the Special Compliance Unit at the time. He hobbled in on crutches and started to make out a case why we should investigate a certain unknown billionaire named Dave King.

While scouring various publications, Chipps had come across an article about how King had purchased artworks with immensely high values. Chipps became suspicious given this man's low income that had been declared to SARS. He was convinced that some income hadn't been declared for tax purposes.[18]

As part of SARS's Illicit Economy Strategy, the tax authority considered tax and customs duty evasion as a category of economic crime that had been neglected by traditional law-enforcement agencies for years. Part of Manuel and Gordhan's plan was to direct SARS's law-enforcement capabilities towards these types of crimes. Their decision was informed by the knowledge that if one taxpayer didn't pay what was due, he or she would be unfairly subsidised by another who was fully compliant. In any democracy this couldn't be allowed. As a result, SARS set its focus on these types of financial crimes from the very early days.

The King case ended some 13 years later with a settlement between King, the NPA, the South African Reserve Bank, King's trustees and SARS. The settlement included plea and sentence agreements before the High Court, a fine of R3.28 million or 984 months' (82 years') imprisonment, and the payment of R8.75 million into the Criminal Assets Recovery Account. SARS recovered R706.70 million in outstanding taxes.[19]

In a tribute to Chipps after his death in September 2013, Alec Hogg, writing in *Business Day*, described King's 'nemesis' at SARS as 'a frumpy, seemingly distracted SARS-employed chartered accountant'.

Writes Hogg: 'He was the closest person I've met to a real-life Columbo, the dithering TV detective who always got the criminal. Judged by his dingy office at the bottom of Jeppe Street in downtown Johannesburg, Mr Chipps was motivated solely by public service. And, until the media reported it as "Chris", I never knew his first name. Nobody ever used it ...'[20]

The *Sunday Times* would later claim that the 'rogue unit' had played a role in this settlement and for this reason questioned its legality. The reality is, the settlement was entered into and confirmed by a High Court judge during court proceedings that were open to any member of the public (and the media).

The *Sunday Times* also made no effort to reflect on a public statement issued by the NPA in August 2013, which said that not only did the NPA and the Reserve Bank collaborate closely on the settlement, but also set out the reasons and basis for it. The suggestion that a 'rogue unit', in conjunction with Pillay and me, had managed to manipulate the most senior people at the NPA and the Reserve Bank, and bypass their stringent policies and procedures – never mind the internal controls and committees within SARS – is worthy of derision. A 'rogue unit' played no part in the matter whatsoever.[21]

Over time, the service's enforcement actions began to have an impact on organised crime. Another example of our successes, one that was also reported in the media, is the case of a KwaZulu-Natal crime boss, Michael Barnabas, who was convicted for tax evasion in 1999.[22] By 2003 all his assets had been seized and sold by SARS. In 2002 Western Cape crime boss and drug dealer Colin Stanfield was convicted for tax evasion and lost his assets to the state.[23] Since 2004 there have also been significant seizures of illegally harvested abalone and illegal drugs, all as a result of SARS work.

For organised criminals, SARS was suddenly starting to become a force to be reckoned with.

4

Gathering clouds

Over time, the public profile of SARS was growing. The media reported on more cases where SARS was beginning to have a marked impact, cracking the whip on violations of tax and customs laws – and criminal activity. By mid-2000 there had been a number of ongoing high-profile cases, including a major investigation into the electronics industry.

Early in 2000, SARS had been approached by certain concerned foreign-owned and listed players in the electronic industry. They were big names, and they were seriously considering withdrawing their business from South Africa because of large-scale unfair competition and fraud in the industry. According to SARS, the electronics industry at the time consisted of nine major manufacturing firms employing about 9 000 workers. The industry, a SARS statement said, 'contributes about two per cent to the GDP, excluding software and services, and generates a turnover of about R7.7 billion in the retail sector ... The brown goods sector, which has been the focus of investigation, employs roughly 2 500 workers.'[1]

The alleged fraud and unfair competition in the electronics industry posed a serious reputational risk to South Africa, possibly leading to job losses and economic hardship, so something had to be done. We worked very closely with the NPA and the Scorpions in those days. Deploying a number of the old-guard investigators and some of the new faces, a plan was devised to address the entire sector across all segments to achieve maximum impact in as short a time as possible.

On 19 January 2001, there was a breakthrough. It was announced that SARS and electronics and furniture retail giant Profurn had agreed that the group would pay R26 million to settle a tax dispute.[2] Then, on 7 July, another jackpot. The SARS statement hit the media: 'The South African Revenue Service (SARS) has cracked a scam involving local businessmen who served as a conduit supplying the local electronics market with goods that had falsified customs clearance records in an operation that netted the entity a total of R67 million in revenue.[3]

By taking on the electronics industry scandals, SARS was beginning to demonstrate the success of the enforcement part of its operations model – and it was doing so publicly. The approach was a kind of shock treatment that was deliberately applied to defaulting corporate taxpayers and their intermediaries. The messages SARS sent out, and which the media published, signalled to the business world that there would be little tolerance from the new SARS management, led by Gordhan, for corporate tax avoidance or outright evasion.

How long these electronics-industry customs scams had operated and the ultimate losses in revenue they incurred to the fiscus remain unanswered questions. According to a SARS statement, the illegal operations involved 'under-valuation of declared import goods, double invoicing, the importation of semi-knocked-down components and non-payment of VAT ... In some instances, the declared values of the imported goods were as low as fifteen per cent of the actual purchase price.[4]

So-called round tripping was another manifestation of the scam. This involved unscrupulous traders who avoided paying anti-dumping duties on imports from suppliers who were involved in unfair trade practices. The result was not only a considerable loss in customs and VAT income for the state coffers, but also placed huge pressure on the profit margins of legitimate and law-abiding manufacturers and traders, as production and retail costs were seriously undercut through fraudulent competition.

According to SARS, the convictions followed investigations that revealed an intricate web of fraudulent operations, linking manufacturers, importers and exporters, and companies that supplied retailers.[5]

In one fell swoop, various companies and individuals were convicted of 133 criminal charges and agreed to pay SARS over R67 million in outstanding taxes, penalties and duties. The effect these shady operations had on the electronics industry was immense. But, as Gordhan emphasised, the impact of the SARS investigations was 'an extremely positive one ... A new stable business climate has been created facilitating open and fair competition between firms.'[6]

Despite its success, it was during this particular project that I, and perhaps Gordhan and Ivan too, made our first real enemy – and this was in the form of an individual inside SARS.

Karel[7] hailed from the pre-SARS old guard; he had been a rising star in Special Investigations in the pre-Gordhan era. I have always considered him one of the technically most experienced and skilled customs investigators in the country. However, over the years, he would surface every now and then with the same old complaints, usually when life at SARS got too much for him. This time, he stated that he believed we had let the miscreants in the electronics industry off the hook too easily.

Karel voiced his initial allegations against a whole host of SARS management – Gordhan and Ivan, my mentor Shirish Soni, Gene Ravele and others – who, he alleged, were corrupt. But, in the end, his issue was actually with me. The problem he had was that I was making headway in my career at SARS, unduly so in his view, whereas he wasn't. In his mind, I had sold out to the enemy, the new guys; I was a 'joiner', he said. Although we were both white Afrikaner males of a similar age and background, we clearly espoused totally opposing political ideologies. Karel and a small group of his cronies had even been involved in a ludicrous attempt to contractually enforce SARS to allow its criminal investigators to discard the practice of using English as the administrative language. They held it as their right to use Afrikaans to draft their affidavits and papers in their cases.

On 8 February 2001, SARS was compelled to issue a lengthy press statement. Karel and his pals had approached the media with their gripes about the electronics industry cases and over the manner in which SARS had dealt with tax and customs disputes. Following their comments to the media, SARS urgently needed to quell the issue and 'publicly restate its approach to these matters'.[8] SARS justified its strategies and procedures for arriving at the settlements with delinquent taxpayers:

> SARS aims to be a more business-orientated organisation, whose focus is on being effective, efficient and taxpayer-friendly. It is this approach that resulted in a negotiated settlement with Metcash. In the past, the organisation tended to be involved in prolonged litigation, which tied up resources for long stretches. SARS was confident that further litigation would only delay the recovery of outstanding taxes and duties. SARS also wanted to expedite the civil side of litigation in order to focus on the criminal investigation.[9]

As part of this new strategy, the statement continued, SARS had reached settlements with a number of entities, among them Metcash, Accord Technologies and Profurn:

> The factors that lead to these agreements are as follows: The length of time of engaging in litigation, the cost of litigation to date, results of litigation to date could not assure SARS of any substantial recovery of taxes and duties [and] continuous litigation would prolong the recovery of taxes and duties indefinitely and increase costs. SARS appointed an internal legal expert to assess the proceedings [and] the recommendation was that SARS should agree to a settlement but that an independent external opinion should be obtained to confirm the advice.[10]

These principles formed the sound basis for changes to tax legislation that would enable formal settlements to be reached between SARS and tax-payers with greater expedience in later years.

SARS had always acted within the confines of the law, but, for Karel and his group of allies, these events were evidence to include in a 'dossier' they were starting to build. As part of the later investigation into the 'rogue unit', Karel would advance that such settlements were unlawful. For many years, Karel remained a disaffected SARS employee and in 2014 he would pop out of the woodwork to become one of the unnamed 'star witnesses' for the Sikhakhane Panel of Inquiry into the so-called rogue unit.[11]

The first clouds had already started to accumulate on the horizon, albeit ones originating from a distant past. Now, more clouds were appearing, also in the form of another 'dossier' – this time compiled by auditors in Durban.

In 2002 a number of auditors were moonlighting as tax advisers for taxpayers. So, while they were auditing taxpayers on behalf of SARS, after hours they would offer to help taxpayers who had a tax dispute with SARS by providing their services for a fee. Of course, this was a conflict of interests and unethical, and when these activities were discovered, the officials were disciplined. Some of them reacted with great anger. They all happened to be black, and they accused Ivan, who is of Indian descent, of being a racist. Their position was that they were being targeted and persecuted because of their skin colour. Over the years they also compiled a 'dossier', which was distributed to politicians and the media, and to whoever else may have shown an interest in it. At the time, their case gained little traction because it didn't deal with all the facts surrounding the events and the claims were easy to refute – at the time …[12]

The claim that Ivan is a racist also formed part of the 'rogue-unit' narrative and it seems to have partially originated in this incident. In the years that followed, charges of racism permeated the organisation and found a fertile breeding ground among disaffected current and former SARS officials. It would become a pernicious basis for complaints against

Ivan and Gordhan in particular. Such claims would almost always under-lie attempts to discredit the SARS management when corrective actions had been instituted against employees found to be involved in corrupt or undesirable activities. In their eyes, the fact that Ivan, Gordhan and others in the SARS executive had played an active part in the political struggle against white oppression and were participants in negotiating our consti-tutional democracy seemed to matter very little.

This practice of compiling 'dossiers' and distributing them to influen-tial recipients became a veritable cottage industry for detractors of SARS over the years. But we had always managed to fend off the attacks by rely-ing on the facts, by ensuring that politicians and the media were properly briefed when SARS was asked for comment and, in some instances, by providing written refutations with formal supporting documentation.

Most of these dossiers contained similar elements, although they came in various guises. They were usually aimed at Gordhan and Pillay, and I would sometimes be dragged in. They often claimed anti-black senti-ments, sometimes that there were 'apartheid spies' at work, most of the time alluding to a secret unit of some kind, and often claiming that we were intercepting communications or were scheming against politicians. From the mid-2000s they began to include the suggestion that we were conspiring against Zuma.

Another warning signal of what was to come was the growing number of instances where SARS officials would be approached by go-betweens, purporting to act on behalf of some politician or other. These would always concern some particular case SARS was working on and the request was always the same: lay off the case. We consistently refused.

In my experience alone, I can count more than 20 instances where I was approached in this manner about cases I worked on. It was by no means easy investigating someone, trying to uphold the law, but knowing full well that there were powerful people out there, plotting to place undue pressure and influence on you, or others above you, to sway the outcome of a case.

During those early years at SARS my private life was dull, if not downright unbalanced. When I joined SARS, I had virtually no friends. I was estranged from my family with whom I had had very little contact for several years because of my duties as a deep-cover police agent.

My work completely defined me. At SARS, I worked virtually every day of the week, sometimes even sleeping in my office and showering at the local gym the next morning. I didn't socialise much and couldn't even make small talk with people.

I was also rather intolerant towards colleagues who had families and social lives. I recall how, early in 2002 or thereabouts, a group of investigators at the Special Compliance Unit came to see me on a Monday morning and complained that I only greeted people on Monday mornings and Friday afternoons. I realised then that days and nights had become blurred and a whole week would seem like a day.

I also remember receiving a call late on a Saturday evening from the angry wife of one of the investigators. We were conducting a raid at a clearing agent's premises. These operations were time-consuming because every product that was seized had to be itemised and recorded. Some of our raids would take all night. Clearly upset, the woman said to me: 'If my husband isn't home soon, his work is going to affect our family.' Later, I realised that the husband hadn't wanted to raise the fact that he had an important family commitment that weekend because it might have created the impression that he wasn't committed to his work.

This event brought home to me how disassociated I had become from the things that should matter to ordinary people. All I thought of, and busied myself with, was work. I came across as aloof and unapproachable, and I know my colleagues found me difficult at times. I started to realise just how far removed I had let myself become from a balanced and normal life.

5

The birth of the unit

Our successes began to give rise to a growing negative sentiment among certain other state institutions towards SARS. Institutional rivalry with other law-enforcement agencies and state intelligence became pronounced and some relationships even started to break down. From around the mid-2000s, we were becoming increasingly isolated within the broader law-enforcement community.

Organised criminals were also beginning to view SARS as a credible threat to their activities and they started to fight back. And they fought dirty. This brought our officials into the pathway of harm and risk.

On the positive side, parliamentarians and members of the public started to view SARS as a highly effective institution and an alternative solution to broader law enforcement. Often, members of the public, rather than reporting crimes to the police would approach SARS instead. I attended several portfolio committee meetings in Parliament where the near impossible was expected of us. We had to start curbing drug dealing, and abalone and tobacco smuggling, reduce job losses in the textile sector, and more.

There was pressure on SARS to participate in various committees, projects and initiatives.

Unfortunately, though, we simply didn't have sufficient resources to deal with everything. We were spreading ourselves too thinly.

As SARS came up with new ways to address organised crime, organised criminals also began to reinvent themselves. The structures of organised crime no longer took the traditional form of a single head with reportees and henchmen, in a top-down hierarchy like the mafia-type syndicates of old. They began to regroup into horizontal networking structures. They no longer worked as teams any more, but were connected across geographical borders and engaged in different types of crimes. Organised criminals started to function, and often sought to 'legitimise' themselves, under the guise of genuine business enterprises.

Consequently, crime began to overlap with business interests and become enmeshed with politics and state activities. Players would associate with one another and conspire together depending on the particular crime or racket. This pattern began to threaten the independence of SARS as efforts to unduly influence the institution over certain cases under investigation began to increase.

The criminals' methods of operation also mutated in response to law-enforcement activities. There had been cases where criminals would infiltrate law-enforcement agencies, posing as informants and bribe officials, and some even went as far as to act as 'complainants' in an attempt to discredit officials with false information. They also started to cotton on to how effective anonymous dossiers could be in discrediting someone when distributed to a gullible media or to state agencies that struggle to distinguish fact from fiction.

Syndicates, particularly in the area of economic crimes, no longer operated in dedicated groups but rather as individuals who, from time to time, collaborated with one another when it suited them. This phenomenon is not unique to South Africa and led to, among other things, the intergovernmental Financial Action Task Force (of which South Africa is a member state) in 2013 declaring tax evasion a predicate offence to money laundering. This move widened the definition of smuggling as a predicate offence to include under-evaluation and customs fraud.[1]

There can be no doubt that organised-crime syndicates have come to consider revenue authorities as a serious threat to their survival. Since the mid-2000s, there have been instances of SARS investigators being assaulted, kidnapped, shot at, injured in drive-by shootings, blackmailed, and threatened, and they have found themselves all too often as suspects in police investigations that were instigated by people who were under investigation themselves and who laid false complaints against our officials. In 2010 a SARS official involved in investigating illicit cigarettes was shot and seriously injured. Tragically, just a year later, another SARS employee working on a five-year-long investigation into illegal tobacco was shot and killed at his home.[2]

In 2012 a number of unarmed SARS officials were investigating the tax affairs of certain taxi owners when they were cornered in an apartment in Hillbrow.[3] A lead had lured them into the apartment and then locked them inside. One official tried to escape through a window and by pure chance managed to attract the attention of a police officer, who came to their rescue. I have absolutely no doubt that the fortuitous presence of that policeman saved those officials from serious physical harm, or worse.

On another occasion I had to arrange legal representation and bail for a SARS official who was arrested in front of his wife and children late on a Friday afternoon on trumped-up charges. We had to move fast to ensure he didn't spend the weekend in jail.

In May 2016 it was revealed during the criminal trial of Radovan Krejcir that he and others had planned to bomb SARS branch offices. We had learnt of this when it was planned, thanks to SARS's HRIU, the so-called rogue unit. Unit personnel had managed to gain access to someone who was close to Krejcir's inner circle. Krejcir had even hatched a plan to steal luxury vehicles that we had seized from him. We also had information that he was planning to break out of prison.

The nature of the game was changing dramatically, and the SARS labour unions began to call for danger pay for certain categories of SARS officials. This was something SARS could not afford. SARS personnel then began to make demands for bullet-proof vests, personal security and bodyguards.[4]

In some cases, provisions for these were made where the risk was considered to be serious. I was also confronted by a number of investigators in my area who complained that they did not want to work on certain cases that presented a risk to them or their families. I always allowed those who did not want to expose themselves to risk to work on other files instead.

Against this backdrop of increasing demands placed on SARS and the growing level of threat from organised crime, the proposal was made that SARS should work more closely with the state intelligence agencies in combating organised crime. It was always understood that SARS did not have a direct role to play in the security interests of the country – the National Strategic Intelligence Act of 1994 reserves this role for the intelligence services and state security forces. However, we recognised that SARS did have a tangential role in so far as it was responsible for administering the control of movement and the manufacture of certain goods under customs legislation. For instance, SARS is required to prevent harmful or illegal goods from moving into or out of the country. And, in a broader sense, the protection of South Africa's tax base serves to strengthen security interests by helping to ensure the country's fiscal sovereignty.

The idea that state agencies should cooperate in fighting crime and, broadly, collaborate on intelligence sharing was first formally postulated at an intergovernmental workshop in 1998 and further investigated in the years that followed.[5] While I wasn't involved back then, I understand a task team met at the Intelligence Academy of the NIA in Mafeking (today Mahikeng) and this gave rise to an intergovernmental task team, chaired by Peter Richer on behalf of the NIA. Richer was a former ANC underground operative, who had joined the ANC in 1975 and went into exile in 1976.[6]

Ivan would later represented SARS on this task team and the Cabinet was continually briefed on the outcomes of their sessions.

From 2006 onwards, SARS and the NIA formally discussed ways in which the two institutions could collaborate. At the time, a number of joint projects had been quite successful and some were still operational. From 2002 to around 2005, investigators from various SARS enforcement divisions had been trained at the Intelligence Academy on the basics of intelligence-driven investigations and how to convert intelligence to render it permissible as evidence before a court.[7]

Various models for a joint team were considered, as well as the question of where such an outfit should be housed – in SARS, at the NIA or elsewhere. This was resolved towards the end of 2006. Just as SARS had done years before with the NPA, the agreement was that SARS would recruit and train a number of people, who would ultimately be transferred to the NIA. This specialist team, although housed within the NIA, would be dedicated to supporting SARS in its efforts to combat organised crime. The plan envisaged that SARS would provide for the personnel cost of the unit, just like it had in the past for the NPA's Special Tax Units.

A small unit was subsequently formed in SARS in anticipation of the joint SARS–NIA initiative. Ivan, as General Manager: Enforcement and Risk, recommended in February 2007 that SARS create specialised capabilities to focus on the illicit economy by appointing 14 external applicants and transferring 12 internal SARS employees from the Enforcement and Risk divisions.[8]

Given the role they were expected to play, the recruits had to have the skills needed to avoid or counter physical and other threats, and had to be willing to accept the risks that came with their work. They would be required not to attract much attention from the subjects of their operations. This was for their protection, as they would be investigating areas of organised crime that posed challenges that were greater than normal. To my knowledge, the recruits to the new unit were mostly headhunted for their specific skills, experience and expertise, and subjected to several tests as part of the recruitment process.[9]

This unit – which existed in different forms over the years and went by different names, as mentioned (SPU, NRG and HRIU) – initially had no formal name and was referred to simply as 'the unit'.[10] At its height, 'the unit' was staffed by 26 members – 12 existing SARS officials, six former staff members of the DSO, one former private investigator, who was also a former NIA official, one Metro Police official, one SAPS official, one SANDF soldier, one Council for Scientific and Industrial Research employee and, later, three SANDF members.[11]

SARS was ready to go ahead with the plan and had fulfilled its part of the agreement, but then Richer left the NIA and joined SARS. Suddenly, the NIA officials who had originally been involved in conceptualising the unit went cold on us. There were no more talks; we received no replies to our letters.[12] Nothing.

SARS was left in the lurch by the NIA with a unit without a name, even though there was a business need for it, and the kind of crime it was set up to combat was rampant. Something had to be done. Ivan decided to seek legal opinion on how best SARS might be able to put the new capacity to use in a lawful manner, and to a certain degree I helped him with this.

The conclusion was that, as long as the new unit was not involved in the covert collection of intelligence that related to national security, and as long as it didn't engage in matters defined in the National Strategic Intelligence Act, then its capacity could be beneficial to SARS's efforts to help combat crime. The aim of those involved in establishing the unit was clear – to advance the cause of the state and improve SARS's capability to deal with dangerous offenders who presented a risk to SARS officials.

The legal view on how the unit should be deployed was that the Constitution does not purport to dictate how government departments function or organise themselves operationally. Nothing in law precluded SARS from creating such a capability. It would not contravene any national legislation. Although the National Strategic Intelligence Act 39 of 1994 prohibits other departments from collecting intelligence pertaining to national security in a covert manner, these provisions pertained specifically to 'national security' and 'covert' intelligence gathering. Neither of these applied to the unit's intended activities.[13]

A hastily drawn-up policy document entitled 'Rules of Play' was compiled with the assistance of SARS's legal staff.[14] These rules were adhered to by the unit from its inception until the day it was closed down. In light of the later *Sunday Times* reports, which claimed that the 'rogue unit' was a secret entity that operated covertly, it must be pointed out that this policy document clearly sets out that the unit may not conduct covert intelligence. It could only conduct investigations that were approved, and the document states that 'such investigations had to be tax and customs related'. At the time we had so many discussions about the legal definition of 'covert intelligence gathering' that the officials eventually grew tired and rolled their eyes whenever I raised the matter.

Since claims have been made in the media that the unit had supposedly spied on taxpayers, let me be clear on this: although it may originally have been conceptualised as a covert unit to be housed within the NIA, by the time it had become a fully incorporated SARS unit, there were no such intentions any more.

Furthermore, while it was also claimed that the unit was unknown and secret, and SARS at times even denied its existence, it featured prominently in a chapter of Julian Rademeyer's top-selling book *Killing for Profit: Exposing the Illegal Rhino Horn Trade*, published in 2012.[15] The unit was named in this book, its mandate was described and it was openly associated with SARS.

On the point of what constitutes a covert operation, while at SARS, I completed a law degree part-time. In my final-year dissertation I chose a subject that I felt wasn't given much prominence in legal circles. It was also an ode of sorts to my career before joining SARS. The paper, titled 'A South African legal framework applicable to covert activities conducted by state intelligence agencies', examines the primary elements that make up covert structures in state agencies and the legal framework that guides these.

Given my research for this paper, together with my background in the police as an undercover agent, I am well informed on the processes and legal aspects concerning covert activities used by state agencies. I emphasise this because, during the events that eventually led to the fall of the unit, it was assumed that it was using 'covert intelligence practices' and was considered to be a 'covert unit'. This was definitely not the case.

Covert units and operations in state intelligence agencies have certain key features that distinguish them from normal detective work and from the kinds of discreet investigations carried out by law-enforcement agencies in this country. First, state employees who operate covertly hide who they work for, sometimes using fictitious identities and so-called 'legends', which project a cover. The SARS unit did not have these features. All the unit members were identifiable SARS officials and this would have been easy to determine.

None of the unit's members had legends or false identities – almost half of the original unit consisted of well-known SARS officials who were transferred to the unit. If anybody asked them who they worked for, they would have identified themselves as members of SARS.

In law, the term 'covert collection' has a rider that refers to information 'for which complete and continuous secrecy is a requirement'.[16] Because the information and evidence collected by the unit could at any time have been used in any of our cases, and because its personnel might have been required to testify in court (as indeed was the case on occasion), nothing they did fell within this description.

Secondly, in South Africa, agents and informants need statutory approval to infiltrate the groups they are investigating, usually with a view to collecting evidence or intelligence that can be used by the state to combat crime. In light of their intended outcome (i.e. criminal proceedings in an open court), such undercover operations are not and cannot be considered 'covert' because complete and continuous secrecy is automatically ruled out. The SARS unit never conducted covert or undercover investigations and never infiltrated crime syndicates.

Another methodology used by covert state units is to intercept telephone calls or emails and sometimes to plant listening devices, or 'bugs'. This practice is strictly controlled and requires the approval of a High Court judge. The unit never used any such interception methods (including the planting of listening devices) in any of its investigations. Self-recording of a conversation by a participant or doing so with a participant's knowledge in the process of collecting evidence of a crime is deemed lawful and doesn't require any form of prior legal approval.[17]

The last weapon in the armoury of covert state activities is the surveillance of subjects without their knowledge with a view to obtaining evidence or intelligence. Conducting such surveillance by the state is common practice.

As I pointed out in my dissertation, this aspect was probably the least clearly defined in law, as no proper statutory legislation exists to meaningfully guide it. Section 14 of the Constitution stipulates that everyone has the right to privacy. Various statutory laws also protect the privacy of citizens. To observe someone in a public place is not considered unlawful, especially if it is part of the state's efforts to collect evidence of criminality. In such cases, the balance of the right to privacy falls away in favour of the public interest. Having said that, the moment you enter an area not considered public, like someone's home or office, or observe people through a window in a property that is not public, without permission from a court to do so, you cross a legal line.

The unit never observed individuals other than in public spaces, and always with a view to obtain evidence that would help inform our investigations. For instance, the unit personnel attended public gatherings where we knew key suspects would be, such as in the courtroom where a major case we were covering was being heard. Unit members would also drive past premises to verify addresses and record registration numbers of vehicles parked in driveways.

To emphasise my point here, one only has to consider how surveillance is practised not only by law-enforcement agencies, but often also by private investigators. In July 2016 Eskom advertised for experienced private investigators with access to 'suitable camera equipment to monitor targeted areas, surveillance equipment and cellphone software analysing equipment …'[18]

Furthermore, journalists have revealed criminal activity using this methodology. For instance, the erstwhile investigative television programme *3rd Degree* exposed racism at a Free State picnic resort in 2000 using a hidden camera.[19] Investigative documentary programme *Carte Blanche* advertises itself as being 'known to go undercover in tracking and arresting high-profile criminals'.[20] In 2007, two people were convicted in the Durban Magistrates Court after they were found guilty for having assaulted a *Carte Blanche* presenter and crew following a sting operation by the journalists. The evidence relied upon during the trial was the video and audio secretly recorded by the journalists.[21]

Years later, when the drama around the unit was playing out in the media, constitutional law expert Professor Pierre de Vos from the University of Cape Town gave a detailed legal view confirming the position held by SARS at the time. He said: '[T]he National Strategic Intelligence Act 39 of 1994 (originally invoked by those pointing fingers at SARS officials and Gordhan) does not prohibit a body such as SARS from establishing an investigative unit and gathering intelligence. Nor does it prohibit SARS from gathering intelligence covertly.'[22]

But, in any event, the SARS legal mandate makes no provision for covert activities concerning national security matters. I was particularly strict about this aspect of the unit's activities. The goal of our projects had always been solely to collect or identify potential evidence and witnesses in cases we were investigating and to assist other SARS units or law-enforcement agencies.

In the beginning, there was still hope that the NIA would eventually honour its agreement with SARS. Therefore, the unit kept itself busy with administrative formulations, policy and procedural designs, job descriptions, structural proposals, basic training and operational matters – and with surprisingly good results.

I was asked to help from time to time, and I participated in some of their training sessions, introducing the unit team to the basic aspects of taxpayer types, trader types, tax types, tax processes, tax and customs powers, case studies and case law. I provided them with training material on a number of these subjects for self-study.

The head of the unit was SARS employee Martin,[23] who hailed from the apartheid-era National Intelligence Service. He was an expert in surveillance and had worked in the private sector before joining SARS. Initially, Martin reported directly to Ivan.

SARS continued its efforts to rekindle the agreement with the NIA and eventually approached the police Crime Intelligence Division in the hope that SARS might site the unit there, but nothing came of the endeavours. Everybody made the right noises; everyone agreed that such a unit was needed, but nobody ever came back to SARS with any practical suggestions.

It surprises me today that people in the law-enforcement agencies act as if they were oblivious to this unit. Not only did we extensively canvass various agencies about the creation and purpose of such a unit, but once it was established we also worked very closely with them from the outset – and the same applies to the unit's later versions.

The next logical step was to convert the new unit into a fully fledged SARS unit and Ivan asked me to assist with this process. We held workshop after workshop and looked at legislation, international best practice, case studies and scenarios, before coming up with a final model for the unit in July 2007. We found that most revenue and customs agencies worldwide had units such as these, in some cases with very invasive powers.

The unit, which would function within SARS's legal and policy framework, was also finally christened: the Special Projects Unit. Internally, it had to operate in support of SARS's other units; externally, it had to assist the country's law-enforcement agencies.

The unit derived its mandate from the State of the Nation Address delivered by President Thabo Mbeki in February 2007:

> [G]overnment will this year ... start the process of further modernising the systems of the South African Revenue Services [*sic*], especially in respect of border control, and improve the work of the inter-departmental co-ordinating structures in this regard; intensify intelligence work with regard to organised crime, building on the successes that have been achieved in the last few months in dealing with cash-in-transit heists, drug trafficking and poaching of game and abalone ...[24]

Significantly, this mandate contained approval for three other units that reported to me at the time. Yet none of these units would attract as much attention in later years as the small SPU.

From around November 2007 onwards, Ivan also began to interpose me between him and Martin, with the ultimate aim of having the unit report to me.

After the SPU was established, our primary concern was the safety and security of its personnel and keeping their work confidential. The concept of telecommuting came up while we were considering different models for working, following international best practice. We discovered, for instance, that in Germany tax auditors were encouraged to telecommute, which saved the German revenue authority money on office space.

Consequently, we provided the members of the unit with 'hot desks' – shared workspaces, PCs and telephones in certain SARS offices that were dedicated to the unit's personnel. They also had the opportunity to work from home. The concept appealed because SARS did not have to house them as a group at a single location. We knew that those they were investigating would be targeting them and their offices. In this way, we were able to ensure their safety and security as a group.

The unit was originally allocated two work spaces – one in the SARS Hatfield offices and the other in the SARS Megawatt Park complex in

Sunninghill, Johannesburg. To enter these offices, the unit's employees had to pass through the main SARS security entrance point, then swipe their access cards at the office entrance and walk past several colleagues before reaching their work areas. This could hardly be described as being 'covert' in any way.

I would like to point out two other important aspects regarding the creation of 'the unit'. Firstly, according to the 'rogue unit' narrative, the SPU was created 'illegally and unlawfully'. However, as I have briefly mentioned, the way in which the unit was established had precedence: SARS had earlier followed exactly the same process to constitute a dedicated prosecutorial function in the NPA to focus specifically on tax- and customs-related prosecution.

Secondly, at that time the state's intelligence apparatus noted that other state departments were also responsible for identifying and addressing socio-economic threats to the country. In 2008 a report by the Ministerial Review Commission on Intelligence was submitted to the then Minister for Intelligence Services, Ronnie Kasrils, which stated that this responsibility lay 'with the Executive and with all government departments according to their respective mandates and areas of focus'.[25]

The prevailing practice of constituting units at SARS was fairly straightforward. A new unit could typically be approved at the level of the general manager. I can think of a number of units formed in SARS in the audit and customs divisions over the years that did not have ministerial, or even executive approval from the commissioner. So, if anything, it is ironic, given the claims of the *Sunday Times* articles, that this particular unit had ministerial approval. The unit was approved by not only the Finance Minister, but also by the Deputy Finance Minister. No other unit in SARS can claim such a high level of oversight in its establishment. In my view, the claim that it was established illegally has always just been a smokescreen. If there were any truth in it, the same would apply for every single unit in SARS, and probably every other state institution.

In another stroke of irony, it seems that Moyane himself ascribes to the legal protocol that SARS follows when setting up units and deploying personnel within them. If this is the case, then how could allegations that the SPU was 'illegal' or 'unlawful' be true? A news report published in June 2016 states that the SARS chief apparently believes ministerial approval isn't a requirement for the creation of units in SARS. 'Moyane sought clarity from the law firm on whether SARS had an obligation to seek approval from Gordhan [the Minister of Finance] in respect of SARS's operating model and the deployment and control of staff,' the reports states. 'The law firm said the SARS Act gave Moyane the powers to formulate a new operating model to control, organise and deploy staff, as long as this was done within the scope of the law …'[26]

6

Pearlies

Abalone, sometimes called *perlemoen*, or 'pearlies', is a mollusc found in the cold waters of the most southerly stretches of South Africa's coastline. Australia is the only other coastal territory where the species occurs naturally. Abalone is considered a delicacy at dinner tables by some, and is much sought after in East Asia. Today it is a scarce and protected resource because poaching is rife.

In South Africa abalone is a restricted marine resource, heavily protected by legislation enforced by the Marine Coastal Management (MCM) Surveillance Unit.[1] Most of the abalone that is commercially available is either farmed or supplied by commercial entities that have licences to harvest limited amounts from the sea.

In May 2007 abalone was included on the list of protected species of the Convention on International Trade in Endangered Species of Wild Fauna and Flora, an international agreement between several governments, including South Africa's. Abalone is included in the Prohibited and Restricted Goods list administered in terms of Section 113 of the Customs and Excise Act 91 of 1964, which means that permits are required to export it. Only registered commercial fishers and retailers may sell abalone, and an operating licence from the MCM must be obtained for this purpose.

Due to great foreign demand, abalone has become a very lucrative item for smuggling. In 2006 SARS was called to Parliament, together with other state agencies, to answer to the lawmakers on how this resource should be protected. On 27 October 2007, the issue of the dwindling stock of abalone was debated in Parliament and new legislation was introduced. A joint media statement by various law-enforcement agencies released that year stated that conservative estimates of earnings for smugglers and poachers in 2005 exceeded R1.2 billion. This figure was based on the value of confiscations, which totalled more than 1.1 million tons during that year.

The statement also made the important point that abalone smuggling is linked to a number of other serious crimes: 'This does not only represent the risk of revenue loss to the fiscus but also comprises convergence of other forms of criminal activity, including drug smuggling, money laundering, smuggling, racketeering and human trafficking.'[2]

At the time, an ANC Member of Parliament had this to say:

> The decision by Cabinet to support the suspension of wild abalone commercial fishing will ensure the survival of the species and will ensure that our children will, in generations to come, know what abalone is ... I think this is a step that deserves the support of all parties. Preserving our natural marine resources is critical. In fact, one of South Africa's great advantages in this area is precisely that we have managed our fish stocks very well and, on a scientific basis, we must continue to do this.[3]

In April 2007, autumn came early in Gansbaai.[4] The ever-present cold sea breeze cut right through even the warmest layers of clothing. A small town near the most southern tip of South Africa, Gansbaai is well known for its commercial shark-cage diving activities. The dense population of seals at nearby Dyer Island exist alongside their natural predator, the great white shark.

Back then, 'the unit' had primarily occupied itself with developing procedures and job descriptions, and other mundane administrative tasks while waiting for the go-ahead from the NIA to begin operations. This didn't mean that the team did not conduct investigations – quite the contrary. What they did could be described as discreet investigations and research. For example, the unit, then still managed by Martin, had been scouring areas where abalone was known to occur naturally in the Western Cape. This was its first major operation.[5]

That year, I was managing three other units and was not directly involved with the SPU/NRG. However, I did play a role in seeking legal advice for 'the unit' at its inception and helped the team to develop processes and procedures. I also provided advice to Martin when he sought it from time to time.

For the abalone investigation, Martin and his team would speak to policemen and locals in the small coastal villages and towns, such as Gansbaai, in an attempt to home in on the big smugglers. Everybody they spoke to knew that they were SARS officials. They all asked the same question, 'Do you know who the smugglers are in your town?' Nobody wanted to talk.

The smugglers not only had big money and protection, but they were dangerous too. In these communities their association with gang syndicates on the Cape flats, and the narcotics trade controlled by them, was well known. Even though many knew who the smugglers were, nobody was prepared to blow the whistle. However, by gradually gaining the confidence of a few individuals, slowly but surely a trickle of information started coming through.

Initially it was only whispers, but the officials in the unit at least had something to follow up and they began to gain a picture of how the abalone trade worked. There was a value chain: local folk went out to sea at night to illegally harvest the abalone. The locations of these harvesting spots were identified by the team. Once harvested, the abalone would then be stored in ice boxes, freezers and fridges in certain homes. Then, people known as 'collectors', who weren't locals, would arrive periodically to collect the contraband harvest. The locals would get paid and the collectors would be on their way again. When the team of investigators asked where the collectors went, they always got the same answer: 'We don't know … Nobody knows.'

However, a breakthrough came when one local was willing to explain how the rest of the process worked. He told the team that the collectors, middlemen in the supply chain, came mainly from Gauteng. They would take the abalone to secret storage facilities, where it would be dried out with industrial fans. In its dried form, abalone is far more compact and can be packaged and concealed in larger quantities. Once dry, it would be smuggled out of the country. Some of these middlemen weren't South Africans, the informant told the investigators.

At this point, what we would later refer to as a 'type-1 project'[6] was now beginning to take shape. Typically, this is a project that focused on a particular economic sector or activity. Type-1 projects would usually result in a report or presentation highlighting geographic areas in order of risk, followed by a breakdown of cities and towns, as well as particular business activities and people suspected of having committed tax- or customs-related offences, or where such illicit activities were most prevalent.

Examples of other type-1 projects are the tobacco industry, clothing and textiles, trade in counterfeit DVDs, drug dealing and the like. These projects informed what further actions other SARS units would initiate – for instance, where to conduct inspections and investigations on a systemic level for specific cases that had been identified.

Type-2[7] projects were subject-specific. In other words, the unit officials were expected to conduct investigations and collect evidence on specific individuals and businesses. Such evidence would either be handed over to the other SARS investigative units or be used to direct them towards potential evidence and witnesses in their cases. As can be expected, in some instances type-1 projects led to type-2 projects.

A type-3[8] project usually took the form of an ad hoc task in support of an investigation being conducted by either a SARS unit or an external law-enforcement agency. The methodology used by the unit in such instances would be an Inspector Plod-type investigation. The men and women of the unit would mine the Internet and social media, do credit-bureau checks and gather other publicly available information with a view to building an organogram that might reveal links between people, businesses, addresses, phone numbers and the like.

They would also interview complainants, people who approached SARS with information and, in some cases, use this information to identify key people to approach in the hope of interviewing them. In certain cases, they managed to follow up on a story told by one person, which would direct them to collect information on the next, ultimately seeking credible sources of evidence that would be required to prove our investigations as possible cases of criminal activity. This type of work requires extreme focus, mental discipline, a very good memory, the ability to extract facts from conversations and interviews, and to seek the right leads for evidence, and all the while never becoming distracted or wanting to give up.

Back in the Gansbaai area, two-person teams from the unit would take turns nearly every day and night to watch over the identified abalone harvest spots from their parked cars. One such team consisted of Simba,[9] a former policeman with a legal background, who was big and fit with a clean-shaven head, and Tony,[10] a trained analyst and researcher, who was shorter and slighter in build. While Simba always smiled, Tony was more studious-looking. Together, they made a formidable team.

The nights were cold and their cars littered with used paper coffee cups and takeaway cartons. It was an uncomfortable operation, but they stuck to it, even though it was a matter of hit and miss. Then, finally, a lucky break. Late one evening, under a full moon, they spotted a group of people launching a small dinghy into the sea. The little boat didn't go far. It stopped near a reef known to be teeming with abalone. The poachers used torches as they dived into the shallow ocean and these cast odd shadows every now and again.

A while later the boat came back to shore and the poachers started off-loading their harvest. The dinghy was dragged up the beach and secured, then the poachers walked off towards a parking lot nearby. Simba and Tony followed them to their cars and took down their registration numbers.

The next day, after the team had obtained the names and addresses of the vehicle owners from the police official who was working with them on the project, they went out and started knocking on doors: 'We're from SARS. We have reason to believe that you're involved in the illegal harvesting of abalone. Are you prepared to talk to us about this?'

This kind of cold calling is similar to the approach employed by sales-people in the hope that a small percentage of customers will respond positively. But, at each house, the team was chased away with the usual response: 'Come back if you have a warrant!'

Then, one guy happened to open his door and, before Simba or Tony could identify themselves, said, 'Come in quickly. I don't want people to see me talking to you ...'

Simba and Tony looked at each other and immediately knew they'd hit pay dirt. The local told them that a man living a few houses down the street from him smuggled abalone. 'He's making a lot of money,' he said. 'But if he knows I spoke to you guys, I'm going to be in big trouble. Every Tuesday, different cars with registration plates from other provinces stop there. I'm sure that's when they load the abalone.'

Tony called Martin and the police officer, and briefed them. A type-1 project had suddenly turned into a full-scale type-2 project. The police officer, a member of the Scorpions, had been assigned to investigate aba-lone smuggling. His view was that it would be fruitless to go after the 'little guys'. All the while, Martin, the Scorpions officer and a representa-tive from the MCM had been liaising about the information coming in. They all agreed that they had to find who the big guys were. They had to identify the collectors and the location of the drying plant. Armed with that information, they could bring an end to the smugglers' game.

Martin, the Scorpions man and the MCM team scrambled to get

everything in place for the following Tuesday when the next abalone collection was set to take place. They briefed the NPA prosecutor and a special task team of the police was placed on standby, ready to take off in a helicopter at a moment's notice.

Tuesday evening came. Other than Simba and Tony, members of the unit involved in the bust were Gertjie, Hector and Pitsa.[11] Gertjie, an ex-soldier with a typical military gait, and usually unshaven, is a somewhat serious character who hardly ever smiles, but he is also an excellent analyst and interviewer who produces very good reports. Sharp and witty, Hector is always instantly liked by nearly everyone who meets him. He is a former cop who cut his teeth investigating gang-related activities. Pitsa, a former underground operative of the ANC, is often underestimated because she is soft-spoken and because of the way she flips her braided locks when she is thinking about something. Yet she is as sharp as they come and one of the best interviewers on the team.

They strategically positioned themselves in their cars at the exits to the town. The next moment, Simba, who was with the informant, called. He'd just identified a car that had stopped at the suspected smuggler's house and supplied its details. The chase was on. The team members' plan was to follow the car to its destination, taking great care not to be noticed. They took turns to drive behind the 'collector', sometimes passing each other, driving ahead and beyond, but all the time making sure the suspect remained in plain sight. When the collector stopped to refuel or for a bite to eat, the others continued ahead, while some pulled back.

And so the chase went all the way from Gansbaai, through the dry Karoo interior, across more than half the length of the country, via Bloemfontein and on to KwaZulu-Natal. It was a drive of almost 12 hours through the night and into the next morning. The destination turned out to be Camperdown, a town just outside Pietermaritzburg with good access to Durban.

Camperdown was small enough for unfamiliar cars and foreign faces to stand out, so most of the team pulled back and drove off in different directions, so as not to draw attention to themselves. It had been agreed that the Scorpions would do the search and make the arrests. The collector turned into a smallholding and entered a nondescript residential building. The Scorpions man had a hunch that this was the drying facility and notified the police task team.

The team of investigators had only a few hours before the planned raid and had to move quickly. Nothing was to be left to chance. When entering premises, there was always the likelihood that the suspects would flee. The property was surrounded by dense sugar-cane plantations. To give you a sense of the extent of their planning, it was anticipated that a suspect could flee into the plantation and be struck by a venomous snake – KZN sugar-cane fields are habitats for mambas. Therefore, the team had to identify a suitable area where a helicopter could make an emergency landing, as well as the nearest medical facility with a snake-poison treatment centre. Again, hardly the sort of thing one would expect in a covert operation.

In the meantime, the police task force had arrived. Once at the property, they secured the building on all sides – if anybody came out, they would see them. A combined team of police officers, the Scorpions, SARS representatives and MCM officials approached the building. As they entered, they found racks of drying abalone, with overhead fans running at full power. That day almost six tons of abalone were seized by the police.

The early successes attributed to the unit were fairly well known both within SARS and externally, primarily because these hits were widely discussed and reported on in the media. On 11 April 2007, the NPA, SAPS, the Scorpions, the MCM and SARS issued a joint media statement: 'An intensive joint investigation by various government agencies today uncovered a sophisticated network of abalone smuggling in the largest seizure of abalone in KwaZulu-Natal to date. Six suspects, four of whom are foreign nationals, were arrested during an early-morning raid on a farm in Camperdown outside Durban.'[12]

According to the statement, the abalone had an estimated street value of between R10 million and R12 million. The location of the drying facility can be explained by its proximity to Durban harbour, through which the abalone would most probably have been smuggled out of the country. Six people were arrested and charged by the NPA.

Barely two months old, the unit had already made its first mark against organised crime. All the unit members who participated in the investigation were considered potential witnesses for the case, and any or all of them could have been subpoenaed by the NPA to testify during the trial. Those required to do so submitted affidavits to the police and the NPA. For obvious reasons, state employees doing covert work would never testify in criminal trials because this would blow their cover. In the end, however, the unit members didn't testify – not because it was a covert project, but simply because they were not called to do so by the NPA.

On 12 October 2007 the Minister of Environmental Affairs and Tourism, in response to a parliamentary question, stated that over a million abalone had been seized in the 2006/07 financial year and that over 400 000 had been seized during the period April 2007 to October 2007. The minister made reference to 32 criminal cases before various courts at the time, one of which was the Camperdown case in the Pietermaritzburg Magistrates Court.

Another abalone-related project in 2007 ensued after SARS customs division had stopped a truck leaving South Africa en route to Swaziland.[13] They discovered a substantial quantity of abalone hidden in the back, undeclared of course. The suspects and the haul were promptly handed over to the police, who took the matter further.

As part of their efforts to identify links between these suspects and others, members of the unit attended court appearances. They quickly developed a tactic that they put to great effect in other investigations, too. When suspects appear in court, people associated with the accused (and, in fact, the activities they are charged for) also tend to go to the hearings. Simply by being in court, watching the suspects and who they associated with, and then checking the vehicle registrations of those people when they left the court building, the team found they could not only build profiles of the suspects, but also demonstrate links between them and other individuals and business entities.

As a result of these efforts, a link chart and profiles of such persons were handed to the police investigating the matter at the time. The same profiles also helped the SARS office in Durban[14] to begin with tax investigations into some of those identified.

In an unrelated income-tax fraud case, also in 2007, which was being investigated by the SARS Criminal Investigations Unit in conjunction with the then SAPS Commercial Crime Unit, the investigators expressed frustration at not being able to track down a suspect to effect the warrant of arrest. The suspect, who lived in the East Rand, had been evading the police and SARS investigators for some time. They turned to 'the unit' for help.

Ingeniously, members of the unit asked the local Metro Police, who had many vehicles on the road, to look out for a particular vehicle and registration number. Sure enough, one day, the call came that the police had found the vehicle parked in the area. The investigating officer who had the warrant of arrest was notified and, with the help of the Metro Police, a tracking device, supplied by the police, was placed on the vehicle. This was done because the team weren't yet sure whether the driver was indeed the man the police were looking for.

On 30 July 2007 the Metro Police, assisted by the unit, followed the vehicle when it started moving. The police stopped the vehicle, checked the driver's identity and arrested him. He was taken to the police station and the police investigator took him into custody that same day.

In another 2007 case, the unit assisted the police after reports had reached us from a primary school close to the SARS head office that a suspected paedophile was harassing children before and after school. The school had reported the matter to the police and a description was given of the suspect's car, since none of the children who had been accosted had managed to record the registration number. Some SARS officials, who had children at the school, had expressed concern at work about these incidents. Martin and his team came to hear about it and decided to help the police find the man.

Every morning, before and after school, most of the unit members sat in their cars, parked strategically around the school grounds. Then, one day, the vile man struck again, and one of the teams saw the commotion as the children screamed and ran off.

The vehicle fitted the description, and the registration number was taken down. A call was made to the police, who went to the address where the vehicle was registered and confronted the man. The officer also confiscated his personal computer. The police, when reporting back and thanking SARS for the assistance, explained that they had had difficulty accessing and downloading data from the computer. The investigating officer indicated that he believed it may contain incriminating evidence.

Team member Tony, also a computer expert, was able to help the police access the computer and download the data. They found high volumes of child pornography. The suspect was arrested by the police and charged for a range of crimes.[15]

Not all the unit's projects enjoyed the same degree of success, however. For instance, the then Department of Social Welfare asked SARS in 2007 for assistance because their social-welfare pay points in Durban and surrounding areas were being inundated by people with fraudulent claims. Members of the unit went to Durban and selected the Pinetown pay point, which was identified as the highest risk, and staked it out.[16]

They were hoping to identify the fraudsters by speaking to people at the pay point. They hung out for days on end, but nothing came up. Other than identifying certain high-risk areas and security measures to be considered for these pay points, this project sadly came to naught.[17]

7

Below zero

I have touched on some of the unit's early projects, although my interaction with it at that stage was very limited from an operational perspective.

I attended a workshop with the unit in late 2007 whose aim was to help to develop a SARS mandate and process flow[1] to fit into the SARS legal framework. There I stood, in front of 26 highly talented individuals, all with high hopes for the future and all raring to go with one goal in mind – to fight crime. What an odd bunch, I thought. Most of them considered this nonsense of 'process flows' and 'legal frameworks' a waste of time. At first we spent days and days trying to get some semblance of structure into our discussions.

I had to get to know each one of the team, and understand their way of viewing things and what their expectations were. One enthusiastic team member, Charlie,[2] a psychologist by training, came to me with the idea of a 'Rubik's cube structure' for the unit. This was a mishmash of textbook organisational structure development, combined with what Charlie believed would work. I knew it was doomed to failure. But I couldn't just tell Charlie that.

So, I sought advice from experienced managers and experts in organisational design. I was a part-time student then at the Wits Business School, where I was concluding a management advancement programme, a postgraduate course for mid-level and senior managers. I also tested some of the ideas with experienced managers there. The experts advised me that when starting a new business unit of this size, a very basic hierarchical structure was always best.

This would ensure a clear assignment of tasks, roles and outputs, and guarantee accountability and an equitable division of labour. I was told that only after such a structure was in place and functioning well could one begin to explore alternative structures, such as a matrix design, which co-assigns responsibilities, roles and shared resources. Boy, did I struggle to get these guys to understand this!

But, in time, as we got to know one another and as I met with some of them in smaller groups, we managed to find common ground. In the end, the proposed structure was hierarchical and simple enough to manage.

One guy in particular, Fransman,[3] a former police officer, was very helpful. Before joining SARS, he had been part of a police crack team that used all kinds of sophisticated tools and analysis to identify and predict patterns involving serial killers. Fransman was a clever guy and very handy when it came to analytical tools and advanced technology, but he was also a loner who preferred working on his own or in a small team.

Fransman got along very well with team member Sibongile,[4] a master's graduate in applied mathematics. The myth that the unit was covert and operated covertly is easily dispelled by the fact that these unit members were both known SARS officials who had been transferred to the unit from other divisions. Also, initially they had been based at the SARS offices in Pretoria and then at the SARS Megawatt Park building, in Johannesburg, before they started telecommuting.

Fransman and Sibongile both understood the principles of business design and planning, and helped to draft the initial flow charts, project planning templates and other documents that eventually came to be placed in a file that they colloquially referred to as 'the Bible'. This was basically a list of processes, procedures, templates and job descriptions that would serve as a guide for the unit's work. Fransman and Sibongile helped greatly in their interactions and discussions with co-members of the unit, apprising them on how things would have to operate. Charlie's Rubik's cube structure was consigned to the rubbish heap.

In those days, the members of the unit had very high hopes and expectations because they believed the NIA might still keep to its side of the bargain. Numerous proposals were drawn up and many ideas were developed by them, all within the context of this continued hope for a combined SARS–NIA initiative. Some ideas were workable; others were not.

It was also around this time that I met another team member – one who would later turn out to be one of the instigators of the 'rogue-unit' story. Michael Peega was a former Special Forces operative and, I imagined, a real tough guy. He had to be – it's no mean feat to be selected for and pass Special Forces training.[5]

In one of the sessions, which I still recall vividly, Peega had quite a lot to say.[6] He started to relate the strangest story imaginable, about how he had been an undercover agent who had helped the South African Government infiltrate terrorist cells in Saudi Arabia. He explained to us how he managed to accomplish this by donning Arabian garb and walking vast distances across the desert. When he was accosted by locals, he claimed to be Islamic and, apparently, was welcomed with open arms by these cells. This ostensibly enabled him to access all sorts of intelligence, which he then passed on to the South African Government which, in turn, passed it on to other states.

From what I had heard, the selection process for the Special Forces doesn't test only your physical fitness, but also your mental agility. I imagined that some basic psychometric testing would also form part of these tests, so it came as quite a surprise when Peega began to tell these truly unbelievable stories. I found it rather worrying for several reasons. First, because they were clearly figments of Peega's imagination and he clearly had no qualms talking about them openly. Secondly, he seemed to believe that we believed him and, thirdly, it appeared to me that there were in fact some in the group who did believe these flights of fantasy. But, at the time, it wasn't for me to judge, and I let it go.

Much later, it would become clear to me that Peega did possess some abilities to infiltrate groups of people and was quite adept at doing so, even if they weren't terrorist cells in the desert. A few years down the line, I would also find out that some of the initial notes and documents compiled by the unit at its inception had seemingly found their way into yet another dossier, referred to as the 'Peega dossier'. Peega distributed this dossier publicly in late 2009, again in early 2010 and, eventually, his dossier featured in the *Sunday Times* in 2014 as part of the 'rogue-unit' narrative.

These notes and documents contained, among other things, suggestions as to funds required, equipment sought, housing, office space and so forth – all based on the assumption that ultimately the unit was going to be housed within the NIA. However, none of these suggestions were ever put forward for serious consideration. They were simply distributed among members and never passed muster beyond that. Sadly, this didn't deter the *Sunday Times* from viewing the Peega dossier as fact, or the suggestions discussed in it as approved, funded and executed.

Peega is a character we'll meet again later in this book.

As I have indicated, there was close cooperation between primarily the Scorpions, the police, the NPA and the unit. Another combined project was the investigation into a new drug that had just hit the streets. Resembling fragments of ice, this narcotic – a potent, smokable form of methamphetamine – was known as ice.

The scientific name for this concoction is methamphetamine hydrochloride but in the drug scene it was also known as 'poor man's crack cocaine'. Methamphetamine is the base chemical used to manufacture the drug and quasi-laboratory conditions are also needed. Rumour had it that given the volumes of ice that were becoming available in Gauteng, there had to be a factory in operation somewhere.

The law-enforcement agencies therefore started putting their heads together and shared whatever information they had. The unit also participated in this process and, pretty soon, by simply following the value chain from user to seller, and from seller to supplier, they came to meet an individual called Jack,[7] who had fallen out with a group of people believed to have been involved in the manufacture of ice. It wasn't long before Martin and the men and women of the unit managed to persuade Jack to work with the joint law-enforcement team.

The information Jack shared with them was revelatory. He confirmed that there was indeed a laboratory manufacturing ice and he explained where it was. Furthermore, he told them who was involved and supplied them with their books and accounting records. Martin and members of the unit, together with some of the police officers involved, immediately set off to the identified location, with the police task force in tow.

The result? A drug laboratory manufacturing methamphetamines was busted in Mooinooi, near Brits, and ice with a value of R270 million was seized. Four individuals were arrested by the police. The unit also handed Jack to the NPA as a potential state witness, together with a host of photos and documents to be considered as evidence in the trial. Some of the SARS officials in the unit at the time were subpoenaed by the NPA to testify in the criminal trial in an open court of law but, in the end, their evidence was not required.

At the time, little of all this was reported in the press but the story made the news sometime later when it transpired that some of the accused in the case had been colluding with police officers and a court interpreter to unduly influence the trial.[8]

In 2007 the unit also helped the police in another case involving illegal drug manufacturing. Quite by accident, while scouring the streets and speaking to people in the drug trade, Martin and members of his team came across a lead that pointed to a possible storage facility for Mandrax in Johannesburg. Mandrax is the trade name[9] of a sleeping medication that had been available on the commercial markets since the late 1960s and its main ingredient is a chemical known as methaqualone.[10]

In the early 1970s, these tablets were starting to be abused in a rather curious manner in South Africa. Users smoke a so-called white pipe consisting of crushed Mandrax tablets mixed with cannabis. Methaqualone was banned in South Africa in 1976 and since then these tablets had no longer been commercially available here. Because of the continued demand for 'white pipe', however, particularly in the 1980s (after which cocaine and other drugs began to dominate the narcotics market), Mandrax tablets were either smuggled into South Africa in large volumes or, in some cases, manufactured in underground laboratories.

Members of the unit did several drive-bys past the suspected drugs facility to determine the movement of people before they called in the police. They found not only a Mandrax storage facility, but also a manufacturing press. Two people were arrested. The search also led them to another address where 17 000 Mandrax tablets were seized in September 2007. SARS reported this in its annual report that year.[11]

Another drug-related type-1 project that the unit worked on (this was at a later stage when it was operating as the NRG), was to create a 'drug map' of South Africa. Fransman and Sibongile oversaw this project, which came about when SARS was asked to appear before an oversight committee in Parliament in 2008, together with other law-enforcement agencies, to account for what the organisation was doing to combat illegal drug dealing and use.

I was one of several representatives who attended. A question posed by a parliamentarian struck me in particular. The MP wanted to know how come, when people in her constituency knew who the drug dealers were, and would even tell her their names, the state agencies didn't do anything about it.

Good point, I thought.

Our task was simple. Unit members had to go to the main cities and engage with the local police, community members and community leaders by asking questions about the drug trade and alleged drug dealers in their community. Then we had to map the information. The first part of the project resulted in a map of South Africa with little dots indicating possible drug dealers and the types of drugs they allegedly dealt in. The second part entailed the whole team going back to the police and other law-enforcement agencies, in an attempt to confirm the information supplied by the local communities. Fransman and Sibongile held the master map and would update it as the information came in.

As part of phase three, they had to liaise with law enforcement to establish which of those dots could be matched with past, current or existing registered criminal cases or convictions. In this way, slowly but surely, the map evolved and became more detailed in its information.

At the same time, Fransman and Sibongile began to build profiles of the primary dealers who had been identified. They relied mainly on data available to SARS by way of SARS records and third-party data, such as bank, credit and municipal records, and the like. Google Maps provided photos of the homes or premises corresponding to the dots. In addition, depending on the drug type, more information was gleaned from customs systems, the World Customs Organisation Regional Intelligence Liaison Offices (of which SARS was a member) and from other information sources that law-enforcement agencies were prepared to share with SARS.

The final product, in my view, was truly a masterpiece. All the information Fransman and Sibongile had put together was transferred onto compact disks, which we distributed to the various enforcement units in SARS and to other law-enforcement agencies. When you inserted the disk, a page would open that informed you about the different drug types, their scientific formulas, and how these illicit substances were used and abused.

The disk also contained the drug map of South Africa, where each dot represented the location of a suspected drug dealer or his associates, or a drug-smuggling operation. The map contained links that provided a detailed profile of the location, and the person or syndicate at that location. More links allowed you to see their past convictions, and their groups' organograms and financial profiles and the like.

More such type-1 projects ensued, some of which took several years to complete.[12] One particular project dealt with high-risk areas in the clothing and textile industry. By 2008 SARS had come under substantial pressure from the labour unions to deal with illegally imported and under-valued stock. By then, it was estimated that over a million people had lost their jobs in the local textile manufacturing sector in the preceding years and a significant number of factories had closed down.

We developed a product similar to the drug map, which mapped areas, towns, shopping malls, flea markets and other spots where counterfeit clothing was sold. With this technology, SARS was able to direct enforcement units to suspected premises where they conducted inspections and raids. Countless tons of smuggled, under-valued counterfeit clothing and footwear were seized by SARS on an annual basis from many of the areas we identified.

We had envisaged that the drug map would be updated every five years or so. Unfortunately, by the time the 'Peega dossier' struck in 2009, the unit's capacity had dwindled, the officials had been exposed to the people they had been investigating and detailed updates were simply impossible. It was a near impossible task with a team of just 26 officials.

Nevertheless, I was extremely proud of this technology, which was ultimately used, to some extent, by the SARS National Enforcement Unit (a different SARS unit that reported to me) in some of their investigations and I believe in certain police investigations too.

Sadly, I didn't participate any further in the parliamentary committee meetings I mentioned earlier. But if I had, I would have been able to answer, on behalf of SARS, the very poignant question that the MP had posed, by giving her the CD with the drug map.

Towards the end of 2007 and the beginning of 2008, things began to come to a head with Martin, who had managed the unit up to that point. From the outset, I found him a difficult person to read and relate to. After Ivan started to bring me in on the unit, Martin and I differed on strategic approaches as to how it should be structured and deployed.

Martin still had very high hopes that the NIA would eventually come to the party, whereas I had come to terms with the fact that this wasn't likely to happen. I wanted the unit to focus more on seeking a solution that would benefit SARS immediately.

After experiencing the first of a series of family tragedies, Martin started taking great strain. However, empathising with what he and his family were going through, I always tried to be understanding. Then, more tragedy struck his family in early 2008 and Martin was by then seriously traumatised.

Early in 2007 Martin took it upon himself to instruct Fransman to engage the supplier of SARS identity cards. The unit was supposed to be issued with normal SARS ID cards but Martin also wanted each unit member to have an additional set of SARS ID cards under an alias. At the time, Martin still believed the NIA would honour the agreement to house the unit, and if that were to happen, then this second set of ID cards would provide fake identities as a cover, which is how some NIA operatives worked.

Fransman followed Martin's instructions and the service provider made sample cards for some of the officials. But the supplier became suspicious of the second set and approached the Scorpions, asking them to engage SARS for clarity on the order. The Scorpions contacted SARS, after which Ivan instructed me to determine the facts surrounding the events.

After I spoke to all the people involved, I advised Ivan that SARS should institute disciplinary proceedings against Martin and Fransman because I believed their actions could have led to unnecessary expenditure. Ivan agreed and the outcome was that both received final written warnings and the order was cancelled. The few who had been given sample ID cards were instructed to hand them in to be destroyed.

Much later, it would turn out that Dippie,[13] one of the unit officials who had worked with me at the Special Compliance Unit, had kept his sample card. A close friend of Peega, Dippie would later play a key role in advancing the 'rogue-unit' story by producing this sample card and claiming it to be something it was not.

The *Sunday Times* later used this information to suggest that the entire unit had been issued with fake IDs and names, and had used them to infiltrate certain groups of ANC politicians. I can unequivocally say that if any official used a fake ID card for any purpose, no such person had any authority to do so and it was never approved by me or SARS. That is not how the unit operated and I, for one, would never have allowed it. The unit's operating procedures, set out in the 'Rules of Play' document, clearly stated that no covert intelligence gathering was allowed. Whoever claims otherwise will have to explain why they didn't hand in the sample cards or destroy them, as instructed at the time.

In early 2008, Ivan, Martin and human resources came to an agreement whereby the remainder of Martin's contract would be paid out and his services terminated.[14] In March 2008, I therefore became the de facto manager of the unit, which had by then been named the Special Projects Unit. (At the time, another division that also reported to me was called Special Projects. To avoid confusion, we changed the name of the SPU to the National Research Group. The rationale behind the new name was simple: its mandate was national in scope and the work the unit carried out was best defined as research, so the name said it all.)

The NRG was a small, low-maintenance outfit comprising fearless, hard-working civil servants, who were prepared to work day and night, with little or no support, to fight real crime. It is pertinent to note that the NRG was funded by a normal SARS cost centre, and the personnel who worked in the unit featured on structural organograms, had standard job descriptions and were on the SARS payroll system. They received a monthly SARS salary, like their colleagues, were issued with SARS IRP5s and SARS was indicated as their employer in their credit applications or related financial transactions.

Moreover, the team members often frequented my office and were known to many people in SARS, as well as by the people they investigated and by other law-enforcement officials with whom they worked. The NRG's finances, performance files, assets and cost centres were audited annually by the Auditor-General of South Africa and underwent SARS internal audits. The human-resources and finance divisions managed their affairs, like any other division in SARS. Once again, this hardly matches the description of what the *Sunday Times* called a 'covert intelligence unit'.

It would be remiss of me not to mention what was later dubbed 'Project Sunday Evenings'. From what I can gather, this relates to events that took place around October 2007, before the unit started reporting to me. 'Project Sunday Evenings' was reported on initially by the *Mail & Guardian* and *Beeld*, and then the *Sunday Times* in May and June 2015.

Media reports suggest multiple versions of what took place. Some imply that the offices of the NPA were unlawfully bugged by these officials to gain information about the possible abuse of power by the NPA in their investigations into Zuma at the time when he was deputy president, and information on the late former police commissioner, Jackie Selebi, who was eventually convicted for corruption, as well as others.

Other versions suggest that these officials acted at the behest of NPA prosecutor Advocate Gerrie Nel – well known for his prosecution of Selebi and Oscar Pistorius – and his colleague, a former member of the Scorpions and later NPA investigator, Andrew Leask. According to reports, Nel allegedly approved payment to a member of 'the unit' to install spy equipment in the offices of the NPA.[15]

As I've mentioned, I wasn't responsible for the unit at the time this project allegedly took place and I don't know anything about the events related to it. But I can say that in my 16 years at SARS, I officially dealt with Nel on only four occasions, and with Leask perhaps three times. On no occasion did we interact in respect of the unit in any manner or form.

This case now seems to form part of an investigation by the Hawks and the NPA. The allegations around 'Project Sunday Evenings' appear also to be part of the efforts to prosecute Finance Minister Pravin Gordhan. In February 2016 the Hawks sought to invoke criminal proceedings against Gordhan based on either the controversial KPMG report into the 'rogue unit' or the equally flawed Sikhakhane report (I'll return to both these reports in later chapters), or reports in the media about 'Sunday Evenings' and a list of so-called 'spy equipment'. Either way, on 18 February, Gordhan received a letter from the Hawks instructing him that he had to answer three pages of questions.[16]

However, other than recommending the establishment of the unit to Trevor Manuel, the Finance Minister, and Jabu Moleketi, Manuel's deputy, in early 2007, Gordhan never had anything to do with the unit in any manner or form. He didn't meet the officials, he didn't directly task the unit and he certainly never received any reports from them. This is not how SARS worked and I would know this better than anybody else, because I managed the unit and its work.

There were at least three to four management layers between Gordhan as commissioner and the unit at any given point in time, and even more after Gordhan became Finance Minister in 2009. So it seems very strange that the questions from the Hawks were directed only to Gordhan, and not to Manuel, Moleketi, Oupa Magashula, who succeeded Gordhan as SARS commissioner, Nene as former Minister of Finance or his deputy, Mcebisi Jonas. All of these individuals presided over SARS during the lifespan of the unit.

All my attempts to ascertain more specifics about Project Sunday Evenings have failed and, from what I could gather, none of the original members who are still at SARS have any knowledge of it. To my knowledge, only three people were involved in this matter anyway.

8

The case of the mysterious blue file

Tobacco smuggling in South Africa is a lucrative business. With the continued increases in excise taxes since 1994, the ban on advertising and legislation limiting smoking to designated public areas, the consumer market was shrinking fast and the price of cigarettes was becoming expensive for many smokers.

Smugglers took advantage of a gap to provide cheaper cigarettes and make huge profits, since the demand for cigarettes did not fall in proportion to the increase in pricing. Whereas counterfeit cigarettes used to be the main headache for the major brand holders, smaller local manufacturers started popping up with new, lesser-known brands. Smokers were becoming less brand conscious and more price aware.

The main illegal schemes in the tobacco industry in the 1990s and early 2000s involved either the smuggling of counterfeit cigarettes or of raw tobacco into South Africa, which would have meant that lower, or zero taxes and duties were paid by the criminals.

Later, counterfeits that had previously been smuggled into the country had all but disappeared. Instead, smaller manufacturers started smuggling more tobacco into South Africa than they recorded and declared in their production volumes, and introduced a whole host of new brand names, which are sold for much less.

This meant that the smaller manufacturers effectively ran two production lines – a legitimate one during the day, for which duties and taxes were paid, and then the so-called B-stock, or undeclared manufacturing, usually produced at night. They not only sold cheaper brands, but also made millions on a monthly basis through the evasion of duties and taxes. The so-called 'cheapies' began to eat into the market share traditionally held by the larger, more established brand holders. Soon the situation was getting out of hand.

In October 2008, the *Mail & Guardian* reported that 'a yellow-jacketed national enforcement unit from the South African Revenue Service … launched an inspection at the Johannesburg premises of Masters International Tobacco Manufacturing, confiscating about 4 500 master cases of cigarettes, comprising 45-million cigarettes'. The article stated that it was the biggest SARS seizure to take place in the country, part of a project that had been launched earlier that year to crack down on the illicit trade in tobacco products.[1]

The bust was a massive success.

The 'yellow-jacketed national enforcement unit' that conducted the SARS raid was a reference to the National Enforcement Unit (NEU), which also reported to me at the time. Its manager was a character known as Tall Pete[2] (the name is self-explanatory), who had practically grown up at SARS as an auditor in the Johannesburg office. Tall Pete had worked his way up through the ranks and knew his work inside out.

The NEU was made up of a combination of experts in auditing, customs and excise, legal people and criminal investigators. They had been slaving away at this case, looking for scraps of evidence to advance SARS's investigation.

On the face of it, Masters International Tobacco Manufacturing was a tobacco plant that relied on imported tobacco for local manufacturing and local consumption, as well as for exports. But facts that would later become public told another story. The numbers weren't adding up – more products were on the streets than could be accounted for by the declared export or manufacturing figures.

Masters International was owned by a company called Breco, which, in turn, was owned by Zimbabwean businessman John Bredenkamp.[3] Bredenkamp, whom the *Mail & Guardian* described as 'one of the most controversial and influential players in the South African arms deal', was no stranger to controversy.[4] The paper also stated that Bredenkamp had business relationships with individuals who were allegedly part of a contraband network that was being investigated by SARS and the Scorpions.

According to the article, the raid on Masters International Tobacco Manufacturing had been informed by earlier raids carried out by SARS on another company with Zimbabwean connections, Mavambo Coaches, a subsidiary of Pioneer Corporation Africa, a listed entity on the Zimbabwe Stock Exchange.

In 2008 the Scorpions and the NPA came to SARS to ask for our help. We actioned our units immediately. Tall Pete and the NEU needed as much evidence as possible to conclude their case against the tobacco manufacturer and immediately started an in-depth investigation. In anticipation of what was coming, Masters International placed itself in voluntary liquidation to prevent its directors and connected persons from being held personally liable for the actions of the company.

By this time, the unit (now the NRG) reported to me. I instructed them to see what they could do to assist Tall Pete and the NEU. We needed critical evidence that would seal SARS's case. In the meantime, Tall Pete and his team went to court and challenged the voluntary-liquidation process.

Members of the NRG hit the streets. They spoke to people in the tobacco industry – importers, transporters, employees in companies, but to no avail. Ato,[5] who had a background in law, was the legal mind in the unit. He was a deep thinker, a man who always remained calm under pressure and could be seen stroking his goatee when thinking. The rule in the unit was, when in doubt about something, don't do it. Ato fiercely enforced this rule and the 'Rules of Play' guidelines.

Frustratingly, weeks of hard work by the NRG turned up nothing.

They did, however, manage to scrounge some publicly available information and, piece by piece, put together a link chart depicting how the process at the Johannesburg factory of Masters International Tobacco Manufacturing worked, how tobacco was probably smuggled, how people were connected, and so on. This information was handed to Tall Pete, who fed it into his teams as the NEU continued to build its own case.

Then, one day, Pitsa and Johnny decided to speak to the security officials who guarded the gates at the factory. Identifying themselves as SARS officials, they asked the guards whether they were aware of anything odd or suspicious going on at the factory.

'No, nothing,' came the response. However, one guard mumbled something about a foreign-registered vehicle that visited the factory occasionally.

'Really?' Pitsa asked, going with a hunch. 'Tell us more – do you perhaps have the details of this car?'

They did, because they had to record the registration details of every vehicle that entered the premises. So the NRG managed to identify a sedan with a Botswanan[6] registration. This information was quickly followed up within SARS and we managed to get a profile, including information from customs border control, of the number of times this vehicle had entered and left South Africa, as well as the details of the driver, a foreign national.

We checked his details and found that he had consistently declared a particular address in downtown Johannesburg[7] as a destination whenever he entered South Africa. The next step was to determine who lived there. First, Pitsa and Johnny and, later, Gertjie and Simba took turns to wait outside the flat until someone arrived. Days and nights went by; they waited patiently.

Then, one evening, Johnny and Simba noticed that the lights in the flat were on. They knocked at the door. Seconds later an elderly gentleman opened the door and introduced himself as Mr Wong.[8]

He invited them in and, over a cup of green tea, Simba and Johnny got down to business. 'Sir, we are investigating a case at a tobacco factory, and we believe you may have visited the factory on occasion. Can you please tell us if this is so and, if so, why? What is your connection to this factory?'

Mr Wong took his time to respond and then said, 'Look, I don't know anything and don't want to say anything but ...' Patiently, according to Simba and Johnny, he took a sip of his tea, before he continued, 'If you were to go into the main building,' and then another sip, 'to the second floor,' sip ... 'to the last office to your right,' sip ... 'you will find a cabinet.' He lifted his cup again: 'Look in the top drawer of the cabinet. There will be lots of documents ...'

Mr Wong took the final sip before placing his teacup on the table before him. He looked straight at Simba. 'But look right towards the back. You will find a thin blue file. Everything you need is in that thin blue file.'

Simba and Johnny tried their level best to draw more from the man but Mr Wong had said what he was prepared to say and nothing more was forthcoming. So off they went into the night.

'Thin blue file? What does that mean?' Johnny wondered out loud as they drove to their homes in Pretoria. As was the norm, they drew up their update report that night and sent it to me. Johnny and Simba's report effectively set out the directions to find the thin blue file, as per Mr Wong's instructions. 'NFPK' – no further particulars known – the report stated.

I had a meeting with Tall Pete and conveyed the information to him. That very day, he and his team conducted an on-site inspection at the factory. Together with the proprietor, Tall Pete and a few of his trusted investigators went on site, all dressed in their yellow jackets. On the second floor, in the last office on the right, they found the cabinet and opened it. There, among several files and documents, right at the back of the drawer was a thin blue file.

Tall Pete opened the file. They had found what they were looking for – a neat, handwritten document recorded the evidence of how tobacco was smuggled into South Africa by the company. The NEU succeeded in its court application to reverse Masters International's self-liquidation and convinced the Master of the High Court to assign an independent liquidator to oversee the liquidation process. They were able to quantify and prove a claim against the estate of the tobacco manufacturer to the tune of R78 million. One crucial piece of evidence relied upon by the NEU during the court proceedings was a certain thin blue file ...

On 5 October 2010, *The Times* reported:

> The auction of 84 200 kg of raw tobacco leaves in Pomona, near Kempton Park, follows a liquidation order obtained in October 2008 against a company owned by [John] Bredenkamp. Aucor auctioneer Matthew Henderson sold the tobacco, which has been stored in a warehouse for the past two years, at R15 a kilogram ... the South African Revenue Service maintains it is owed by Bredenkamp. Henderson said he last year also auctioned off property and assets belonging to Masters International in Elandsfontein in Johannesburg to the value of about R4-million ... *The Times* has learnt that 480 tons of tobacco belonging to Bredenkamp's companies is being stored in three warehouses in and around Johannesburg ... 'Other normal liquidation processes will follow to recoup monies owed to SARS,' said an official.[9]

Again, the members of the NRG could have been called at any time to testify before the court in the matter. The fact that they were not was not of their doing. The evidence they managed to gather overtly for the NEU was seemingly sufficient to conclude the case.

In a project that spanned 2008 and 2009, the NRG made history in South African tax investigations. We had heard rumours of what people referred to as a 'phantom accounting system', also called zappers and phantom ware. This phenomenon was unheard of in South Africa at the time. The more formal term used to describe this kind of criminal financial-management software is a 'sales-suppression system'. The Organisation for Economic Cooperation and Development (OECD), in which South Africa has observer status, issued a guide on these systems in 2013.[10] On the surface, the technology seems like a supposedly normal accounting system, used mainly by retailers. It has all the expected features: it records stock, sales, invoices, receipts and taxes. It can print daily, weekly and monthly accounting records. Yet the software has a feature that can blank out certain sales and receipts. You can set it to suppress, for instance, every fourth sale, or random sales of a particular value, whichever you prefer.

The effect is that, on paper, your stock, sales and receipts would balance for tax purposes. All you would have to do is click on a secret place on the screen, or type a particular code on the keyboard, and the unrecorded sales and receipts would reflect. One would then be able to take this money out of the company's takings for the day, week or month, and people would be none the wiser.

By 2008, SARS was locked in a litigious battle with a large cash-and-carry business. Rumour had it that the company had such a sales-suppression system in place but since this type of fraud was unheard of at the time and not really understood, SARS didn't have much to go on.

The SARS audit of this business had reached the stage of a tax inquiry – a legal process conducted in camera. A tax inquiry is authorised by a high-court judge and the court appoints independent external counsel to serve as chairperson. SARS would sit on one side and pose questions that the taxpayer, subpoenaed to testify under oath, had to answer. Witnesses could also be called by either party.

While the inquiry continued, the NRG was called upon for assistance. Tony came up with the idea of scanning newspapers and the web to see if such phantom systems were being marketed somewhere. His logic was sound: someone had to be producing these systems and someone had to sell them, presumably by advertising them.

So, for months, Tony and the rest of the NRG team followed every single advertisement in all the mainstream newspapers that promoted accounting software and they identified similar offers on the Internet. We eliminated those we knew were reputable software companies. We reckoned that companies with well-known brands and reputations wouldn't involve themselves in such practices.

A number of players landed on Tony's list and the NRG went cold calling. One day in 2009 Tony and Josey[11] met with a guy in downtown Johannesburg.[12] Josey, soft-spoken and unassuming, hailed from the former Scorpions. They asked him the question they had been asking the other companies: are you aware of such systems and, if so, where can they be found?

'Yes,' he said, 'I know these systems.' He continued, 'I've bought a package like this myself, and have sold a few. It's not illegal is it?'

Tony and Josey recorded the entire conversation. 'So, who did you sell this to?' asked Josey.

Lo and behold, one of the buyers happened to be the very same cash-and-carry retailer that was the subject of the SARS audit. So, back we went to the auditors and gave them the evidence. The man whom Tony and Josey had interviewed testified at the inquiry. The cash-and-carry retailer's game was up.

The NRG made history with this operation not only because it was the first of its kind in South African tax investigations, but also because it enabled SARS to provide the operation as a case study in an OECD report entitled *Electronic Sales Suppression: A Threat to Tax Revenues*.[13] OECD member countries across the world now use this guide as part of their training and manuals for tax audits where such systems are believed to be prevalent.

9

Of brothels and dossiers

In 2007 an event took place that I was made aware of only much later but which would have significant consequences and reverberate into 2014 when the *Sunday Times* first starting writing about the 'rogue unit'. The circumstances gave rise to the *Sunday Times* 9 November 2014 headline, 'Taxman's rogue unit ran brothel'.[1] Next to the headline was a large photo of me. That was the day I had to rush out to calm the wife of unit member Johnny.

Stoffel,[2] a former policeman and member of the Scorpions, was part of the original SPU and later the NRG. He was based in Durban. Our paths had crossed many years before when he and his police colleagues had severely manhandled me while I was an undercover police agent. It was known that I had been associating with criminals, but none of the police officers were aware that I was an undercover agent. Stoffel and his colleagues were investigating a case and wrongly regarded me as a suspect because the crime had been committed in the residential complex where I lived.

When I met Stoffel again in 2007 my appearance had changed so much that he didn't recognise me immediately. It was only some months later that he recognised who I was. Stoffel was a difficult fellow, in my view, and hardly ever allowed anybody to complete a conversation. He left the NRG in early 2010 to join the local SARS investigations office.

But back in 2007, Stoffel decided one evening to have his colleagues from the unit over for a braai. They were in town on business and staying at a hotel. He took them to a house in the northern suburbs of Durban. Johnny later told me what happened that night.[3] 'We get to this house … It was right on the beach, a perfect venue for a braai. I think it was Tony, Gertjie, Dippie, Josey, Michael Peega and me who were there, together with Stoffel.'

I asked Johnny to describe the venue. 'It was a fancy house, but sparsely furnished,' Johnny said, adding, 'Immediately after we got there, the hair on the back of my neck stood up.'

'Why?' I asked.

'Because … there were television sets – all showing porn movies. I remember Tony saying to Gertjie and me that we better get the hell out of there. "This feels like a setup; our wives are not going to like this," he said.'

But, according to Johnny, Stoffel told the guys, in his usual abrasive manner, to hang on, and that 'the meat was almost ready'.

The next moment, Johnny discovered that the front door was locked.

'JvL, we couldn't get out of the house. It was so embarrassing. Tony, Gertjie, Josey and I stuck to each other like little girls. I wanted to go to the bathroom and even asked Gertjie to come with me to avoid any situation where we would be alone in that house. So there we stood, in the bathroom, side by side, doing our thing. It was extremely uncomfortable.

'Minutes later, I'm standing in the bar area and suddenly a woman, topless, appears and walks up to me. She asks me in a thick foreign accent, "So, do you think I'm prrretty?"'

It was Tony who took the lead and spoke up: 'Stoffel, open this door! I want to go,' he commanded. 'This is crap.'

Stoffel obliged and, according to both Tony and Johnny, they, together with Gertjie and Josey were out of the house in a flash and on their way back to their hotel. But it seems that Dippie and Peega remained and eventually ended up 'entertaining' the female companions present. The story gets slightly murky here, but it would seem that one of them, or perhaps both, took some of the women to their hotel room for further 'entertainment'.

However, this stage of the 'entertainment' came at a cost and the men had to pay for it. One version of events has it that no payment was made; another version has it that they did pay, but that the money was taken out of the wallets belonging to the woman or women later that night.

The entire team returned to Gauteng the next day, while the women apparently complained to Stoffel, insisting that he pay them. Stoffel then called Dippie or Peega – or both – and demanded that they pay the money owed.

None of this ever came out at the time. However, later, when the stories started featuring in the media, and the *Sunday Times* used this incident as the basis to run its report about the 'rogue-unit' brothel, it became imperative for me to find out the origins of these rumours.

Early in 2015, during a telephone discussion soon after I had left SARS, I asked Jonas Makwakwa, then the newly appointed SARS chief operating officer, why they weren't doing anything about the brothel claims and why they were allowing the stories to stay in the public domain. Makwakwa was a member of the so-called SARS Kroon board, tasked to look into these allegations. 'You know these guys never ran a brothel. You know it's nonsense. This story is harming SARS's reputation, Jonas,' I told him.

Makwakwa answered with a giggle, 'No, there was a brothel. It was a mobile brothel.'

Mobile brothel – I still do not know what he meant by this. One thing, however, was clear by then: SARS wasn't going to do anything to dispel these allegations or even attempt to establish the true facts surrounding the *Sunday Times* articles. To me, this was a clear indication that it suited certain individuals that the public believed this lie.

After I had left SARS, Stoffel called to tell me that Makwakwa and Moyane had flown to Durban to meet with him. My response to him was that he had better put things right with everybody affected and clarify in writing to Moyane what the true origin of the brothel story was.

Stoffel did write a letter, even if half-heartedly. He sent me a copy, which I have kept. In it he basically refutes the allegation of a brothel and bemoans how it had affected his family and reputation. I would have expected him to say more but, for some reason, he didn't.

A second set of events involving Peega, which I believe really pushed the 'rogue unit' narrative, started in 2008. On 25 December, while on leave, Peega was travelling, together with another person, to Modimolle, north of Pretoria. The police and South African National Parks (SANParks) personnel were conducting a routine roadblock, when they were stopped. Both men jumped out of the car and ran off. Peega ended up being arrested.[4]

When the police searched the vehicle, a .303 hunting rifle and other poaching paraphernalia were discovered, including a French Special Forces jacket that belonged to Peega. The jacket was covered in blood, which turned out to be that of a rhino that had been poached earlier, its horn brutally chopped off. At first, Peega claimed to be working undercover for SANParks, but the SANParks authorities who were present readily dismissed this.[5]

Peega then made a confession in his mother tongue to the police investigating officer through another police officer who acted as his interpreter. Peega admitted having been recruited by a rhino-poaching syndicate, identified the syndicate members and said that he had been paid R10 000 as recruitment fee to participate in scoping out poaching sites and, going on poaching hunts; he also admitted having shot at a baby rhino. He took the police to several of these sites, pointed out where they had hidden in wait of rhino, and revealed the location of an AK-47 rifle and ammunition, and so forth.[6]

He was promptly arrested and held in the local police cells pending his appearance before a court. Not once did he contact anybody at SARS to notify us of his predicament.

In January 2009 Peega was due to attend a meeting of the NRG. His absence was reported to me, as he was meant to have been back from leave by then. I became worried and sent guys to his home and to visit his friends to find out what had happened. Later we contacted the police and the mortuaries.

In response to our enquiries, I received a phone call from a police officer, informing me of the events that had led to Peega's arrest. SARS then instituted disciplinary charges against Peega and he was dismissed by a disciplinary panel, with an outside counsel as chairperson. He appealed against the dismissal, which was also heard by an outside counsel, but the appeal failed.

Witnesses during his hearing included police officers who had arrested him, several of his NRG colleagues, and colleagues from SARS's ACAS division. During these formal proceedings the NRG's mandate was openly presented and formed part of the records released by SARS in 2010.[7] The NRG and its work were openly discussed during the proceedings.

This is an important point because, later, the *Sunday Times* maintained that the SPU/NRG, the so-called 'rogue unit', operated covertly and secretly.

Some time went by, then Peega struck back. From the end of 2009 towards early 2010 he released a dossier to the media and various politicians, including firebrand politician Julius Malema, then the president of the ANC Youth League. The 'Peega dossier', as it became known, was titled 'Project Broken Arrow' and made all kinds of outlandish claims.

In it Peega alleged that the SPU/NRG had 'spied on politicians' and conspired to 'overthrow government'. Peega claimed that 'Post-Polokwane we [as in the SPU] were given projects and subjects named as tax offenders but on close inspection we realised that the concerned targets were JZ sympathisers'.[8]

According to the *Mail & Guardian*, Peega listed in his dossier the individuals he claimed had been targeted, but nowhere in his supporting documents is any evidence presented to support these claims. 'Minutes of National Research Group meetings refer only to six projects, none apparently linked to the Zuma sympathisers he names,' the article states.[9]

Probably the most ludicrous allegation was that the unit had been conducting so-called lifestyle audits on certain people, including politicians Fikile Mbalula, Tokyo Sexwale, Zizi Kodwa and Malema. I can assure you, not a single member of the SPU/NRG was suitably skilled or equipped, or capable of conducting an in-depth tax audit. The unit never conducted such audits and none of the people mentioned by Peega had, to my knowledge, ever been subjected to such audits.

The nature of a lifestyle audit is that it requires significant interaction between the SARS auditor and the taxpayer. If any of these individuals were subjected to such audits they definitely would have known about it. But Peega wanted things both ways – on the one hand, he claimed the unit was covert and unknown, and, on the other, that its members openly conducted 'lifestyle audits' – an impossibility for a secret unit.

Late in 2009 a newspaper approached SARS with a copy of Peega's 'dossier' asking for comment. SARS compiled a line-by-line refutation of each and every allegation in this dossier. Attached to the line-by-line refutation were annexures, including the original memoranda setting out the mandate, structure and workflows of the SPU/NRG. In February 2010 SARS then formally released certain facts about Peega, refuting the allegations he had been advancing to journalists and politicians.

We knew this was coming because, before his dismissal, Peega had threatened to publicly release all the names of his colleagues who worked on high-risk investigations. It later bcame public knowledge that we were tipped off that Peega was colluding with people within and outside of SARS, seeking to 'recruit' more people to assist him in what he then referred to as 'Project Broken Arrow' (his later 'dossier' was called Operation Snowman). Two people, independently of each other, reported this to SARS and provided written reports stating the facts to their knowledge.

In the end, we had this big file, which SARS used from then on to brief anyone who came knocking on our door with Peega's 'dossier'. In the months that followed, we briefed Members of Parliament, politicians, journalists and editors. I recall speaking to journalists at *Beeld*, the *Mail & Guardian*, *The Sunday Independent*, *City Press* and, yes, the *Sunday Times*.

In February 2010, Adrian, as SARS spokesperson, and another SARS colleague and I went to the offices of the *Sunday Times* in Johannesburg. We were met by Phylicia Oppelt, then editor of daily newspaper *The Times*, who would later become editor of the *Sunday Times*, and gave them the same briefing.

Quite amazingly, as part of developing the 'rogue-unit' narrative, the *Sunday Times* published a report on 12 October 2014 stating that 'not all of Peega's claims were far-fetched'.[10] Even more astounding is the fact that the *Sunday Times* acknowledged in the same article that they knew of, and had in their possession, the document issued by SARS refuting Peega's claims, but their report reflected nothing of its contents.[11]

In 2015 the media shed more light on Project Broken Arrow/Operation Snowman when *Beeld* reported that

> Pravin Gordhan [then Minister of Cooperative Governance and Traditional Affairs] was the target of a secret misinformation campaign aimed at bringing him into discredit with President Jacob Zuma as well as destabilising the taxman ... the bitter fruits of this campaign, already six years under way, are clear from the past few months' chaos at the South African Revenue Service (SARS). Project Broken Arrow, an 'organised effort' by ousted SARS employees, involved the spreading of rumours of a 'covert and surreptitious investigation unit' within SARS, documents seen by *Beeld* show.

According to the *Beeld* report, Project Broken Arrow's goal was to 'destabilise and disorganise' SARS, and to eventually 'create chaos to target the reputations and stability' of certain officials. 'The so-called Peega file, which flowed from Broken Arrow, set out to "prove" that a "covert investigation unit" within SARS would have supposedly spied on former Zuma loyalists, like Julius Malema and Fikile Mbalula. Mike Peega and the late

Leonard Radebe, the dissatisfied and discarded SARS employees, were fingered in a confidential 2009 report as the alleged conspirators,' *Beeld* reported.[12]

A number of disgruntled former SARS employees, some of whom had been part of the NRG, were identified as having set up this dossier to discredit their ex-colleagues. The dossier was meant for the eyes of Zuma and former police boss Bheki Cele. According to a report in *The Citizen*, the former SARS staff members aligned to Broken Arrow were 'very dissatisfied' with the appointment of Gordhan as Minister of Finance, and Broken Arrow was managed as a secret project with a budget, a 'safe house', borrowed cars and equipment. Further reports confirmed this.[13] In January 2016, *The Citizen* reported on the conspiracy as follows:

> A 2009 plot detailing how to 'expose' and 'take care of' then South African Revenue Service (Sars) boss Pravin Gordhan, former deputy commissioner Ivan Pillay, former group executive Johan [*sic*] van Loggerenberg, and 'a host of other significant individuals' in Sars' National Research Group (NRG) appears to be in full flow.
>
> Project Broken Arrow names President Jacob Zuma as the 'Old Man' who was to receive a report of the NRG – which has been accused of being a 'rogue unit' in some media – for perusal. The report would be handed to Zuma by former Sars head of customs, Leonard Radebe, who quit in 2008 before he could face a disciplinary inquiry for possibly issuing a false settlement agreement in the Dave King saga ...[14]

In his dossier, Peega mentioned every single member of the NRG by name, and in one stroke placed all his former colleagues in harm's way. Management at SARS were unanimous in their decision that the NRG personnel had to be protected. As a result, most of the officials were placed in various other enforcement units in SARS in early 2010.

Only seven remained in the unit – which was then renamed the High-Risk Investigations Unit – and from this point onwards they all telecommuted. Most of the larger projects were brought to a close and we had to start afresh. With this small complement of staff, we were simply unable to conduct projects of the same scale and magnitude as before. In 2011 the HRIU lost Simba to another government department and that left the unit further depleted.

During this time SARS cooperated with the NIA in their investigation into Peega's allegations. We provided them with everything they asked for but never received any formal feedback on the progress or the eventual outcome of the investigation. We also engaged the police, asking them to investigate the matter too, but year after year our formal requests for feedback were unanswered.[15]

Since the matter of the late Leonard Radebe would be used by the *Sunday Times* as a basis to prove the existence of the 'rogue unit' and because Radebe worked with Peega, his story warrants mentioning. In 2010 Eyewitness News reported that

> the man allegedly spying for the ANC Youth League [Peega] could be receiving help from other former South African Revenue Service (Sars) employees with an axe to grind against the organisation ...
>
> It is understood Peega may not be working alone in drawing up dossiers on the Youth League's enemies. Two allies, Leonard Radebe and Kenneth Fitoyi[16] are also allegedly part of his operation. The three all worked at Sars but left under a cloud. Now it appears they are using their political contacts in the League to pursue their agenda against Sars.[17]

Radebe had been General Manager: Customs before he resigned from SARS in the wake of a sequence of events that concerned Dave King, the multibillionaire businessman who was embroiled in one of the longest legal battles with SARS. In 2008 King's counsel made representations to the High Court that he had entered into a tax settlement with SARS but didn't wish to disclose the details.

At that time, SARS and the NPA had held a worldwide preservation order over all of King's assets, associated entities, family trusts and the like. Legally, something like this had never been achieved before in South Africa. It meant that even funds held offshore in suspected tax havens were frozen by the state. If there was a settlement with SARS for a multimillion-rand tax debt, it would have enabled King to have these funds released. The legal team representing SARS and the state on this matter had no knowledge of the alleged settlement and this was questioned publicly. My role in this affair was limited but it is a matter of public record, as set out in an affidavit that was submitted to the police.

By pure coincidence, one Sunday, Oupa Magashula, then SARS head of Corporate Services, went to a well-known restaurant in Muldersdrift. The manager of the Casalinga Ristorante Italiano expressed his satisfaction that so many senior SARS officials visited his establishment.

Magashula asked the natural question, 'Who else was here?'

Quite innocuously, the manager explained how Radebe and King had been meeting there some time before. By that time, the litigation between SARS, King and other state institutions was the biggest, most protracted, costliest and possibly the most legally complex tax dispute in South Africa's democratic history.

Magashula immediately reported this information to Gordhan, the commissioner, and to the SARS executive. If the restaurant manager's story was true, it would have meant a major breach in Radebe's professional conduct. Radebe was a SARS executive member at the time and was heading customs operations. He had no interest in the King matter whatsoever or the processes of litigation that had been before various courts for close to a decade. It was highly irregular for a SARS official, let alone a senior manager, to meet alone with a taxpayer, particularly one involved in a legal case.

I went to the restaurant, together with Magashula, and interviewed the manager. I brought with me photos of the general managers, with their names concealed. I asked the manager to identify Radebe, which he was able to do without hesitation.

Together with the head of the SARS Anti-Corruption Security Division, Clifford Collings, I interviewed Radebe. At first, he denied ever having met with King. He then proceeded to do so under oath by way of an affidavit. I then put it to him that a witness had seen him at the restaurant, together with King, on a specific date.

At that point Radebe acknowledged that he had lied. As the *Mail & Guardian* reported in November 2008,

> Radebe quit the revenue service ahead of pending disciplinary action last month after it emerged that he had a meeting with King at a Johannesburg restaurant. Radebe was questioned about the meeting and provided an affidavit outlining his version of events. This formed the basis for the internal investigation at Sars. 'I resigned because I wanted to protect the reputation of Sars and because it was the honourable thing to do,' Radebe told the *M&G*.[18]

The criminal case against Radebe never progressed beyond that stage, for reasons unknown to me. The *Sunday Times* would later report, as fact, that the 'rogue unit had spied on Radebe' and was 'deployed to destroy his career' and had 'used CCTV' to do so.[19]

If the *Sunday Times* had bothered to conduct elementary research, such as reading news articles from around that time, or had bothered to access the police docket or the affidavits contained therein, it would have been able to determine the true facts. The paper's 'investigative journalists' clearly didn't care to reflect on any of these facts at all.

As for Peega, this wasn't the last we heard of him. He would feature a year or two down the line, this time as a 'secret agent' for the tobacco industry.

And in 2015 he managed to dupe the producers of current affairs TV programme *Carte Blanche*, who filmed him during a documentary claiming
that SARS had instructed him to infiltrate a rhino-poaching syndicate
and that he had therefore been wrongfully arrested.

10

To catch a crime boss – Krejcir

SARS had a long-standing case against colourful and outspoken strip club owner Lolly Jackson. I was one of the initial SARS employees involved in investigating this case. In his biography, *Stripped: The King of Teaze*, Jackson devotes an entire chapter to lament what a hassle SARS had become to his growing empire of strip clubs, called Teazers.[1] At the time he had hoped the SARS investigation would just go away.

Over the years, Jackson got to know me quite well and, needless to say, he did not like me at all and even said so publicly whenever presented with an opportunity. SARS did not go away, though. Instead, Jackson's tax troubles got worse. In 2010 he was murdered at a house in Kempton Park, on the East Rand, but the SARS investigation continued.[2]

After various court actions, mainly overseen by Tall Pete and the NEU, it was eventually revealed in court in 2013 that Jackson owed SARS in excess of R100 million in unpaid taxes. His case came to a very dramatic conclusion when SARS was granted a final order against his estate that year. SARS had by then taken judgments and was in the process of pre-serving some of the strip clubs and other assets, and selling them off in lieu of the debt. So, quite ironically, in this sense SARS 'owned' a strip club or two, albeit through a court-appointed curator.

A news report at the time quoted Adrian, as SARS spokesperson, saying that the court had given the revenue service the right to start valuing Jackson's assets: 'The estate owes us more than R100 million in outstanding taxes and these tax debts are made up of a number of companies, some of which are still operational, who over the years have built up substantial tax debts individually.'[3]

The same article mentions that a company owned by Czech fugitive and businessman Radovan Krejcir in June 2012 reportedly claimed close to R9 million from Jackson's estate. As would become publicly known only in 2013, by that time we had been investigating Krejcir for nearly three years.

Krejcir, a Czech national, was pursued by the law-enforcement authorities in his home country for money laundering. In June 2005, following a raid at his mansion in Cernosice, near Prague, he was arrested for conspiracy to murder a customs official, fraud and a host of other alleged crimes. During the bust, he asked to use the bathroom, jumped out of a small window and disappeared.

In September 2005, Interpol issued an international warrant for his arrest. But Krejcir was gone. He popped up again in the Seychelles but he would soon head for other shores. In April 2007 he arrived in South Africa with a fictitious passport under the name of Egbert Jules Savy.

Despite his new ID, he was arrested the moment he arrived in South Africa. The South African authorities wanted to extradite Krejcir, but he managed to avoid it on various legal technicalities. Soon he began to play a role in organised crime. A *Mail & Guardian* report from 2013 gives a chilling description of how 'the bodies around Krejcir keep piling up'.[4] More than seven gruesome murders were directly tied to him. It was quite clear that he operated with absolute impunity in our country, had done so for a number of years and nothing seemed to be happening in the general law-enforcement environment to stop him.

Tall Pete and the NEU started investigating Krejcir in 2010 but shortly after this he was tasked to head up a new unit and my office manager Paulina[5] took over the NEU. I had always considered Paulina, who was an excellent manager, to be my successor.

For major projects, I would set up a meeting in my office with the investigators and then put down what we already knew, drawing up our plans on a whiteboard. In this way, we could establish the gaps in our information and do scenario planning. My team members used to call our sketched plans 'JvL drawings'.

In 2010 we developed a JvL drawing about Krejcir. It was evident that there were many gaps. We didn't know this man at all. Our first stop was to ask law-enforcement agencies, both locally and abroad, to help us fill those gaps, but they weren't of much use, so I asked permission for Paulina, Tall Pete and some other investigators to go to Europe to glean first-hand information about Krejcir from the authorities there. This was the first time in the history of SARS that investigators had travelled to Europe for an investigation of this nature.

They came back with a veritable treasure trove of information, which helped us to complete one part of the JvL drawing on my whiteboard and contributed greatly to our asset-freezing order that was to follow. The units under me began to engage all the third parties we had managed to identify and in the years that followed we slowly completed the rest of the JvL drawing.

Throughout 2011 the NEU investigators relentlessly worked on their case against Krejcir. We used every tool available in legislation to get to the bottom of his activities. The men and women often worked on the case until late at night. Unfortunately, for legal reasons, I cannot elaborate much on the detail but, as would become publicly known later, we also conducted an in-depth tax inquiry against Krejcir that year. Tax inquiries are similar to those used in liquidation cases where subjects of investigation can be called upon to testify in camera.

Around this point there were some management changes. In 2012 Ivan appointed Godfrey Baloyi as the new head of the unit, replacing me. Baloyi reported to the Chief Officer for Tax and Customs Enforcement

Investigations, Gene Ravele.[6] Addressing over 300 SARS managers and several private guests at the annual SARS National Management Forum that year, Ravele spoke about the HRIU. Aware of the effect that the Peega dossier had had on SARS employees, Ravele explained to the forum exactly what the mandate of the unit was, that it consisted of a mere six people, that it wasn't 'covert' and didn't 'spy on taxpayers or SARS officials', to use his words.

He asked if anybody had any questions. There were none forthcoming. To this day, I am baffled as to why not a single one of those 300 senior managers who listened to that address stood up and spoke out when Moyane joined SARS as the new commissioner and began to suspend a number of people on the basis of unfounded news reports about a 'rogue-unit'. Why didn't anyone say, 'Wait a minute – these stories in the news can't be true, we all knew about this unit'?

Towards the end of that year, reporting to Ravele, I was back to managing five units, including the HRIU and the NEU, now named National Projects.[7] I had a lot on my plate, so during 2012 Guillam[8] took over the day-to-day running of the HRIU. I could no longer meaningfully manage and oversee all the units and projects, 80 of which could be running at any point in time.

If I had to assign a percentage to the amount of effort and time I spent managing each of the units that reported to me, I would say that the HRIU took up only about 5% of my time on average, if that much. I find it ironic that such a small unit, and one that took up so little of my time, would eventually be the cause of all the upheaval.

Guillam, a former soldier, an officer and a true gentleman, was as close to the Peter Guillam character in John le Carré's novels as you will ever get. Once, in the midst of the chaos around the 'rogue unit' late in 2014, he remarked, like a character straight out of a Le Carré espionage novel, 'Johnno,' (as he called me), 'unfortunately, it is the weak who destroy the strong.'

Guillam first caught my attention when I read some of his reports on behalf of SARS, for the Financial Intelligence Centre and the international body the Financial Action Task Force (FATF). They were exceptionally well written and well researched.

The FATF is an independent intergovernmental body that develops and promotes policies to protect the global financial system against money laundering, terrorist financing and the financing of weapons of mass destruction. The FATF recommendations are recognised as the global anti-money-laundering and counter-terrorist financing standards, and South Africa is a member state. Guillam was also the coordinator of the FATF typology study on the illicit tobacco trade,[9] which is now used worldwide by many financial intelligence centres and revenue administrations.

Guillam brought even stricter controls into play for the HRIU, including daily meetings, new reporting templates and weekly reports with greater detail. Nothing happened until he okayed it. I felt comfortable with him in charge.

However, I believe the investigations that were to follow from this point onwards, and the matters uncovered by the HRIU during this time, often in conjunction with the other units under me, ultimately led us straight into the eye of the storm …

After I was reappointed as manager of the HRIU, the unit was tasked to get whatever information it could on Krejcir to assist the National Projects Unit.

The HRIU immediately began to mine any data and information publicly available on Krejcir. As would later be revealed publicly, the first real breakthrough for the HRIU came when Tony and Gertjie managed to identify a Facebook profile used by Krejcir under the name Russel Knight. Most likely this was used to communicate anonymously with his associates. The Facebook profile led them to a number of links to various people we didn't know anything about.

The HRIU built profiles of these people with whatever public information was available. Then the unit hit the streets and began to knock on doors again. At the same time, they started doing daily and nightly drive-bys at various addresses we had identified. Whenever a car was spotted or people identified, this would be recorded and followed up. All the time the link chart and JvL drawing would be updated with new facts at our disposal.

With only a handful of people in the unit, they had to work day and night to identify individuals and find leads. A good example of how the HRIU helped other SARS units and the Hawks was in 2011 when SARS confiscated a Lamborghini and a Ferrari belonging to Krejcir. Thanks to the HRIU team, who drove by Krejcir's house and businesses repeatedly, and attended every court case he appeared in, SARS could zoom in on these vehicles. We had found that when these cars were imported into South Africa, their value had been under-declared, so a lower import duty had been paid to SARS than was due.

It wasn't long before the unit managed to get in contact with someone who was prepared to talk to us about Krejcir. This person pointed them to another individual, whom I'll call Dumisane,[10] who provided us with some specifics that I was able to verify thanks to the investigations of the National Projects Unit.

Dumisane also proved exceptionally helpful when he identified how stolen and laundered gold was purchased and mixed with legitimate molten gold as part of an entirely different scam at an illegal gold-smelting plant operating in a house in Midrand.[11] This scam was also linked to Krejcir, in that he was allegedly a beneficiary of the profits of the scam.

The HRIU drove past the house regularly and whenever a vehicle was parked outside, they would follow up its registration details. Soon enough, they managed to find links between people they had identified. One day Johnny and Hector spotted a 'for sale' and 'to let' sign outside the house.

Inside, the two team members met an estate agent, who offered to show them around. They found a door leading to the garage, where they noticed various gas bottles and other equipment. Hector took photos of the equipment on his cellphone.

Back in Pretoria, their first stop was to meet an expert in gold smelting, who confirmed that what they had found was a makeshift gold-smelting plant complete with the dies and forms, and smelting and mixing equipment. The very same day I assigned the matter to the Tactical Intervention Unit, and asked them to conduct an inspection at the premises. All the equipment was seized and the plant shut down.

A second breakthrough came soon afterwards when the HRIU guys picked up that there was a person awaiting trial in a Pretoria correctional services facility,[12] who we were told had made certain allegations regarding Krejcir to the media, who had then reported on it. Guillam made arrangements to see him. (It's worth noting that when Guillam and another official visited this man in jail, they signed in to the visitors' book in their capacity as SARS officials: no one can possibly claim this was covert work.)

They obtained an affidavit from the man, which set out facts that incriminated Krejcir, facts that I later included in my affidavit. This affidavit was to become material in directing some of the investigations of the National Projects Unit and allowed us to successfully apply for a preservation order of all assets connected to Krejcir.

But the investigation wasn't over yet. Not long afterwards, Guillam and the HRIU managed to identify an entirely different witness, thanks to Dumisane. The unit began to engage this witness and got information about another, entirely different set of criminal activities related to Krejcir. Slowly but surely, they put together a bigger, more connected picture of his operations, which included a complicated VAT fraud scam.

One day in early 2013, a SARS criminal investigator who had been assigned to this fraud case, who didn't work in my division, came to see me. He explained that he was struggling to persuade the witness to agree to testify in their case. The investigator was aware that the witness was also speaking to the HRIU and asked whether I could perhaps help.

I agreed and asked Johnny to speak to the man about why he was reluctant to testify in the VAT fraud case. As it turns out, for some reason, he didn't trust the SARS investigator. Johnny was able to put his mind at ease and I was able to inform the SARS investigator that the witness would testify.

The outcome of these investigations became public in a dramatic fashion in late 2013 when SARS seized all assets associated with Krejcir. As published in the *Mail & Guardian*, a court order placed all of Krejcir's assets, as well as those of his family and associates, under the control of a curator. Effectively, the court granted SARS the means to seize control of all of Krejcir's known assets and any others that we were able to link to him – thanks to the link chart and the JvL drawing we had built up over time. All in all, 15 businesses, including the infamous Money Point shop in Bedfordview, were linked to Krejcir and his wife and son.

Money Point made the headlines in November 2013 when it was bombed and two people died.[13] It was owned by another company, called Crosspoint, which was involved in gold trading and money lending. We had found that a substantial flow of funds had been exchanged through the Crosspoint bank account, although it had submitted an income tax return for 2010 reflecting an assessed loss of only R169 563. The income tax returns for 2011 and 2012 were still outstanding.

We also found that Krejcir had paid over R3.7 million to a man named George Smith, also known as George Louca. This was the man Krejcir claimed to have met in prison when he was first arrested on entry into South Africa in April 2007. Louca was implicated in the murder of Lolly Jackson, after which he fled to Cyprus. He was extradited to South Africa and implicated Krejcir in Jackson's murder during his testimony in the case in 2015.[14] By then, Louca was terminally ill with cancer and died shortly afterwards.[15]

We also discovered that the infamous Glenn Agliotti had 'borrowed' R500 000 from Krejcir to pay his legal fees. If that weren't enough, we also found multiple instances where law-enforcement officers had been paid by Krejcir, ostensibly in the form of loans or gifts. By the time we moved against Krejcir's assets, there were four separate cases in the Czech

Republic for which Krejcir was sought to stand trial.[16]

Although he initially indicated his intention to oppose our asset seizure, by 2015 Krejcir had thrown in the towel, which meant that SARS was able to sell off the assets in lieu of his tax debts. His sumptuous mansion in Bedfordview was eventually sold at auction by SARS. So, in a strange way, even though most of us had left SARS by that time, we had still contributed towards SARS's revenue take for that year.[17]

I am convinced that the actions pursued by SARS also spurred on the other law-enforcement agencies to deal with Krejcir. First, my affidavit, presented in court by the NPA, brought many facts out into the open and the momentum we created helped other authorities to act. Secondly, we also made life very difficult for Krejcir because we had managed to cut off his access to his virtually unlimited sources of cash.

Shortly after the SARS asset freeze, the Hawks and the NPA swooped on Krejcir in November 2013 and he was arrested for the first in a series of offences, including kidnapping and attempted murder, for which he would later be convicted. An able NPA prosecutor, Advocate Lethabo Mashiane, was in charge of the first criminal trial against him. Among other things, Mashiane relied on my affidavit, which was submitted as part of the SARS asset preservation order.

Krejcir applied for bail the minute he was arrested but Magistrate Reginald Dama denied bail, citing Krejcir's history of falsifying passports, committing fraud, absconding from prison and fleeing his country of birth as reasons.[18]

I want to pause here to reflect on the impact that investigations, such as those SARS conducted into Krejcir, had on the HRIU and other units involved. The men and women who were part of these units dealt with organised crime and sophisticated criminals, who were generally dangerous people. At night, while most of us were asleep, or during the day when we were going about our normal business, they worked tirelessly to combat crime. All the while their lives were in danger. No case proves this better than this one.

This is why I find it totally irresponsible that the *Sunday Times* and the panels that SARS instituted to investigate the so-called rogue unit named these officials and published their details. If any harm were ever to come to any of these officials or their families, how would we know that it weren't as a result of their identities being revealed to the people they investigated?

At the time, little was known of what happened behind the scenes during our investigations. But, since then, researcher Simone Haysom of the University of Cape Town's Centre of Criminology has researched and written about the contributions of the HRIU to the Krejcir case as part of her studies into South Africa's underworld. In an article published in April 2016, 'Sars, Krejcir and the destruction of state capacity', she wrote:

> On 22 February this year, Krejcir – now representing himself – stood before Judge Colin Lamont for sentencing ... The next day he gave Krejcir 35 years ...
>
> Lamont had convicted Krejcir despite – not because of – the Hawks investigation, whose policemen he lambasted for torturing their suspects and for lying under oath. Yet those policemen continue to have careers in the SAPS, while Sars's NRG [National Research Group] has been all but eviscerated.
>
> Since December 2014, when the *Sunday Times* broke allegations of the existence of a 'Rogue Unit' – more or less identified as the HRIU – supposedly using illegal methods for illegal ends, Sars has been purged of senior staff associated with the NRG ... Of the investigators in the HRIU, only three out of six remain in Sars, redeployed to other teams ...
>
> Sars cases that were on the books when the scandal broke are feared to be mothballed, or worse, settled for negligible amounts. They include audits or investigations of the Guptas, Julius Malema, alleged underworld figure Mark Lifman and various tobacco barons,

together with Zuma-linked matters such as those involving family friend Thoshan Panday, ANC donor Robert Huang, and Nkandla.

The NPA is severely compromised, and crime intelligence and the Hawks are consumed with factional battles – battles that are directly linked to criminal interests. With Sars's capacity decimated, there now exists no part of the State with the independence or skill to pursue serious organised and commercial crime cases. The bill for that damage can only grow ...[19]

When I read this, I thought I would cry.

11

Project Honey Badger

By 2013 tobacco smuggling had reached epidemic proportions. A host of small local manufacturers, wholesalers and importers had sprouted up across South Africa and they were raking in billions, while the state was not receiving the revenue it was due from excise, income tax, VAT and customs duties.

A study by the Department of Economics at Stellenbosch University found that trade in illicit cigarettes in South Africa at the time was 'between 40% and 50% of the total market, and that cigarette tax increases had, to a large extent, contributed to its continued existence and growth by creating a financial incentive to smuggle'.[1] In 2013 South Africa also became a co-signatory to the World Health Organization's Protocol to Eliminate Illicit Trade in Tobacco Products.[2]

By then, several of the units that reported to me, together with the SARS Large Business Centre and the customs and excise divisions, were involved in a range of separate investigations, audits and inspections, focusing on a number of role players in the tobacco industry. In an effort to bring some structure to these investigations and to emulate the success-ful impact we had had on the electronics industry in the early 2000s, we decided to group all our cases and projects under a single umbrella.

The project was called Honey Badger and was widely covered by the press. I believe this project played an important role in the eventual demise of the HRIU and the character assassination of key figures at SARS. The tobacco industry is a dirty business. If a case study were to be done on how business interests, organised crime and influence over state officials overlap, then this sector in our economy would be a prime example. I would soon discover exactly how unsavoury it really was.

In the second half of 2013, I spent hours studying our existing cases. Meanwhile, independently from our investigation, Pete Richer, then Group Executive: Risk Strategy and Planning, had assembled a team that consisted of various officials from across SARS who were analysing the numbers in the tobacco trade. They looked at data relating to volumes of imports and exports, breaking down the entire value chain. For example, they analysed the volumes of paper imported for manufacturing cigarettes and measured this data against production levels reported to SARS.

Richer's team also looked at VAT and income-tax ratios, and compared these with excise duties and exports declared to SARS. It was evident that none of the numbers added up. By then, the units under my management were involved in several cases involving players in the industry. For instance, the Tactical Intervention Unit had made significant detentions and seizures of smuggled tobacco, the National Projects Unit had over 20 cases going against numerous companies and individuals, and the HRIU was slowly putting together the connections and associations on a link chart that covered up three large office walls. We were beginning to understand the gamesmanship. And we were getting ready to strike.

Our first shot across the bows at the tobacco industry took the form of an open letter I compiled in November 2013 addressed to the two primary representative groups in the industry – the Tobacco Institute of Southern Africa (TISA), which represented the big multinational manufacturers and tobacco growers, and a smaller industry body, the Fair-Trade Independent Tobacco Association (FITA). Collectively, these two organisations represented about 90% of all tobacco manufacturers in South Africa. In the letter I explained that SARS would be asking the NPA to prosecute 15 local tobacco manufacturers and importers for tax evasion and smuggling.[3]

Those who were at risk for non-compliance were issued a warning of regular and random audits, and verification exercises by SARS. I warned that our investigations were not restricted to the smaller independent manufacturers and importers and that we were also probing concealed international transactions by some of the larger tobacco manufacturers, including listed companies. I stated that SARS would apply the most appropriate punitive measures in law to deal with serious offences, including the withdrawal or refusal to grant registrations and licences. SARS meant business, and we were clear in our warnings that we expected those in the industry to comply with tax laws.

A joint team comprising some of the most experienced customs and excise officials in my units, together with experts in the excise division, the audit division and the SARS Large Business Centre began to conduct inspections nationwide. At the same time, we took a closer look at the smaller players. They were 'small' in respect of what they declared to SARS, but big when it came to smuggling.

What we didn't realise at the time, and it only emerged later, was that we were up against interests and people with influence and power way beyond our imagination.

At this point we need to take a step back in time to 2010. Late that year the media reported that a multi-agency task team, called the Illicit-Tobacco Task Team (often referred to as the Tobacco Task Team and sometimes the Anti-Illicit Tobacco Task Team) had been formed to deal with the illegal trade in tobacco.[4] Strangely enough, SARS was not included as a permanent member on the team.

As I understand, the management team was made up of a senior Hawks official, who headed it, an official from the State Security Agency (SSA), who was later replaced by someone else from the same agency, an official from the police Crime Intelligence Division, Lieutenant Colonel

Hennie Niemann, an NPA prosecutor and a few members of the Financial Intelligence Centre, which is an organ of state.[5] In turn, this team had a number of informants who worked closely with primarily Niemann and the official from the SSA, and several lower ranking police officials who conducted criminal investigations for them. It would seem that, from time to time, this task team was also augmented by representatives from tobacco manufacturers and private investigators who worked on some matters.

Late in 2013, I wrote to the task team to express concerns I had about certain cases we were working on, in particular those where commercial interests of certain companies apparently overlapped with what the team seemed to have involved themselves with. I never received any meaningful reply and the relationship was strained from the beginning.

Why we were never invited to be part of the team is open to speculation. But my own view is that it is because we were not prepared to advance the agenda of certain industry groups over others. In March 2014, the amaBhungane Centre for Investigative Journalism reported that its investigation into the R5 billion a year illicit tobacco industry revealed how 'two major multinational companies used their considerable resources to influence South African state security agencies to protect their commercial interests'. According to the article,

> African conglomerate Lonrho was able to sidetrack a criminal investigation of its logistics subsidiary, Rollex, which in 2010 had been caught smuggling truckloads of illegal cigarettes across the border from Zimbabwe … In another case, the dominant South African cigarette producer, British American Tobacco (BAT), appears to have parlayed its support for law enforcement into preferential access to state security structures – and, with that, the alleged capacity to spy on its competitors. Both companies have denied any wrongdoing.[6]

That we were not included in the Illicit-Tobacco Task Team in 2010 should have been an early-warning signal. So much was at stake. Exactly how much was highlighted by amaBhungane's probe. According to their report,

> The big players, particularly BAT, have hit back by pursuing an aggressive campaign to support action against the traffickers, including by funding Tisa's favoured private investigations firm, Forensic Security Services (FSS), to the tune of about R50-million a year.
>
> That campaign includes a seat on the Illicit Tobacco Task Team, which includes representatives from BAT, the Hawks, crime intelligence, the SSA and the National Prosecuting Authority (NPA), but not Sars.[7]

The report states much of the focus is on the small players, 'who are blamed for most of the contraband activity. But, controversially, the structure gives BAT access to state intelligence and the ability to influence who the state targets among its direct competitors.'[8]

Another familiar name popped up again in the report: none other than Michael Peega. The amaBhungane report states that Peega was recruited in December 2011 by Forensic Security Services, which was providing investigative services to TISA. The report states:

> Peega emerged as one of a number of BAT agents paid in a roundabout way: direct deposits are made into untraceable foreign currency cards by BAT's global head office in London.
>
> The evidence may prove embarrassing for the cigarette giant, which appears to be running a private intelligence network in Southern Africa enjoying active support from the SSA and other law enforcement entities.
>
> Tisa is said to spend roughly R50-million a year on services provided by Forensic Security Services, though neither it nor BAT would confirm the figure. BAT and Forensic Security Services representatives,

through Tisa, also sit on the multi-agency Illicit Tobacco Task Team, where critics say they get to drive the law enforcement agenda.[9]

This news report is in line with an important output of the HRIU's tobacco industry investigation that uncovered an entire network of 'private spies' who were employed in the industry. At first, around November 2013, we were able to identify a few such spies, but soon afterwards we discovered many more fairly easily.

We found that these people were being paid off the books, so to speak. This meant that none of these spies declared the income they earned in this manner and neither did the companies that paid them. This alone amounted to money laundering and tax evasion. It also pointed to possible corruption-related offences, because they were being paid for information about competitors that wouldn't ordinarily be available publicly. All this was being done under the guise of 'private investigations'.

But there was more. The HRIU identified how investigators of a large tobacco manufacturer used so-called cash passport debit cards in the names of others to pay money into accounts in another country, to be withdrawn by these 'spies' in South Africa. My guess is that this practice wasn't just limited to South Africa. These practices amounted to tax evasion, money laundering and corruption, as well as bribery and corrupt practices in other jurisdictions.

We warned the tobacco industry in April 2014 that these activities contravened certain laws. An obligation also rested on SARS to report this to the Hawks. However, between late December 2013 and early 2014 it turned out we had a little problem on our hands. It appeared that some state officials were in on this, in particular some members of the Illicit-Tobacco Task Team.

There appeared to be open collaboration between certain officials of the Illicit-Tobacco Task Team, employees of certain tobacco manufacturers and private investigators. It was a veritable free-for-all, whereby the position of some role players in the industry was being advanced to the detriment of others. We discovered that a mishmash of spies reported to state officials, that some were also reporting to one tobacco manufacturer or their private investigative firm, and that they were getting paid by all parties!

In February 2014 we briefed the head of the Hawks, at the time Lieutenant General Anwa Dramat, and then head of the SAPS Detective Service, Lieutenant General Vinesh Moonoo, about what we had discovered. Present at the briefing was a member of the Illicit-Tobacco Task Team, so I had to pull my punches. In March 2014, Pillay, armed with a briefing note that I compiled from the HRIU reports, raised these issues with high office (I am not allowed to identify of which institution). Nothing ever came of it.

On 30 March 2014 *Business Day* ran a scoop by journalist Malcolm Rees, under the headline 'BAT's smoke and mirrors war on rivals'.[10] We will meet Rees again later in the book. Rees reported on 'sensational recordings and documents' that he had uncovered that 'show how South Africa's largest JSE-listed company, cigarette giant British American Tobacco (BAT), appears to be committing "industrial espionage" on a grand scale, running a network of "agents" placed to spy inside rival organisations'.[11]

According to the article, personnel from BAT's London headquarters allegedly gave their South African agents Travelex cards in return for information. These cards were registered in the UK under different names, then recharged with cash over the Internet, so they could be used at South African ATMs. 'One agent,' according to the report, 'who was placed in a senior position within BAT's rivals, said that BAT's "worldwide" practice of making secret payments to agents could be considered "international money-laundering".'[12]

Rees quotes this agent as saying: 'They had a deal to pay me for industrial espionage, and may I say I'm not the only one in our little circle. There are [government intelligence agents] who have left the state, and gone to work for BAT ...'[13]

According to the report, BAT's South African managing director,

Brian Finch, denied any knowledge of spying on rivals or of payments to 'agents'. However, he did acknowledge that SARS had launched an audit into BAT's South African operation.

With the HRIU closed down by October 2014 and so many key SARS officials who had resigned in the six months that followed, I cannot help wonder whatever has happened to this case ...

In August 2016 information was leaked on Twitter that seemed to confirm the findings of the HRIU's investigation into private spies in the tobacco industry. The leaks point to a network of over a hundred informants and spies, overseen by 'handlers', who were allegedly involved in illegal surveillance (photos, videos and illegal audio interceptions). These informants and spies apparently had access to millions in funding, bought expensive equipment that has interception and surveillance capabilities, illegally placed and used tracking devices on their competitors and gained illegal entry to premises.[14]

This network of spies appears to have been created at the behest of, and was funded by, tobacco firms in conjunction with officials associated with the Illicit-Tobacco Task Team. The leaks were based on records of Forensic Security Services and private companies, as well as affidavits by individuals who had allegedly done work for BAT and TISA. This documentary evidence was seemingly obtained by FITA and tobacco manufacturer Carnilinx in what appears to have been an effort on their part to expose the collusion between BAT and TISA and their undue influence over law-enforcement agencies.

Even though it wasn't part of the Illicit-Tobacco Task Team, SARS went ahead with its own investigations. In late 2013, the team members of the HRIU decided to begin a step-by-step assessment of each suspected tobacco manufacturer. They worked in alphabetical order, beginning with ABC Tobacco Co Ltd,[15] which was based in an industrial area in Tshwane.[16]

The team had driven past the company's factory a few times, and tried to find witnesses or anyone who might be able to tell us more about what was going on inside, but nothing credible came up. However, we were convinced they were running a 'B-stock' manufacturing line – in other words, making certain batches of cigarettes, usually at night, that were not recorded or declared to SARS and therefore no taxes were paid on this stock.

One day, one of the team members noticed that municipal CCTV cameras, owned by the Metro Police, were installed throughout the area, and one happened to focus on the entrance to ABC Tobacco. Then, a type-2 project was initiated, which entailed an ingenious plan by the HRIU. Because the cameras covered only public areas, and because we were collecting actual evidence of suspected offences, it was legally permissible to monitor what the cameras recorded at Metro Police's operations centre. We counted every truck that entered the gates at ABC Tobacco, which enabled us to compare the estimated volumes delivered against the volumes declared for tax. The Metro Police helped us in our investigations and we made it clear to them that they were working with SARS officials, so once again, we were certainly not operating covertly.

Day in and day out, for weeks and months, the team members of the HRIU sat with police officers and took turns to keep watch in the operations centre. They did not want to miss a single offload. The Tactical Intervention Unit assisted by conducting weekly inspections and comparing the amount of stock that was delivered with what was declared. In this way, we tried to obtain evidence that more tobacco was delivered than the declared amount of cigarettes that were manufactured.

One day in December 2013, I got a call from HRIU team member Johnny, who told me that Forensic Security Services, the private security firm working for TISA (which, as mentioned, represented the big multinational manufacturers and tobacco growers), had also cottoned on to the idea of monitoring the deliveries at ABC Tobacco at the Metro Police's operations centre. This appears to have been part of their own efforts to curb the illicit trade in tobacco.

Soon the private investigators were ensconcing themselves at the centre. When Johnny told me this, I instructed our team to withdraw immediately. The reason was simple: I didn't want SARS to be seen working hand in glove with private investigators who were being paid by one faction of the industry while we were trying to deal with non-compliance among all the role players. In the past, SARS had been accused too many times of taking sides with one part of the industry against the other. More than a decade before, it had been widely reported that a tobacco importer, Phoebus Apollo, had obtained and executed an Anton Piller search warrant against the police, BAT, SARS and others on the argument that the state was working to advance the interests of certain commercial competitors over others. (An Anton Piller is a private search and seizure warrant that allows one to execute searches and seize documents from state institutions and businesses.)

Even though the HRIU had to abandon the Metro Police's operations centre, its investigation yielded good results. In December 2013, the Tactical Intervention Unit confiscated tobacco worth more than R300 million in KwaZulu-Natal[17] based on information the HRIU provided.

Shortly thereafter we had ABC Tobacco exactly where we wanted them. Their problem was that they couldn't lay claim to the tobacco, because, on paper, it wasn't theirs. If ABC Tobacco were to lay claim to it, they would have had to admit committing fraud. They were in a tight squeeze because the suppliers of the tobacco wanted to be paid, but they had lost their stock to SARS. I do not know how this case ended, because soon after all hell broke out.

Another kind of criminal activity we came across in the tobacco industry was the practice by 'go-betweens' to extort money from the subjects of SARS investigations. Once such a go-between (it might have been a lawyer, accountant, business consultant or any other) had identified someone who was under investigation, they would approach this person, supposedly on behalf of a SARS official, and then claim that they would act as go-between in return for money – effectively bribery. In several instances, people fell for this trick and forked out hundreds of thousands, believing that these bribes would make the tax case against them go away.

But, of course, the cases were never dropped. The person who had paid the bribe would then insist that the go-between resolved the dispute, at which point the scammers would play for extra time by suggesting that the SARS officials were just 'playing hardball' to create the perception that they were doing their work. The ingenuity of this scam was that the person or entity under investigation could never admit having paid a bribe.

The scammers would use the most devious means possible to demonstrate their close connections with and influence over SARS officials. Invariably, the scammer would, in the presence of the individual under investigation, call a SARS official and have an arbitrary discussion, usually ending with ambiguous words such as 'okay, remember that other thing we discussed? We will talk soon. I will come and see you.'

Sometimes they even arranged a meeting with a SARS official under some pretext and invited the person under investigation to go to the same venue to observe the meeting from afar. The SARS official would be totally oblivious to the fact that he was being used as part of a scam.

By 2013 these scams had got so bad that someone in Durban started impersonating Ivan Pillay.[18] This conman would meet with taxpayers to assure them their cases would be dropped in exchange for a fee. In another case I would later discover that someone collected at least R800 000 from an unsuspecting tobacco manufacturer by claiming this money was being 'collected' on behalf of Ivan and me.

The scammers would capitalise on the fact that investigations took time to reach fruition. When it finally dawned on their victims that they had been taken for a ride, there was nothing they could do – someone who had paid a bribe to make their tax problems disappear could hardly lay a criminal complaint against a fraudster without incriminating himself.

I strongly believe that some of the last projects the HRIU was involved in – a number of which related to the tobacco industry – further contributed to its demise. In the course of fulfilling their duties, the team stumbled upon several sensitive matters, which I believe made certain people in prominent positions very nervous.

As I have mentioned, I am limited by law as to how much detail I may divulge. While my description of the following cases may appear innocuous and vague at times, they concern prominent individuals and should more details about them become public, there may be wide-reaching consequences.

For instance, in an earlier project, which came to fruition only in 2013, the HRIU had managed to unearth business links between certain individuals we were investigating for tax evasion. This particular case involved hundreds of millions of rands. During the tax investigation the HRIU had, purely by accident, found evidence of massive sums that were being laundered offshore by way of fictitious front companies. These activities were linked to government officials and politicians whom I cannot identify.

At one point, my manager, Ravele, also asked me to meet with and debrief two men who had offered information to SARS about the tobacco industry. This task was assigned to the HRIU, who debriefed them in detail with a view to compiling affidavits that they could sign.

It was a long and arduous task for, mainly, Johnny, Tony and Gertjie, who had to examine details for a period spanning more than a decade. We expected these two men to back up what they claimed with specific details and evidence that would allow us to use their allegations in tax, customs and criminal proceedings.

I knew we were going to be in trouble when Johnny called me one day after a session with one of these men saying there was 'big trouble'. Johnny was never one for drama, so I knew something was up.

What they had given us was extremely sensitive because it showed how money received from tobacco-smuggling operations was paid directly to influential businessmen, gangsters and politically connected individuals.

I told Johnny to hand the sensitive material provided by them – notes, details of payments, fraudulent bank accounts, text messages, money flows, chequebook stubs, memory sticks – the whole lot – over to me. I sealed it all in a box and locked it away in my office safe.

I had decided that, as a unit and as SARS, we would stick to the matters that concerned the tobacco industry. We could always go back to the other information and evidence the two men had supplied at a later stage and then decide how best to deal with it. However, just to be safe, I briefed Ivan and Ravele on the matter. I have no doubt that scratching around in this affair put the unit in harm's way. We were also never able to conclude this investigation.

Probably one of the last projects the unit was involved in occurred when I was privately given two recordings made by people in the tobacco industry. They recorded two conversations they had had with convicted drug dealer Glenn Agliotti. The man who gave me the recordings told me that he was giving them to me because he believed I should be aware of how people were abusing my name to extort money from taxpayers. He said I could use the recordings in any manner I chose.[19]

I asked the HRIU to make transcripts of the recordings and was truly astounded by what I read. It seemed Agliotti presented two main schemes to these men. On the one hand, Agliotti claimed he had permission from the Presidency, the NPA, the Hawks and national intelligence, to set up an illegal tobacco-smuggling operation, supposedly as a way to counter other smuggling operations. He then wanted these men to help him set this operation up and claimed that they all stood to make a lot of money through this process.

On the other hand, he (falsely) told them that he was in constant contact with me, and that, if they paid him enough money, he would get me to help them with their tax problems. He claimed to have met me, quoted me as if I had spoken to him about certain cases, and suggested that these men would basically get a free pass to commit any crime they wished under the auspices of this smuggling operation.[20] We were never able to conclude this investigation.

In late 2013 and early 2014 a few other matters were also assigned to the HRIU, most notably cases that related to significant tender fraud and an influential family whom I cannot identify. These cases were still in the conceptualisation phase when the storm struck the unit.

Whenever we stumbled across sensitive matters I would compile notes for Ivan on cases that concerned other state departments. He always went to brief high office about it and continually requested the respective agencies to collaborate with us on such matters. But nothing ever came of Ivan's briefings.

While we thought we were upholding the interests of the state, other agencies and our country as a whole, in hindsight, I think some of these briefing notes helped seal our fate. By trying to nurture cooperation between SARS and other agencies, we came across things others didn't want us to know about. It must also have been quite embarrassing for certain officials in other agencies. Clearly, some people did not believe us any more when we said that we had come across certain matters *by accident*. In their minds, we deliberately went looking for these things and that might have been why they started assuming we had a covert intelligence unit – because, otherwise, how else could SARS have known about all these things?

I suspect all of the projects I've mentioned came to an end when the unit was closed down in October 2014. However, all of the information is still with SARS, and I would like to believe that SARS will still act on it in terms of its statutory mandate.

12

Double game

I first met Pretoria-based attorney Belinda Walter at my office on 4 September 2013 in my official capacity. She attended the meeting, where a colleague of mine was also present, as chair of the Fair-Trade Independent Tobacco Association (FITA). I ended up referring her to another state department to address the query she had raised.[1]

Almost two months later on 25 October 2013, out of the blue, she asked me out on a date. Thereafter a brief yet damaging relationship ensued. A report in the *Sunday Times* about our relationship several months later would be the first in a series of articles the newspaper would run on me.

When we met I knew nothing about Walter. She told me that she had recently established a law firm that specialised in family and matrimonial law. I had no inkling then of the depth of her involvement in the tobacco industry. We were both single at the time, so media reports that labelled it an 'affair' are wrong. We only really saw each other at weekends and usually communicated by text and telephone during the week.

For the past two years, I have deliberately avoided making the intricate details of this brief relationship public. The relationship was not the finest moment in my life and it is something I deeply regret. I thought that by keeping the details of our relationship private I might be able to retain some of my dignity after the gross character assassination I have had to endure since Walter and I broke up. Furthermore, the matter is a subject of ongoing litigation and I would rather use that platform to state my case. Having said that, I do believe it is in the public interest to explain certain aspects of the relationship that are relevant to this story.[2]

Because of her role as the FITA chairperson and SARS's investigations into the tobacco industry, I declared the relationship to my line manager and two other senior SARS officials. When potential conflicts of interest presented themselves during the course of the relationship, I dealt with them immediately and decisively.

In letters addressed to the *Sunday Times* on 5 and 7 February 2014, in her capacity as an attorney, Walter explained the genesis of our relationship and pointed out that we were both intent on avoiding any conflicts of interest:

> The possibility of a misunderstanding regarding my romantic relationship was discussed at length and thought through with my partner at its inception. Even these original discussions placed the possibility of a relationship under strain and contributed to my personal stress and what later transpired.
>
> We went out of our way to precisely avoid any perceived prejudice to any third party, associated person, employer etc. This should not be construed that we have anything to hide or that we were doing anything wrong. We primarily did so particularly to protect the integrity of the institution for whom my partner works. My partner and I both take our careers very seriously and the responsibilities entrusted to us.[3]

I believe Walter's letters accurately sum up how the relationship unfolded and therefore I have added an extract from one of these letters as an annexure to this book.

Within the first days of the relationship, Walter revealed to me that she acted as lawyer for a certain tobacco manufacturer while simultaneously acting as a 'State Security Agency agent' for the Illicit-Tobacco Task Team and was tasked to spy on the very company she was representing.

Besides the ethical and legal concerns this situation gave rise to, I was adamant that we could not continue our relationship if she chose to remain the legal counsel for this tobacco manufacturer. Since I was busy with investigations into the tobacco industry, it presented a clear conflict of interest for me.

So I put that choice to her. She claimed that she felt in a quandary anyway because of her role as both informant/agent and attorney and that she welcomed the opportunity to withdraw from her client. All of our conversations about this are recorded in text exchanges between us.

By 16 November 2013, barely two weeks after our first date, and after several delays from her side, I sent the following text message to her: 'I am allowing you to do what you think best. Ultimately you must decide. What we cant [sic] continue doing is always going back to them in any conversation we have. You must decide. You say you have. So then do what you need to do. Since last week you have been delaying this.'

She stepped down as lawyer for the client on the same day and notified SARS. She sent me copies of both letters to my private email address.[4] Walter would later falsely claim that I forced her to relinquish this client against her will.

Walter would later tell the Sikhakhane Panel (which investigated her allegations against me and to which we return in a later chapter) that she had established FITA with the assistance and approval of the State Security Agency (SSA) and the Illicit-Tobacco Task Team.[5] I doubt this assertion because not only would it have been illegal, but I cannot imagine that either the legal advisers for the Hawks, police and SSA or a judge (who would have had to authorise it) would have allowed such an operation, especially where it concerns a lawyer as agent.

Walter would later also confirm to the Sikhakhane Panel that she acted as an agent for the Illicit-Tobacco Task Team. Furthermore, in an interview with *Carte Blanche* in February 2015, she was pertinently asked, 'Were you an agent?' To which she replied: 'Yes, I'm not going to lie about that, yes I was.'[6] Walter furthermore told me how she was tasked by her handler to surreptitiously record our first meeting and how disappointed they were with the results of the recording because I had not implicated myself.

I have often reflected on the early days of this relationship and why I got involved with someone so fraught with these types of issues. It's a difficult question to answer. Unfortunately, when it comes to relationships that end badly, hindsight is a perfect science. I think that, ironically, partly because of my background as a deep-cover police agent many years before, I probably felt that I understood the situation. I think that, at the time, I considered her as one of 'us' – people in the state that fought crime.

But our similar backgrounds also became the source of one of our very first disagreements because I would question how she could justify her role as an attorney who gets paid by a client but spies on that client. At first she disagreed with me but a little later agreed, admitting she wasn't legally covered for her actions.

My advice to her was that she should reconsider her position and, at that time, she claimed that she did. (Much later I was to discover that she had been informed by her Illicit-Tobacco Task Team handler in late 2012 that she wasn't legally covered, but she never conveyed any of this to me.)

After Walter withdrew as legal counsel for the tobacco manufacturer, I believed that the perceived or potential conflict of interest was thereby removed. A few days later, she also resigned as chairperson of FITA after we had a similar discussion about this. Perhaps naively, I trusted Walter when she led me to believe that she had ended her associations with these tobacco-related entities and individuals, including the Illicit-Tobacco Task Team.

Another significant exchange took place about two weeks into our relationship. She sent me a text message in which she claimed that SARS or other law-enforcement agencies were intercepting communications of certain people in the tobacco industry. I made the terrible mistake of not correcting her on this. At the time I believed it was to the state's advantage if people who were involved in crime believed that they were being subjected to such scrutiny. Our correspondence over this would later come back to haunt me.

But this wasn't all I came to discover about Walter during our relationship. In January 2014 she told me that she was also an informant for a multinational tobacco manufacturer who paid her to spy on her clients and on FITA members, and that she did so with the full knowledge and permission of the Illicit-Tobacco Task Team. She told me how the task team was in fact instrumental in setting up this arrangement.

Once again, I pointed out the legal and ethical pitfalls of her involvement in this and she assured me that she was in the process of terminating her arrangement with the multinational tobacco company. We had countless disagreements about the various professional roles she played and the fact that she didn't have sufficient legal cover from the state to expose herself in this manner. That she was an attorney, I pointed out, made it even worse.

During this time, Walter claimed that she knew things about some officials in the Illicit-Tobacco Task Team and certain private companies that pointed to unlawful actions on their part. She expressed a desire to expose this in several text messages that she sent me. She wanted to meet with certain journalists to divulge everything she knew.

In further text exchanges in January 2014, she offered to testify against various people. She began to tell me about – but only to a limited extent, as I was to discover later – certain instances in which she believed some of the members of the Illicit-Tobacco Task Team, tobacco manufacturers and private investigators were acting illegally and unethically. In her text messages, Walter continually lamented the fact that she had been used by the Illicit-Tobacco Task Team and private business, and claimed she didn't know any better. According to her, they were the bad guys and SARS were the good guys.

I sent her text messages in which I offered to help her set up meetings with law-enforcement officials who could take down an affidavit from her. Her response to this was that she wanted certain assurances from the state upfront.

In January 2014 she recorded two conversations with her London-based handlers and gave me copies. She then approached a company to download records from her old mobile handsets and data from a data cloud that she wanted to use to support her claims. The fact that I advised her to record these conversations flies in the face of her later allegations that I and/or SARS were intercepting her conversations. Why would I have suggested this to her if we were intercepting her communications?

Walter not only gave me the recordings of the two conversations in my private capacity, but also allowed me to photograph two cash passports that she had used to receive payment from the multinational company she spied for, emails between her and the company, and a letter she later received from them that confirmed the payments made to her by way of these anonymised cash passports. At the time she said I could use this as I wished.

She openly discussed with me and others (including journalists) what she discovered in the downloaded data. However, Walter wasn't entirely happy with the information the company retrieved for her because they couldn't access the deleted data, so she asked me whether I could help her retrieve the data, including the deleted data. I knew someone who could do this, and in March 2014 I gave her two memory sticks containing the downloaded data.

She said I could keep one copy and again said I could use it as I wished. Perhaps she had hoped I wouldn't look at the data, or alternatively believed that even if I did, I would have protected her in any event. I will never know.

Either way, at that stage, I didn't really make much of the information that had been retrieved. I knew she was talking to the media and I thought the issues it raised were limited to what was being reported on. Later I wished I had looked at it at the time.

All of these events led me to believe that she was sincere about wanting to expose corruption in the tobacco industry.

Since this matter was raised often in the media, I want to state that after Walter told me me about her role as informant and lawyer for a tobacco manufacturer we did have conversations about the tobacco industry from time to time. At times she was also present at my home when Guillam or others briefed me after hours on certain matters and when I took or made work-related phone calls with colleagues.

She would later use these conversations as part of her complaint against me, claiming that I had repeatedly and unlawfully shared confidential information with her. However, I would be very surprised if any current or former SARS official can claim he or she has never discussed aspects of their work with or in the presence of their spouses, partners, families or friends. I considered our conversations private.

Furthermore, I could hardly have ignored what she told me. I believed she was genuine in sharing with me what she referred to as acts of criminality and unethical activities in the tobacco industry. But every now and then, I found her to be less than frank about particular matters that I happened to be aware of. I had a nagging feeling she was hiding things from me. Whenever this occurred, I would – as a test – share matters with her that were not factually accurate to ascertain whether she was being completely honest with me.

Soon the initial trust that existed between us started to fade. Over time I began to develop an increasing discomfort with how she raised certain matters with me and how she responded to what I put to her. This was exacerbated by the fact that I discovered she had gone through my phone messages in December 2013 on two occasions without my permission.

I also have to ask why Walter, if she believed certain conversations were problematic, chose to raise this only some days after I had ended our relationship. Her later allegation that I had discussed the tax affairs of politicians and political parties is simply untrue.

Our relationship was already rocky before it reached breaking point on 31 January 2014, when we had a big argument after I found that she had gone through my phone messages and emails without my permission for the third time. The next day, Walter arranged to meet with her erstwhile legal client, their (new) lawyers and a senior advocate, effectively telling them she wanted to return to their fold. *Sunday Times* journalist Malcolm Rees was also present at the meeting, during which she confessed that she had acted as an informant for the Illicit-Tobacco Task Team, the SSA and the multinational tobacco firm. She also made various allegations against me, although there was no mention at that stage of a 'rogue unit', or any other SARS unit. In fact, it seems that very little of what would later be alleged by her was put to the participants at this meeting.

Throughout the day I tried to make contact with her via text exchanges because she wasn't taking my calls. She brushed me off with rude responses and accused me of having used her to obtain incriminating information about her clients. That evening I got the following message: 'I have to live with the consequences of all my bad choices and allowing people to manipulate me. I don't have a clue how to even start. I damaged other people, exposed [name removed] to risk and at the same time destroyed myself. I can't even begin to make it all right. When I'm threatened I panic and do stupid things ... I pissed off the wrong people and in trying to make it right now I've made it worse ...'

I tried to calm her down, aware that she had done something terrible when she said this, but she would have nothing of it.

Although she didn't tell me outright what she had done, by then I knew that, whatever it was, it was going to present a problem when she sent this message: 'You don't know what I did. This time they will do terrible things. I only blame myself.'

Later I drove to her place to see if she was there and to check on her. She let me in and then told me about the meeting. She didn't want to go into much detail about what she had said about me, other than to say she had confessed to everyone present about her role as informant and that she had made certain allegations about me.

I tried to be understanding and ascribed her behaviour to the stress I believed she suffered from as a result of having to act as a triple agent. We reconciled, but I realised we would now have to deal with the consequences of her actions.

Walter decided to write letters to her former client's attorneys, the tobacco manufacturer, the senior advocate and the *Sunday Times*, in which she withdrew the allegations she had made. In these letters, written between 2 and 7 February 2014, she stated under legal letterhead that she had lied, had defamed me, had made up stories based on rumours in the tobacco industry and apologised to all concerned (see Annexure 2). Most significantly, in a letter to me she asked my forgiveness and apologised for defaming me (see Annexure 1).

I wrote and submitted a detailed report to SARS on 3 February 2014 setting out precisely what had happened.[7]

Walter would also later claim that I had forced or coerced her to write these retractions and apologies or authored them myself. Again, not so. Since I haven't had an opportunity to respond to these claims I would like to quote a message she sent me on 3 February:

> I feel so disgusted and disappointed in myself that not only did I betray you, but the types of things I said to those scumbags. I don't understand how you can ever look at me. You should hate me ... Just hectically ashamed of what I did. I need to get through my difficulties so that I can have all this behind me. It was so far already and now I have made things so much worse. I have caused so much kak.

I then asked her to email me a copy of her retraction to the advocate, to which she replied, 'Hi, sure. Will do. Just got home. I am mailing now ... Did you get it?'

Clearly, then, I was not with her when she wrote the letter. Furthermore, why would I have asked for a copy of this particular letter if I had written it? In another example she told me in a text message on 3 February that she intended to send a letter to the *Sunday Times* and she subsequently sent me a copy of what she had sent to the newspaper. Again, I wasn't with her when she did that.

Truth be told, this was the beginning of the end of the relationship for me. In the first week of May 2014, I saw Walter for the last time and on 13 May 2014 informed her that the relationship was over. We remained in contact via text messages until the fateful day of 27 May 2014, during which time I always tried to remain civil. In the months that were to follow, I would discover many more surprising aspects about Walter.

I believe the data retrieved from Walter's old cellphones and from the data cloud lies at the heart of at least the initial attacks on me and SARS. In the events that were to follow much has been made of how I came to possess records of her communications pre-dating the time I met her.

Walter has consistently claimed that she never gave me her handsets to have the data downloaded for her. She even challenged me by way of a legal notice to produce photographs of the handsets and her written approval. In addition, she claimed that for three years before we met, her communications were illegally intercepted by SARS. However, initially she made no mention of a 'rogue unit' or, for that matter, any SARS unit. It was only much later, in late 2014 that she would imply the alleged interceptions were done by the 'rogue unit'.

Why the issue of how I came to possess the data is significant will shortly become clear. What I can say is that I have photos of each handset, including their batteries and serial numbers, and an envelope with Walter's handwriting on it, which gives the details of the data cloud. She handed me this envelope, which contained the cellphones, at her home on a Sunday in February 2014. There are also text messages between us in which she refers to the phones and discusses the extracted data with me.

After the data was downloaded, I was given two sets of it on two memory sticks. I gave both to Walter in March, but, as explained, she told me to keep a copy. I put the memory stick in a basket I kept on top of my fridge, thinking I would look at it later when I had a chance.

However, when she publicly denied some weeks later having given me the phones it made me realise that the data was somehow critical to her claim that SARS and/or I had been illegally intercepting her communications for a period of three years *before* we had met. For some reason, it was important to her to discredit the data in my possession.

It was at this point that I started working through the material. I also gave a copy to the HRIU and asked them to do a more detailed analysis of it for me with a particular focus on anything that linked with the tobacco trade. What I found was shocking, to say the least. It documents precisely how the interests of informants, state officials who were part of the Illicit-Tobacco Task Team, as well as private business overlap way beyond what could be considered proper. In some instances their activities were clearly unlawful.

As I expect that I might have to rely on this data in pending litigation, I can't divulge too much, but to give a sense of the type of collusion that took place, I will provide a few examples. In a text exchange on 2 September 2011 between Walter and her Illicit-Tobacco Task Team handler at the time, he describes their relationship as follows:

> **Handler to Walter:** You and I know exactly what and who we are/were from the start … our ability to do what we do, I think was the initial attraction between us. We are birds of a feather. We even, around the time we nailed [name of person in tobacco industry's] ass, agreed that we make a *moerse* good team to push people to do what we wanted them to do … whether it was [person in tobacco industry], [initials of senior manager in SSA], SARS, NPA or Lonrho!! Our strength to get things done lies in our joint ability … why would I fuck with that!?

In another text exchange, on 9 September 2012, between Walter and her later handler in the Illicit-Tobacco Task Team, a SARS official who was investigating illegally imported cigarettes and had confiscated a batch pending the outcome of her investigation becomes the focus of her ire:

> **Walter to handler:** [Name of a SARS official] needs to let my [cigarette brand] cigarettes go. If I gun hard at [name of the SARS official] – will I be ok personally. [SARS official] is fucking idiot and I can't help myself.

Just days later the same SARS official is again discussed, and this time her career seems to be at risk:

> **Walter to handler:** What was [SARS official's] attitude? Do we help [SARS official] or sink the bitch?
> **Handler to Walter:** No. Nobody. Also decided not going to speak to the stupid bitch again. Don't sink her. Will find our own way in.
> **Walter to handler:** Ok. But do I carry on with matters that will hurt her career?

In another conversation they talk about creating evidence to counter a SARS investigation:

> **Walter to handler:** I think I have created enough paper trail and evidence to win in a court on [SARS-related] issue and the [SARS criminal case].

I know this particular case well. SARS was unable to counter the 'paper trail' and, with it, lost over R25 million in revenue that was due to the state. I also appear in some of Walter's text exchanges that took place in 2012 and 2013 – before I had met her. She seemed to know quite a bit about me, though. On 6 February 2013 the following exchange took place:

Handler to Walter: Do you have any evidence, with the emphasis on evidence, that JvL is on the take [accepts bribes]?
Walter to handler: No. None.
Handler to Walter: Ok thx. His name came up in a conversation and just want my ducks in a row. Will talk later.

The manner in which state officials were discussed, the nature of these discussions and the tone speak for themselves. Suddenly it was crystal clear to me why Walter had to discredit the data retrieved from her phones and the data cloud at all costs.

There is another discussion I can refer to here. This time, it occurred among Walter and her clients in a so-called chat group:

Participant: I'm good ... aggravated that [initials of person in tobacco industry] seems to be getting away with everything ... but I don't think it's a good idea to go to Moneyweb [Online financial news agency] ...
Participant: I agree. [Foreign tobacco baron]'s son wants all his details ...
Participant: He loves me. Be [*sic*] will pull political strings with Zuma? May be worth a try.
Participant: Does he have contacts? ... can he bring in a hitman?
Participant: Do it!!!!
Participant: He says he may have someone who can force Zuma's hand to squash him.
Participant: They don't hurt people. I said it's the first person I want dead.
Participant: I don't hurt people either ... but he is a cockroach ...
Participant: I agree.
Participant: So we can exterminate him ...

Given these types of exchanges, and in retrospect, I believe Walter had wanted to do the right thing at the time when she gave me the data. But I believe her dilemma was that she couldn't make a full disclosure because that would expose how complicit she was. I believe that is why, when she realised how the data could potentially expose her, she denied having given her phones to me and, just in case I might make the information public, she claimed her communications had been illegally intercepted by SARS.

On 1 August 2016, SARS finally conceded to the police that I did indeed obtain this data in my own private capacity, and not in the course of my duties as a SARS official. I was therefore also free to provide this to the police.[8] Since then I have been in contact with the SAPS about this matter and have offered my full cooperation in any investigations that might follow.

What I would discover only much later was that Walter had instituted legal proceedings against the multinational tobacco firm that she used to spy for on 23 May 2014. That was just ten days after I had ended the relationship. She demanded £5 million as payment for damages she had allegedly incurred.

In the letter of demand addressed to the company, her attorney made reference to the recordings of the conversations she had with her London-based handler, the payments made using concealed methods and various email exchanges (including a letter confirming the payments made), which Walter also provided to me during happier times. Quite tellingly, the letter pointed out that the arrangement was 'not a bona fide crime fighting initiative' and more specifically put to them that it was in fact for purposes of 'industrial espionage, alternatively to unlawfully compete with its competitors' and to 'sabotage the business of their competitors'. The letter also stated that solicitors were in the process of being appointed in the UK to prosecute the claim and demanded that the funds be paid into a trust account within a few days. It also stated that a similar claim was to be instituted against the SSA on very much the same basis.[9]

If she had gone ahead with the case, it would in all likelihood have exposed instances of corruption and money laundering in South Africa and bribery in the UK. It would also have pointed to complicity between certain South African state officials and private businesses in unethical and criminal activities.

Just days later, on 27 May, Walter apparently met with members of the Illicit-Tobacco Task Team. These are the very same people she had sought to expose to the media and was willing to testify against just about two months before. It appears that they advised her that it would be 'difficult for them to assist her' if she was at 'loggerheads' with the multinational tobacco company and her Illicit-Tobacco Task Team handler, both of whom she was in the process of suing.[10]

Apparently, she was 'made to feel' that she had 'broken rank' and was told that she was 'on her own' due to media reports that were published in March 2014 (the amaBhungane and *Business Day* articles I've referred to elsewhere), which implicated certain officials of the Illicit-Tobacco Task Team and private business interests.[11] They of course knew she was the source for these articles.

Apparently, '[t]he withdrawal of the civil claim was instigated by the South African law enforcement officials assisting me with the complaints against Van Loggerenberg and SARS'.[12]

Shortly afterwards, Walter withdrew the civil claim. In return for this, she claims to have been 'assured' that she would be provided with 'immunity' from prosecution in terms of Section 204 of the Criminal Procedure Act 51 of 1977, 'should it ever become necessary'. To seal the deal, Walter met with two NPA officials and Lieutenant Colonel Hennie Niemann of the Illicit-Tobacco Task Team.[13] (Niemann is the same policeman who had approached an attorney in February 2014 looking for any 'dirt' on me and whom we had reported to the Hawks at the time.)

But there's a glitch here. Under Section 204 of the Criminal Procedure Act 51 of 1977, an NPA official cannot give this kind of unspecific, future-based indemnity from prosecution to anyone. It is only applicable to individuals who stand accused of crimes and who the state wants to use as witnesses against their accomplices in an existing or pending trial. There has to be a criminal investigation and subsequent trial, and specific offences must be described. A person who applies for Section 204 indemnity will only receive indemnity if the judge or magistrate presiding over the trial believes at the end of the trial that the state witness had testified truthfully and honestly. Not only is such a blanket indemnity a legal impossibility in South Africa, but the real question that remains is this – for which crimes did Walter supposedly receive this indefinite 'immunity'?

Most importantly, I believe these events themselves quite possibly amount to various offences described in the Prevention and Combating of Corrupt Activities Act 12 of 2004, the Prevention of Organised Crime Act 121 of 1998 and the Financial Intelligence Centre Act 38 of 2001. All of these pieces of legislation speak to offences where evidence of corruption and money laundering is deliberately concealed.[14] I also believe these events amount to the classic case of the common-law offence of compounding.[15]

Nothing about this 'deal' was disclosed to the subsequent SARS-appointed panels or investigations into the so-called rogue unit. I myself came to know of this 'indemnity offer' by chance in late 2015 and early 2016, long after I had left SARS. I was approached by attorneys who represented local tobacco manufacturing interests in South Africa. They indicated that they believed they had unearthed significant evidence of various criminal practices in the tobacco industry, and sought my assistance and advice.[16]

They had got wind of the fact that I had the data that Walter had given me and they were interested in getting their hands on it. Although I never gave this to them, during our interactions, they gave me certain documents. This was how I discovered that around April 2015 and earlier, Walter had confessed certain things to them, albeit selectively.[17] She had made no mention of the data whatsoever and that was why they then approached me.

Our interaction fizzled out after I asked for certain assurances from them, which they weren't willing or able to provide. I did however point out to them various acts of corruption, money laundering and the concealment of these offences in the tobacco industry, and advised them to report these offences to the Hawks. I'm not holding my breath on any speedy investigations or prosecutions, though.

In February 2016 I learnt that the multinational company had appointed an international law firm to probe allegations of corruption in Africa. This followed a BBC *Panorama* documentary revealing claims from an ex-employee, who said that the company had paid bribes to African officials.[18] This move confirmed the reservation I had always held, namely that the board or management of the company were most probably not aware of what was happening at a lower level in the company.

Following their announcement, I contacted the law firm's London-based offices and offered to help them. They acknowledged my offer of assistance and proposed a meeting that same week in Cape Town. I was unable to attend then, but I asked them whether they had engaged with any South African law-enforcement agencies and, if so, to what extent. They never answered my question but undertook to contact me again at a later stage. This never happened.

13

The Tempest (Act I)

And then the storm was upon us. The first gale that struck came in the form of an email from Walter. This email, dated 28 May 2014 – the day after Walter was apparently given the 'indemnity deal', was soon to be used as part of her complaint against me. The complaint to SARS came a couple of weeks after I ended the relationship.

Various senior managers at SARS were copied in on the email. It was written in a rather emotional manner and didn't take the form of a typical, formal complaint. In effect the 'complaint' was sent as a reply to an earlier email from me, in which I had alerted Walter to the fact that I'd had media enquiries about our relationship. I also set out how I intended to reply to such queries.

That email set off a chain of events that I don't believe even Walter could have foreseen.

Because none of the media reports or the subsequent panels that investigated the complaints elaborated on the full extent of the allegations made against me, I will expand on what I have stood accused of. If one reads the original complaint – and the details that were added to it over time – with a legal eye, it essentially claims that I committed a number of criminal offences.[1]

In the initial complaint, Walter claimed that I had unlawfully shared confidential taxpayer information pertaining to two very prominent politicians, as well as the details of SARS operations. It also stated that I was generally unfit for office and cast a host of negative aspersions on my character.

Walter undertook to provide an affidavit in support of her allegations and all emails and text exchanges between us to SARS in support of these allegations. Importantly, there was no mention of a 'rogue unit' at SARS yet.

By June 2014, the allegation had been augmented. Now, firstly, it was alleged that the relationship was a ruse and that I, in my official capacity, conducted an undercover operation on behalf of SARS without the required legal approval. In other words, that I was spying on Walter illegally. Apparently, I had also intercepted taxpayers' communications, specifically hers, which is a contravention of Section 16 of the Regulation of Interception of Communications and Provision of Communication-Related Information Amendment Act 21 of 2010.

I had then also, allegedly, contravened Section 205 of the Criminal Procedure Act 51 of 1977, since I failed to obtain the required authority to access cellphone records. I have always maintained that these particular allegations were intended to discredit the data retrieved from the phones and data cloud, together with other evidence in the form of recorded conversations and correspondence that I had privately been given by Walter.

As I have already mentioned, she had initially told me to use whatever information from the phones and data cloud as I wished. However, I strongly believe that by then she regretted having given me the evidence and data after we broke up, and knew that I was not going to ignore information that implicated her and certain officials of the Illicit-Tobacco Task Team in illegal and unethical activities. What better way to get out of this sticky situation than to say I had intercepted the communications unlawfully?

Furthermore, it was alleged that during the supposed illegal spying operation that I committed illegal acts, including corruption, that I had improperly or unlawfully caused a SARS audit into Walter's tax affairs and had manipulated or directed the audit in an improper manner. I was also accused of having had unlawful and improper relations with various persons at SARS and elsewhere, and having unlawfully disclosed to Walter various SARS operational matters and cases.

I had ostensibly also caused or participated in an assault on Walter, which had taken place sometime in 2013 on a date before I had met her. Furthermore, I apparently also held 'secret shares' in a wine estate in the Western Cape, and laundered money through a fundraiser club I was part of through a bank account in Liechtenstein, or Switzerland or some other tax haven.

Later, I had also seemingly caused, or influenced a particular tobacco manufacturer or representatives thereof to lodge a false and frivolous criminal complaint against Niemann of the Illicit-Tobacco Task Team sometime in 2013.

Soon further allegations were levelled against me. Now, I had also supposedly conspired with an SSA official to meet with and threaten Walter on 20 July 2014, and had colluded with him to illegally intercept communications. The fact that I had last met this man in my official capacity more than a year and half before didn't seem to matter. Still there was no mention of a 'rogue unit'.

As an aside: In June 2014 I was approached by a senior SSA representative called Toby.[2] He wanted to speak to me about any risk or unlawful activities which may have a bearing on the SSA and which I may have been aware of. He was particularly interested in the data that emanated from Walter's phones. I asked him to address his request to me in writing, but he never did so.

About a month later he arranged that I meet a very senior official of the SSA to brief him about the data. We decided that they would send SARS a formal request to get access to it so I could formally hand over the data to them. Before then I had made parts of the information available to Toby, though. We all agreed that the state's interests had to be protected.

I never had any reason to doubt Toby's bona fides and I believed that he also looked out for my interests. Over the course of the next few months he and I would sometimes meet just to catch up. Often he asked me to brief him on certain matters. Ultimately he also helped me brief high office (I am not allowed to identify of which institution) on the 'rogue-unit' claims and I provided him with a detailed analysis as events unfolded as and when he requested information.

By August 2014 Walter's allegations morphed again.[3] I was now also apparently in possession of unlicensed firearms and had been conspiring with criminals and a tobacco company to bring legal actions against Walter and others in exchange for tax leniency. Shortly before this, the police arrived at my home one day wanting to search it for unlicensed firearms allegedly in my possession. I have never owned a firearm in my personal capacity in my entire life. I had been issued with a 9mm Walther pistol many years ago by the police, and later a .25-calibre pistol. Both were returned to the police when I left.

At SARS, I was issued with the same type of Walther pistol, which was the property of SARS. It was always kept in my safe at the office. I was one of a number of senior officials to receive a firearm from SARS because of potential and actual threats to our lives resulting from high-risk investigations in earlier years.[4]

Interestingly, the description given by Walter of the supposed illegal firearm I kept at home doesn't even closely correspond with a 9mm Walther pistol, which has a very distinct feature, an unusually narrow barrel. It was alleged that I had a silver or black pistol, possibly a Beretta or Glock, neither of which even remotely resembles a 9mm grey Walther pistol.

This allegation might be explained by the fact that, sometime before the police arrived at my home, I had purchased an air pistol (for which I didn't need a licence) from a sports shop. I was by then truly afraid for my life, and this air pistol resembles a real firearm. The one I bought looked like a Colt .45 pistol. It's black and, to the untrained eye, might be mistaken for a black Beretta or Glock 9mm pistol.

The question is, how did anybody know I had an air pistol? I obtained it long after the relationship ended. My view is that it must have been picked up in one of two ways – either I was under constant surveillance, in which case someone could have seen me buy it, or Walter had been given access to my credit-card transactions, as I bought it with my credit card. Either way, it would have been illegal.

The complaint was continually altered to suit changing circumstances at SARS and much later the media story.

In August 2014, Walter would also falsely allege in her opposing affidavit to an interdict application against her and British American Tobacco that SARS and I had offered the applicant, her former client Carnilinx, 'tax leniency'. By May 2016, nearly two years later, I had allegedly also approached and conspired with certain people in the tobacco industry with a 'strategy' aimed at embarrassing the state intelligence agencies. I had, among other things, supposedly also stolen and leaked SARS information to these individuals, caused and helped them to register frivolous criminal complaints against officials associated with the Illicit-Tobacco Task Team, and leaked false information to the media.[5]

My last text interaction with Walter, on 27 June 2014, is significant. That day she contacted me asking me to get SARS to pay her as a 'source of information' and wanted to know how much she would be paid. I explained to her that this was not possible and that SARS didn't do so, in any event. She then texted me saying I should remember that she had kept records of all our interactions and text exchanges throughout our relationship. I saw this as nothing other than attempted blackmail. She then repeated her request that I should get SARS to pay her. I answered by telling her I wasn't open to blackmail and said she should leave me alone.

As I have already started to show and will continue to do in the chapters that follow, there is no basis for these allegations against me. However, the ever-morphing complaint set into motion a sequence of events that would ultimately lead to the 'rogue-unit' narrative that has since become so firmly entrenched in the public's mind. The claims around a so-called rogue unit have, in turn, seriously harmed the integrity of SARS, led to the departure of almost the entire top management of SARS and, to my mind, are clearly part of the ongoing campaign to discredit Finance Minister Pravin Gordhan.

The Kanyane Panel

I still clearly recall the day when Ivan, Collings, then Group Executive: Anti-Corruption and Security, and I met to discuss the initial 'complaint'. It was a day or two after Walter's email of 28 May 2014.

I saw it as a domestic dispute that had now unfortunately entered my workplace and believed there were two ways to deal with it. Either they could see it as a private matter between two persons, or they could give it air, in which case there was a chance that it could affect my professional reputation. 'I understand that I cannot determine what needs to happen,' I said to them. 'If you, as my employer, believe it should be dealt with, let me take special leave. I will live with the consequences.'

I was uncomfortable with Collings being involved because we had a difficult working relationship. I got the impression that he didn't want to debate the situation at all and simply wished for an investigation to be launched immediately. Although we were at one time on good terms, our relationship had been deteriorating, primarily because I believed his unit – which investigated internal corruption and misconduct at SARS – was intruding on the mandates of units under Ravele (to whom I reported). We also had differences of opinion about the manner in which SARS was sharing taxpayer information with other law-enforcement agencies.

As an aside, much has since been made about sophisticated spyware that was allegedly acquired and used by the SPU/NRG or the HRIU. Most interestingly, that equipment – which wasn't 'spyware' to begin with but was commercially available – was acquired by ACAS, the unit Collings presided over. His was a different unit, it was in a different division and had a different cost centre from that of the HRIU.

Ivan, then still acting SARS commissioner, made the final call and appointed Moeti Kanyane, a reputable attorney from a law firm, to chair an internal panel to look into Walter's complaint. Kanyane was to be assisted by Brian Kgomo as Group Executive: Internal Audit, and Collings. This became known as the Kanyane Panel.

On 15 July 2014, I was asked to appear before the panel the following day. That was the only occasion I appeared before the Kanyane Panel and it was literally only for a few minutes. I was not asked any specific questions about Walter's allegations (there was no mention of a 'rogue-unit' yet) and the discussion was very general in nature. None of the issues set out in the panel's ultimate report were put to me, so that I could properly address them.

I was provided only with a document containing allegations as they stood at that stage and another file containing severely censored WhatsApp text messages, which was intended to serve as 'substantiating evidence' (purportedly spanning the period of the relationship), neither of which I had the opportunity to study when I appeared before the panel. More than 90% of the text exchanges were redacted (blacked out with a marker pen). The next day, I was provided with an additional document containing further severely censored WhatsApp texts after I noted the dates on the first document didn't add up and pointed this out to the panel in an email.

I had some questions for the panel, mostly relating to the legalities of the process and I insisted that Walter should testify under oath. They were unable to answer my questions but undertook to provide answers. This never happened. It was agreed that I would make a written submission to the panel based on the documents presented to me. I immediately started on a line-by-line refutation of the allegations, and began to collect my own evidence in support of my counterclaims.

During my short interview before the panel, and subsequently in writing, I made several attempts to alert the panel (and SARS) to evidence in my possession that was relevant to the complaint, including the role of people involved in the Illicit-Tobacco Task Team, the data from the phones, the data cloud, the recordings, documents and text messages. I stated that the information in my possession had been legally obtained, even if in private, and that it implicated several people in various illegal activities.

I made the point that the data I had in my possession had to be discredited at all costs by those implicated by it and that this was why I stood accused of having illegally intercepted communications. I said that I believed this partly explained why certain persons were seeking to discredit SARS and me. I provided the panel with proof that the phones and data cloud had been given to me voluntarily. Yet the panel didn't even ask me for the data at that time.

A worrying incident that took place early in 2014, which was recorded in an internal SARS memorandum, was also submitted to the Kanyane Panel (and later the Sikhakhane Panel) by me. It happened at a joint governmental workshop attended by HRIU manager Guillam, who was told by a state security official to 'warn JvL, they're coming for him …'[6]

I also passed on to the panel an email sent by Walter to a host of people on 20 July 2014. In it she falsely accused me of having conspired with her first SSA handler to threaten her at a meeting that same day. She also stated that he had told her that he represented individuals who wished to 'replace the leadership of SARS and the Minister of Finance [then Nhlanhla Nene]'.

I worked hard on my formal submission to the panel in the form of an affidavit, but in the end I wasn't afforded the opportunity to submit it to them. I also discovered much later that no one interviewed by the panel had testified under oath.

On 28 July 2014, nearly two weeks after I appeared before the Kanyane Panel, Adrian, SARS spokesperson, and I both received a query from *City Press*. The message was worrying: 'Just received a tip-off from a SSA [State Security Agency] contact that you have been fired for corruption. Unbelievable … Smell a rat. Can we talk?'

I discussed the matter with Ivan and Ravele, and together we decided to brief *City Press* to defend both me and SARS. Walter's complaint and the information I got from her data – the fact that there were apparently people who wanted to remove the leadership of SARS and the sudden leak of misinformation about me being fired to *City Press* by an 'SSA contact' – we believed demonstrated an intention to discredit SARS. Ivan also told Ravele to brief the SSA on what we were going to expose to *City Press*. Adrian released a short statement to the media to say that we believed people involved in the tobacco industry were thought to be behind the attacks on SARS and me.

In a sad turn of events, my father died around this time. By early 2014, he was fatally ill. He had suffered a number of strokes in previous years and had been looked after by my youngest sister for some time. As the eldest son, I had to help with the funeral and other arrangements, which I did to the best of my ability.

His memorial service was on 7 August 2014, three days before the first *Sunday Times* story that would change my life forever. Emotionally, I was dealing with a relationship that had ended acrimoniously, the humiliation of the Kanyane Panel process, the death of my father and the pressure of arranging his funeral. I had to face a panel of investigation that didn't seem to want to hear my side of the story, colleagues were starting to avoid me at work and now the media had become involved. At first I was angry, but this soon turned into feelings of shame and helplessness.

The day after the memorial service for my father, 8 August 2014, two significant meetings took place, one of which I attended.

Present at a meeting at Life Café in Brooklyn, Pretoria, which I did not attend, were Walter, her SSA handler, a Hawks brigadier and Niemann, then still a member of the police Crime Intelligence Division. They were all part of the Illicit-Tobacco Task Team and they had urgent matters to discuss that day.

So, how did I get to know about this meeting and its agenda? you may ask. Walter recorded the details of the conversation in a later email, which was sent to a number of people, and one of the recipients later shared a copy of it with me.

Even though she still maintains publicly that this wasn't the case, at this meeting Walter acknowledged to those present in a roundabout manner that I had access to her phones and that the data in my possession had been handed to me in private, as opposed to having been illegally intercepted. It was also conceded that the relationship between a large multinational tobacco manufacturer and the Illicit-Tobacco Task Team occurred with their knowledge, at their instigation and that they shared information between them, for which Walter was paid twice over. It was clear that they were very concerned and felt something had to be done.

The other significant meeting that day took place after I received a call from *Sunday Times* journalist Malcolm Rees to ask whether I would meet with him. I agreed, since we'd interacted a few times before in the presence of Rob Rose, editor of the *Sunday Times* business section, to whom Rees reported. Both had been liaising with SARS on tobacco-related matters through Adrian and me, and with permission from SARS. I had been asking for a while to meet with them because I was concerned about how things were unfolding. But they kept delaying. Until that day.

Rees told me he couldn't see me straight away because he had to wait for 'something', so we agreed to meet that afternoon at one o'clock, at a restaurant in Midrand. Rees was already there when I arrived. After exchanging pleasantries, he put one or two questions to me. He informed me that he intended to publish a story about my former relationship. I warned him that there was a campaign to discredit me and SARS. I cautioned him not to allow himself to be played by his unnamed sources. It was turning into a very uncomfortable meeting.

It became apparent that Rees didn't really want to hear me out and was in a hurry to leave. I explained to him that the hour he had indicated he had available was insufficient to take him through all the detail.

I reminded him that I had been inviting him for months to meet with SARS and that both he and Rose had ignored my requests. He didn't want to postpone his story and said that his editor, Phylicia Oppelt, had insisted that they run the story that Sunday.

He left to pay his bill but in his haste he forgot an email on the table and rushed off. I noticed the mail, picked it up and read through it as I walked to my car.

The 'something' that Rees had to wait for before meeting me was this email. It was sent to him at 12.00 pm that day and was written by Walter, who had attended the meeting in Brooklyn that same day. Rees had tried to scratch out her name, but it was still clearly visible. It had been emailed to him an hour before our meeting and set out in detail exactly which questions Rees had to ask me, what to publish and what not to disclose.

A short while later, Rees, rather sheepishly, called and asked if I had taken the email, and if he could have it back. Sure, I said. But I told him I had taken photos of the pages and again told him that he was being played. He later sent me some questions by email, which I answered and tried to field, but the die had already been cast.

10 August 2014, The second gale strikes …
I woke up that Sunday to an article about my former relationship on the front page of the *Sunday Times* under the bold and large heading 'Love affair rocks SARS'.[7]

The report, written by Rees, effectively contained everything that was suggested to him in the email sent by Walter and ignored the information he was told to ignore. At this point, there was no mention yet of a 'rogue unit'. Much was quoted from my correspondence with the *Sunday Times*, but other relevant parts that I sent to them were ignored. This was most likely because it didn't fit the storyline.

But that wasn't all. A second article, 'Love turns sour in text messages', made some of my messages to Walter public. In addition, Oppelt wrote an editorial to explain why my private life had suddenly, in August 2014, become a matter of 'public interest' and to assure readers that the *Sunday Times* wasn't being 'played'.

What I found very interesting was what wasn't considered relevant to or in the public interest. First was the fact that the allegations Walter made against me on 28 May 2014 – which the *Sunday Times* now reported on – had been made against me before, on 1 February 2014, and they were aware of this. As I have explained, she had shared these allegations with a number of people at the start of that year, including the *Sunday Times*, but she retracted it over the following days and admitted that she had lied about certain things and defamed me. None of this was reflected, however, in the *Sunday Times* article.

Secondly, I had given Rees the text exchanges between Walter and me in which she offered to testify against a number of parties who were involved in the tobacco industry. This was also conveniently disregarded and not considered to be in 'the public interest'. The various allegations Walter had made against the SSA, the Illicit-Tobacco Task Team and the multinational tobacco manufacturer in her confession (to Rees among others) on 1 February were seemingly also forgotten or not considered in the public interest.

What is even more important, and I believe of equal public interest – even though the *Sunday Times* did not think it relevant to publish – was that Walter accused journalists at the *Sunday Times* of receiving bribes and gifts from tobacco manufacturers in exchange for favourable media coverage or for negative coverage of their competitors. These claims were made in the same correspondence as the retractions and admissions. One journalist allegedly received sponsorships in the form of clothing for a sports team, whereas another had allegedly been 'offered cocaine, a holiday and cash' by a tobacco manufacturer, which he never reported to his bosses at the *Sunday Times*.[8]

The same edition of the *Sunday Times* published an article that attacked Ivan's status as acting SARS commissioner. This probably shouldn't have come as a surprise to us: it was in line with a message I had received earlier that year from a go-between from the hallowed halls of Parliament. The message was addressed to Ivan and said: 'They are going to humiliate you guys, hound you out of SARS, and do so in a manner that none of you will ever get work again ...'

So, the targets were in their sights. However, over the course of the next 18 months developments would show that perhaps indeed the *Sunday Times* had been played.

City Press and the original 'rogues'

That same Sunday, *City Press* carried an exposé about what they described as a 'rogue unit' that allegedly operated within the SSA. Under the headline 'Sex, Sars and rogue spies', investigative journalist Jacques Pauw wrote, 'A *City Press* investigation has revealed the existence of the Special Operations Unit of the SSA, where rogue agents use state resources to conduct dirty tricks campaigns, smuggle cigarettes and disgrace top civil servants.'[9]

By then I was already aware of *City Press*'s investigation, having met with their team on 30 July 2014 after they contacted SARS and me directly. I did so with written permission from my manager and with Ivan's approval. The *City Press* team wanted to verify information relevant to me and we wanted an opportunity to defend SARS.

The *City Press* team put it to SARS, specifically to Adrian, and then to me, that they believed that there were rogue intelligence agents involved in campaigns to discredit certain state officials. They believed SARS, and me in particular, to be victims of such a campaign. They showed me some of the evidence they had uncovered and I provided them with more details in an effort to help defend myself from false accusations.

According to *City Press*, the activities of the supposed 'rogue agents' in the SSA included 'running a campaign against Hawks head Lieutenant General Anwa Dramat for his role in [police Crime Intelligence chief Richard] Mdluli's fraud and murder investigations, by leaking a police dossier to the media, implicating Dramat in *perlemoen* smuggling and the illegal rendition of Zimbabwean criminals.'[10] Sometime later, Dramat was suspended and charged for the alleged 'illegal renditions'.

These 'rogue elements' were also 'working to replace Sars' top management, from acting Commissioner Ivan Pillay to Van Loggenberg [*sic*] – because the service was investigating tobacco smugglers with close links to the unit,' the report said. '*City Press* is in possession of hundreds of SMSes, emails and tape recordings that date from 2011 to 2014 ... The SMSes and emails were forensically extracted from cellphones and have been handed over to the office of State Security Minister David Mahlobo and to Sars' top managers.'[11]

The first media story about a 'rogue unit' in a state institution therefore didn't even relate to SARS. The first time the *Sunday Times* used this term in relation to SARS was later, on 12 October 2014, in a lead article with the heading 'SARS bugged Zuma'.[12]

In response to the *City Press* articles, the Minister of State Security, David Mahlobo, asked the Inspector General of Intelligence to 'establish the facts and get to the bottom of allegations made about members of the State Security Agency'.[13] Mahlobo had then just been appointed as the minister and I felt somewhat sorry for him to have been saddled with what was clearly going to be a mess.

I appeared before the Inspector General of Intelligence twice. At the first meeting I presented over 30 instances of possible unlawful or illegal activities that I was aware of and believed to be relevant to their mandate. I also identified over 60 people I believed should be interviewed or be of interest to their investigation.

But I detected some reticence that day. This was confirmed very soon when I was given an 'informal message' from SARS's company secretary, which reached me via Guillam. It went something like this: 'Don't rock the boat. When you go there again, say sorry and only answer questions posed. Don't be difficult.'

I didn't understand why this message had been passed to me but I sent a message back to the effect that I would oblige. So, at my second appearance, I apologised to the Inspector General if I had offended anybody and declared myself ready to only answer questions posed to me. I was asked virtually nothing regarding the 30-plus instances I had raised in the first meeting. Most of the questions posed to me related to SARS only.

But my conscience forced me to ensure that at least some documentary and data records that I had in my possession were delivered to the office of the Inspector General of Intelligence. I followed this up with a lawyer's letter to confirm what I had given them. This included the text messages between Walter and her SSA handler, also a member of the Illicit-Tobacco Task Team, where they described themselves as a '*moerse* good team' who could manipulate the SSA, NPA and SARS to do what they wanted.

I had assumed this would be sufficient evidence to demonstrate that not all was well in the State of Denmark. And these were just some messages out of hundreds more illustrating wrongdoing.

However, on 5 May 2015, in a brief news article it was reported that Mahlobo said an investigation had found no evidence that rogue state intelligence operatives of the SSA were trying to destabilise SARS.[14] I was gobsmacked.

Nearly two years later, in mid-2016, I had an opportunity to discuss the matter with one of the spies identified as one of the rogue intelligence agents in the *City Press* articles. Let's call him Boris. He turned out to be quite willing to talk openly to me and to answer all my questions. Boris, who I understand is no longer working for the SSA and is living abroad, actually seemed like quite a nice guy.

He told me he was the person who had tipped off *City Press* but never explained whether he did so on orders or of his own accord. But he did admit that they were instructed to 'look at us' (myself and the HRIU) with, in his words, 'a microscope'.[15] He told me in no uncertain terms that they had been given the official instruction to 'find whatever they could' against us.

Between us, we managed to piece together what had really happened after *City Press* reported on a 'rogue unit' within the SSA and the *Sunday Times* started with the first of their series of articles fingering me. What seems to have transpired is that various individuals, some from within the tobacco industry and others from the Illicit-Tobacco Task Team, had been played off against one another.[16]

When Boris and I had our little chat I had asked him about his experiences before the Inspector General of Intelligence – assuming he would've been called. After all, *City Press* identified some of the members of what they claimed was a special operations unit in the SSA that was allegedly responsible for disinformation campaigns against certain state officials. Most interestingly, Boris then told me he never appeared before the inspector general. I had to ask him twice just to be sure.[17]

It now perhaps becomes easier to understand the *Sunday Times* article 'Love affair rocks SARS', the email Rees left behind when he met with me that day and the meeting at Life Café in Brooklyn between members of the Illicit-Tobacco Task Team. Clearly, *City Press* had been asking uncomfortable questions to some members of the Illicit-Tobacco Task Team, which left them very concerned.

They knew the *City Press* report was coming. It is my contention that, for them, there could be no better counter-offensive than to get the *Sunday Times* to run a counter-narrative that same Sunday.

Shortly after these reports appeared the *Sunday Times* would take the 'rogue-unit' label and aim it right back at us. There were certainly enough people who had been waiting for an opportunity like this to pounce on many at SARS, including me and the HRIU. After all, as I have illustrated, we had made many enemies along the way. All of a sudden Peega's old 'Operation Snowman' dossier became very relevant and convenient to some. There was blood in the water and the sharks were circling.

And so began the media storm. The *Sunday Times* was on a roll, and was only too eager to listen to any source willing to advance the narrative that I was corrupt and, shortly after, that I had managed a 'rogue unit'.

And, boy, did the 'sources' line up.

14

The Tempest (Act II)

Between August 2014 and April 2016, more than 30 articles were published by the *Sunday Times* about me, the so-called rogue unit, Ivan Pillay and, ultimately, Pravin Gordhan. Here I examine some of the articles that created and helped to advance the SARS 'rogue-unit' story. These reports also cast aspersions on a number of other key SARS employees and led to SARS replacing virtually the entire top management of a once-proud state institution.

First, I'd like to share a key piece of history that you should keep in the back of your mind as this 'rogue-unit' narrative develops. To me, some striking similarities are apparent if one compares what happened to us at SARS with the disinformation campaigns that the state intelligence machinery used against liberation movements before 1994. During the 1980s, the 'total onslaught' years, the apartheid regime had a very powerful and secret weapon, a unit known by its acronym Stratcom (Strategic Communications). It was a shadowy unit, buried deep in the recesses of the Security Branch. Even today, very little is known about their operations.

This unit, among other things, was engaged in what militarists would call 'psych-ops', or psychological operations. They paid journalists to plant and advance stories, placed and managed journalists in media houses, issued leaks and rumours, and put together seemingly credible dossiers and stories – all aimed solely at discrediting the 'enemy'.

The most famous Stratcom operation was called Romulus. This came to light at the hearings of the Truth and Reconciliation Commission (TRC) in the mid-1990s. According to a South African Press Agency (SAPA) report on the testimonies of Stratcom head Vic McPherson and operative Paul Erasmus in 1997, Operation Romulus had sought to bring Winnie Madikizela-Mandela into disrepute with the aim of discrediting the ANC and to 'sow division within the ranks of the liberation movement':

> Articles were placed in South African and international newspapers discrediting Madikizela-Mandela with 'several notable successes', according to documents submitted to the TRC from a Stratcom disinformation campaign known as Operation Romulus. A document entitled 'Dissemination of suitable material re Winnie Mandela abroad: Discreditation of the ANC' said a 'veritable mass of material' was forwarded to the media 'with the specific objective of using Winnie Mandela … to discredit the ANC as a whole.'
>
> Articles highly critical of Madikizela-Mandela appeared in early 1991 in leading British newspapers the *Sunday Times*, *The Times*, *The Independent*, *Daily Express* and other newspapers. An article appeared in the United States *Vanity Fair* entitled 'How bad is Winnie Mandela?' The document was written by former Stratcom operative Paul Erasmus, who took the stand with McPherson …[1]

This report describes Stratcom as 'the propaganda apparatus of the apartheid security police'. McPherson explained to the TRC exactly what Stratcom did:

> Strategic communications is the planned, coordinated execution of a deed and/or the presentation of a message by means of various communication instruments to: change the attitudes, values and views of

individuals, and/or a group of persons and/or to create the required attitude and/or to maintain an existing attitude; to neutralise hostile propaganda and/or to utilise hostile propaganda; and to reach national objectives.

Stratcom can be seen as political warfare as utilised in the Republic of China or psychological warfare as utilised in Europe or civic action as utilised by the Americans or active measures as utilised by the old Soviet Union. Stratcom was a covert operation and was conducted in secret ... [T]he way we have trained our people and instructed our people is usually *to work on an actual or a factual incident or event and then perhaps add on and that will eventually lead, say, to disinformation or [falsehood], something extra to a story ...*[2]

Over the years I kept an ever expanding file of all the dossiers and allegations that had surfaced from before and since inception of the SPU/NRG and HRIU. These maintained that Gordhan, Pillay and I were racists, that we were opposed to Zuma, that we had entered into unlawful tax settlements, spied on taxpayers, intercepted communications, and so forth. There was a common thread to all of these allegations: they relied on a little bit of fact, which lent a veneer of credibility to their content. The rest was fiction, just like Stratcom's propaganda communications.

I called this file 'Bedknobs and broomsticks', as it reminded me of the eponymous movie from my childhood. *Bedknobs and Broomsticks* used special effects, with both real-life actors and animated characters. As a child, the combined effect seemed very real to me, even though it was just fiction. I saw an analogy there.

I first came to learn that the Kanyane report had been completed when I got a call from *Sunday Times* journalists Malcolm Rees and Stephan Hofstatter on 16 August 2014. I was still in the process of finalising my formal submission to the panel and had no idea that it had already wrapped up its proceedings and produced its report.

When they called to ask for my comment on the report, I was so surprised that the process had been concluded without my having been given the chance to be properly heard that initially I did not believe them. They told me the Kanyane Panel had completed their report the day before. In the end, I didn't receive it until a week later but somehow it was leaked to the *Sunday Times* within 24 hours.

Although the panel's report contained no definite adverse findings against me, and found that it was unable to conclude that the information and evidence placed before it established even a prima facie basis for further action, the panel did make certain comments and expressed certain views that were critical of me. And they made these assertions without giving me an opportunity to place any information or evidence before them. Needless to say, I wasn't afforded the right to reply to the comments or findings.

Paragraph 6.23 of the report states that the panel assumed that I had stopped preparing a response to the complaint 'after I was informed on 21 July 2014 that the panel had been instructed to conclude its work and report on the facts established' up to that stage.[3] This is simply not true. I wasn't informed on 21 July, or any other day, for that matter, that the panel had been 'instructed to conclude its work'.[4] All the while I was still preparing my submission to the panel.

The panel proceeded to justify its failure to afford me an opportunity to respond by suggesting that I would not be adversely affected by the report, since it 'makes no definitive adverse findings against' me. Well, in fact, history would prove that I was 'adversely affected' by the report.

In the end I submitted two formal replies to SARS in response to the report, even if after the fact. I pointed out factual flaws in their findings, asking that my response should accompany the Kanyane report on record. SARS acknowledged it would do so, but the report and my replies were conveniently cast aside.

Also, by August 2014 the complaint against me had morphed once again. Now doubts had been cast over a fundraiser club that I was part of. There was a further set of allegations to the effect that I had been advancing the agendas of criminals and criminal syndicates, and had caused these criminals and syndicates to threaten Walter. It was also claimed that I had contacted the media with the aim of slandering her and caused parties to bring certain legal actions in exchange for tax leniency.

Allegedly, I had also caused Walter to act against her will by influencing her to withdraw from particular clients of her 'long-standing' legal practice (even though the practice had been established only in mid-2013), had caused her to resign as chairperson of the Fair-Trade Independent Tobacco Association (FITA), and had influenced her to issue various communications to an advocate, the *Sunday Times* and others. Furthermore, I had allegedly shared confidential information about taxpayers and, in particular, her own confidential information in the form of a 'secret affidavit', to the media, specifically to journalist and author Jacques Pauw.

It was at this point that Walter first made reference to a SARS unit in her allegations (it was in her opposing affidavit to the interdict application sought against her and British American Tobacco by tobacco manufacturer Carnilinx).[5]

17 August 2014
Sunday Times headline: SARS sleuth sidelined in aftermath of love affair
By Stephan Hofstatter, Mzilikazi wa Afrika and Malcolm Rees

The Kanyane report is leaked to the *Sunday Times*. The front-page story states that I was 'set to be removed from dozens of high-profile cases following a damning report by a panel that investigated allegations of serious misconduct'.[6]

The article then goes on to reflect on some of the comments made by the Kanyane Panel about my former relationship, including that it was a 'patent conflict of interest' and that I had disclosed it only four months after the relationship began. Had the Kanyane Panel afforded me an opportunity to respond to their comments, I would have been able to demonstrate that I did in fact disclose the existence of the relationship within days to my line manager and two other senior SARS officials.

Significantly, this article fails to reflect on numerous key details: the fact that the Kanyane Panel stated that it was unable to conclude that the evidentiary material presented in support of the allegations was credible or reliable; that no affidavit was provided by Walter; that similar allegations had been made against me before, only to be recanted; that no data was provided to the panel as had been promised; and that whatever was provided in text was heavily redacted.

The article goes on to state that a source 'close to the investigation' said there would also be an investigation into 'donations channelled through Wachizungu, a charity Van Loggerenberg champions. The donations were from taxpayers under investigation by SARS and law and auditing firms regularly used by the revenue authority.'[7]

'Given his role in Wachizungu, there is a potential conflict of interest in so far as some of the donors are entities and persons that either have disputes with SARS or remain or have been SARS's service providers.'[8] But no such persons were ever identified.

Firstly, I was never given a chance by Hofstatter to properly respond to these allegations. I was still trying to explain to him how the fundraiser functioned when, mid-sentence, he shouted, 'Have to go, we are running to print!' and put down the phone.

Secondly, many people 'championed' the work of this fundraiser – not only me. So, to attribute all its fundraising to me alone was factually incorrect. Furthermore, most people associated with this fundraising club weren't even SARS officials. The fundraiser never received donations, as the story implied, and never 'channelled' any donations from 'taxpayers under investigation by SARS' or 'law and auditing firms regularly used by the revenue authority'.

For the sake of transparency, we created what we called 'donor rolls' on the Wachizungu website, which show clearly who made donations to which charity. Each donation was also acknowledged on Facebook and Twitter, showing clearly who had made a donation, when, and to which charitable organisation. Wachizungu itself was never reflected as a recipient of any donation.

In 2015 I took it upon myself to obtain the services of a very reputable auditing firm at a cost of over R87 000 to audit the account. We did test payments through the online platforms to demonstrate how donations reflected. My ultimate goal was to demonstrate that whatever went into that account from any donor, went straight out of that account to the relevant charity that the donation was intended for. Wachizungu got a clean and unqualified audit report.

31 August 2014
Sunday Times headline: SARS to foot love scandal bill
BY PIET RAMPEDI, MZILIKAZI WA AFRIKA, STEPHAN HOFSTATTER AND MALCOLM REES

At this point, I was instructed by SARS to refer all media enquiries to Adrian. The headline suggests that SARS was footing my entire legal bill, even though Adrian is quoted as denying this. Only those parts relevant to my duties and related to my actions in the course of my duties were paid for. I paid significant portions of my legal bill myself.

In this article, the *Sunday Times* reports that SARS was paying for a public-relations company for me. I have never used the services of a public-relations company and consequently this claim is emphatically denied, in writing, by Adrian. Nevertheless, the newspaper states this falsehood as fact.

In October 2014 the eye of the storm was upon us. Shortly before, Toby had informally advised me that a new commissioner for SARS was on his way. He assured me that the new man was fully apprised of my situation and realised that it was a private matter that had spilt over into my workplace. I needn't worry.

Up until this point the only mention in the media of so-called rogue agents was the *City Press* article about agents that were allegedly associated with the SSA.[9] But, from October onwards, the *Sunday Times* and its anonymous sources went into overdrive. Although Rees initiated the first story, it would be journalists Stephan Hofstatter, Mzilikazi wa Afrika and Piet Rampedi from the investigative team who would build and expand on the 'rogue-unit' story relentlessly.

Later, Rampedi would identify his sources in his verbal submissions to the Press Ombudsman in December 2015. He claimed they were a combination of 'former SARS employees', 'current SARS employees' and 'intelligence officials'.

On 1 October Tom Moyane arrived at SARS to assume his duties as the new commissioner. In light of all the *Sunday Times* reports I tried to meet him several times because I wanted to explain the background and history of the HRIU to him but I was never given a chance. I firmly believe certain individuals deliberately misled Moyane and withheld crucial facts from him at that time.

After several attempts to set up a meeting, I resorted to writing a letter to Moyane in response to all the articles. My hope was that this would help inform him about the issues that were at stake and enable SARS to refute the allegations about a 'rogue unit'. Later this letter was to surface in the *Sunday Times*, whose reporters for some reason had decided to refer to it as a 'confession'.

From this point onwards, Adrian was increasingly sidelined as spokesperson and Luther Lebelo started taking over the role as SARS spokesperson. All the while, nothing was being done by SARS to counter the lies published in the *Sunday Times*.

By now Walter had also instituted civil proceedings against SARS and me in my official capacity, claiming for damages on the basis that SARS,

I and other unnamed people at the tax authority had allegedly illegally intercepted her communications and provided a copy of these interceptions, as well as a 'secret and confidential' affidavit, to *City Press*. I intend to defend these false allegations made against me in court, however, at the time of writing, the matter had not been enrolled in court.

12 October 2014

Sunday Times headline: SARS bugged Zuma – Tax authority paid agent R3m to hush up illegal spying operation
BY PIET RAMPEDI, MZILIKAZI WA AFRIKA, STEPHAN HOFSTATTER AND MALCOLM REES

The *Sunday Times* now stated as fact that a former 'spy master', referring to Martin, who had been head of the unit at its inception, had blackmailed SARS into paying him R3 million to keep silent about how its 'rogue unit' broke into Jacob Zuma's private home in Forest Town, Johannesburg, and planted listening devices there. According to the report, this was after Zuma had been fired as deputy president in 2005.[10]

The article goes on to say: 'Documents seen by the *Sunday Times* and SARS officials who spoke on condition of anonymity claim that the unit also intercepted a meeting between Zuma and SARS executive Leonard Radebe at the Beverly Hills Hotel in Durban ahead of the ANC's 2007 Polokwane conference ... A senior intelligence official confirmed this week that the cabinet security cluster had independently established that a bug had been planted in Zuma's house.'[11]

Strangely, when this supposed 'bugging' had taken place, the SPU/NRG/HRIU didn't even exist. The SPU was established in 2007. The Scorpions, however, had conducted a much-publicised search of Zuma's Forest Town home in April 2005.[12] The rumour seems to have its origins in one or two SPU officials, who worked at the Scorpions at the time of the raid and who later related their experiences of the raid to their colleagues at SARS.

Even if bugs had been planted at the president's house back then, it had nothing to do with SARS and even less with a unit that didn't exist at the time. No other raid was ever conducted on a residence of Zuma since then. Despite this, the *Sunday Times* was only too happy to state as fact, in the lead story on its front page, that SARS had 'bugged Zuma'. It was all a little *Bedknobs and Broomsticks*, I thought …

As for the meeting at the Beverly Hills Hotel between Zuma and Radebe, I have no knowledge of it.

12 October 2014

Sunday Times headline: Operative's claims not far-fetched now

By Mzilikazi wa Afrika, Piet Rampedi, Stephan Hofstatter and Malcolm Rees

In this article the indomitable Michael Peega features again. The report starts by saying how his dossier claiming that SARS ran a 'rogue unit' was easily discredited at the time it was released in 2009, when 'SARS responded swiftly by issuing a briefing document refuting his claims. The notion of a rogue spy unit was consigned to the dustbin of fabrication. But a lover's quarrel earlier this year brought new evidence suggesting that not all of Peega's claims were far-fetched.'[3]

The evidence supplied in support of this claim are private text messages between me and Walter, which are quoted completely out of context. In a giant leap, the reporters write that these messages support her sworn statements in court proceedings, in which she claims that 'the revenue service was gathering illegal covert intelligence'.

The *Sunday Times* claims that in these messages I referred extensively to SARS phone and mail interceptions, 'including references to "running plenty of lines"', 'watcher and listener ladies' and targets changing their 'phones and e-mails' because they 'know how I operate'.

To give an example of just how badly one quote was taken out of context, in a WhatsApp message sent to Walter on 21 November 2013 I refer to 'my watcher and listener ladies' with reference to staff at SARS whom I worked with. The background to this remark is that, a few days before, she and I had watched a movie called *Tinker Tailor Soldier Spy*. In the film the main character refers to 'watchers and listeners', and I recall that we had a light-hearted discussion about this. It was in this context that I referred to some officials as 'watchers and listeners' – as a joke. If one takes the entire conversation, and not just this snippet, into consideration, you'll see that there is no mention whatsoever of communications being intercepted by SARS or anybody else.

Another text message that the *Sunday Times* elaborated on is one sent on 1 March 2014, in which I shared information about a media enquiry about our relationship and shortly after passed on an email containing the actual enquiry. She asked how I had obtained it. I answered with the word 'intercepted'. The media enquiry I passed on to her had been sent directly to me by someone in the tobacco industry who had been approached by a reporter from *The Sunday Independent* who wanted to find out more about my relationship with Walter.

This message was therefore not intercepted by SARS. Yet, as the *Sunday Times* put it, this shows that 'Van Loggerenberg refers extensively to SARS phone and mail interceptions ...'[14]

Then the *Sunday Times* goes on to say that I had, first, claimed 'messages had been tampered with' and, later, that I had said I had 'deliberately lied to his [my] girlfriend at the time' for reasons I would disclose to investigators.

I never said text messages had been tampered with. This is a figment of the imagination of the person who wrote this part of the article. What I did say was that the snippets of texts put to me were being taken out of context and should be considered within the context of the entire conversation. In fact, I had a long discussion with Rob Rose of the *Sunday Times* just after 10 August 2014 during which I not only explained these texts to him, but also sent him complete sets of the conversations to provide the broader context.

19 October 2014

Sunday Times headline: Pravin's pal scores on early retirement – SARS immediately rehires deputy commissioner

By Piet Rampedi, Mzilikazi wa Afrika, Stephan Hofstatter and Malcolm Rees

Now it was no longer just about me and the so-called rogue unit. Ivan Pillay and Pravin Gordhan were also drawn in and the scope creep had begun.

'Former finance minister Pravin Gordhan allegedly cost taxpayers millions by forcing the South African Revenue Service to bend the rules to clinch a cushy retirement deal for his buddy, Ivan Pillay,' the report states.[15]

The report claims Ivan was improperly rehired by Gordhan at the expense of the taxpayer after his retirement. It continues: 'A *Sunday Times* investigation has established that Gordhan approved deputy commissioner Pillay's early retirement with full benefits and allegedly immediately instructed SARS to rehire him on a three-year contract …'[16]

However, there was no 'investigation' by the *Sunday Times*. The story was based on an internal leak from within SARS and the 'sources' simply presented private employee information concerning Ivan to the *Sunday Times* and put a twist on it.

The newspaper had emailed questions to SARS asking for information about Ivan's pension and retirement benefits, and his current contract with SARS, at 11.00 am on 17 October 2014. SARS was asked to respond to 13 questions from the newspaper by 4.30 pm the same day. The questions related to memorandums and documents that were more than four years old and had to be retrieved from the SARS human-resources system and the archive of formal correspondence between SARS and the Office of the Minister of Finance. The period of time given for SARS to respond was wholly inadequate. Nevertheless, a written response was provided at 4.41 pm.

SARS said that, as far as it was concerned, the institution and the former Minister of Finance, Pravin Gordhan, had complied with all the provisions in law granting early retirement and in retaining Pillay as an employee on a contract basis. Interestingly, there's no mention of the fact that Magashula was SARS Commissioner at the time and Nene was Deputy Minister of Finance, or of any of the senior human-resources staff at SARS, who would have all had to consider the matter.

SARS cautioned the newspaper that it was in possession of confidential employer/employee information and that any publication of the information contained in the documents would constitute a material breach of Ivan's right to privacy and the confidentiality between SARS and its employee.

In the end, one paragraph from the SARS response was quoted in the newspaper on 19 October 2014. Clearly, this wasn't about me or the original 'complaint' any more.

At the time Ivan obtained legal advice and it was suggested that he could sue the *Sunday Times* for publishing this article. When I asked him later why he didn't, Ivan, his usual calm self, said he thought that if he did, it would seem as if he were using state resources to defend himself and he didn't want such a perception to mar SARS's image. He reckoned it would be best to leave things be in the hope that the storm would eventually subside.

9 November 2014

Sunday Times headline: Taxman's rogue unit ran brothel: Secret outfit also posed as guards for ANC heavyweights, spied on top cops and acted for SARS bosses' friends

BY MZILIKAZI WA AFRIKA, PIET RAMPEDI AND STEPHAN HOFSTATTER

Top SARS sleuth admits: we ran a rogue unit – *Sunday Times* reports were true, investigator admits to his boss in 'confession' letter

BY PIET RAMPEDI, MZILIKAZI WA AFRIKA AND STEPHAN HOFSTATTER

In this edition, the *Sunday Times* really went to town with its 'rogue-unit' narrative. There were stories on the front page, and the second, third and fifth pages. All thanks to so-called 'agent reports' by SARS officials that they had been given by their 'sources'.

The front-page story made the now infamous claim that the unit had run a brothel. I have already explained the origins of this story – Stoffel's lewd house party.

At some point, I got to read the 'agent reports' that the newspaper had relied on for its articles. These so-called agent reports appear to have their origin in a request by Moyane to Ravele to obtain 'reports' from former SPU, NRG and HRIU staff.[17] To my knowledge, there were five such reports, all of which I've read. Dippie, Johnny, Ato, Jabulani[18] and Kendo[19] submitted reports based on broad questions posed to them. Josey, Gertjie, Tony and a host of others, who were still working for SARS, weren't asked to submit reports.

A common thread in Dippie and Kendo's reports was the suggestion that certain unit members had apparently acted as 'bodyguards for VIPs' and then 'infiltrated' them in this manner. From what I could gather, Peega appears to have known some politicians from the time before he joined SARS. Apparently, Peega made a bit of pocket money by acting as a bodyguard and driver for them. He continued to do so after he was appointed at SARS and from time to time he gave some 'moonlighting jobs' to his pals, Dippie and Kendo and others in the unit. This is old news and was reported in the media in 2010.[20] Dippie and Kendo remained close friends with Peega after he left SARS.

None of them reported their 'moonlighting' activities in their declarations of private interests to SARS. So, when this little bomb burst I guess they had to cover themselves and cleverly decided to turn their moonlighting into a 'rogue-unit project'.

Kendo and Dippie also convey in their 'agent reports', albeit in very vague terms, conversations during the initial days, when the plan was that the unit would be housed in the NIA, about the possibility of covert mechanisms that were discussed, but eventually decided against. None of them distinguish between fact, discussions and what was ultimately implemented. As an example, nobody got 'new cars and homes', as the newspaper claims.

When I read these reports, I was terribly disappointed, especially by Dippie and Kendo. Had they forgotten how Peega had tried to recruit them in late 2009 to discredit SARS, Gordhan, Pillay and me in his so-called Project Broken Arrow dossier? Back then, both of them submitted written reports to us about Peega's efforts in this regard.

The claim that the unit spied on 'top cops' seems to relate to an incident that, again, took place at the Scorpions before the SPU had been established. Back then, the erstwhile Scorpions conducted surveillance on former police commissioner Jackie Selebi. It seems his security detail picked this up and confronted the Scorpions about it. One of the former Scorpions who had been involved in the surveillance later joined SARS and shared this information in a conversation with some of the NRG officials. This is what set off this particular rumour.

The claim in the news report that members of the unit used 'fake names' can only relate to the incident I described earlier where Martin and Fransman obtained sample identity cards with fictitious names shortly after the unit was started. That was when it wasn't yet clear whether it would be a co-project with the NIA, whose agents use fake names when needed. It seems that someone didn't hand in or destroy his card, as instructed. This card was offered to the new SARS management under Moyane as proof of the allegation that unit members operated under false names: another perfect example of where a detail of factual information was taken and embellished to create a completely fictional story.

Johnny and Ato's reports were fair, but either the newspaper omitted elements that did not suit its story, or the reports they received were altered. Crucially, the *Sunday Times* ignored the fact that these reports emphatically denied that there were house infiltrations, interceptions or bugging, specifically of Zuma. Dippie and Kendo also denied this.

The second article, 'Top SARS sleuth admits: we ran a rogue unit', left me bewildered. As I have mentioned, I wrote a letter to Moyane towards the end of October 2014 when I was on special leave because I believed he was being lied to and facts were being withheld from him. My letter was delivered to him in hard copy; it wasn't emailed. In this letter I denied the claims in each and every *Sunday Times* article to date, including that we ran a 'rogue unit'.

In a misleading introductory sentence, the *Sunday Times* team said I wrote a 'confession letter' and that I admitted that '*Sunday Times* reports were spot-on because the agency did have a rogue unit that followed one of its managers who had several meetings with President Jacob Zuma'.

In a move that wouldn't pass Logic 101, the report goes on to claim that because I admitted that the SPU/NRG had followed Leonard Radebe on one occasion during a 2010 investigation into Radebe's meeting with Dave King, it proves the existence of a 'rogue unit' and implies that it spied on Zuma. Huh? (If Radebe ever had meetings with Zuma I know nothing about it.)

The journalists offer no further proof of the existence of the 'rogue unit', except the claims made by an unnamed source.

How my note ended up at the *Sunday Times* would be interesting to know. Only three people in SARS, to my knowledge, had the initial copies of that note. Aware that this letter might also be leaked to the media, I had asked that it be handed to Moyane in person. It was confirmed to me that it had been given to him in person the week before this article was published.

16 November 2014

Sunday Times headline: SARS chief acts on 'brothel' claims – *Sunday Times'* disclosures of 'rogue' spy unit unleash a storm as top sleuth is suspended

By Piet Rampedi, Mzilikazi wa Afrika, Stephan Hofstatter and Malcolm Rees

In November, three months after the first *Sunday Times* report on me had appeared, the axe came down. The newspaper reported that I had been suspended for my role in the 'rogue unit'.[21] And I wasn't to be the only victim:

> According to a circular and two senior SARS officials, the commissioner also sidelined SARS's executive committee (exco), saying he had lost confidence in its members. The exco included deputy commissioner Ivan Pillay and chief officer for strategy Pete Richer, who set up the unit in 2006. According to senior SARS officials who attended Moyane's 'compulsory' meeting on Monday, the commissioner gave them a dressing-down.
>
> 'He did not take questions. He said it was disgusting that SARS was now running brothels,' said a SARS official. Another said Moyane promised to appoint his own team because the exco suffered from 'analysis paralysis'.[22]

Except, there never was a brothel. The EXCO was suspended for nothing.

The *Sunday Times* again repeats as fact that a former NIA operative had blackmailed SARS into paying him more than R3 million for his silence after he threatened to go public about the rogue unit's actions.

The newspaper then makes a meal of the fact that I demanded an apology and a retraction of the claim published in the newspaper the previous week that I had written a 'confession' to Moyane. 'He has been invited to deliver a summons to our attorneys,' wrote the editor, Phylicia Oppelt. 'We are more than willing to defend our story in any forum he chooses.'[23]

Despite the bravado displayed at the time by Oppelt and the *Sunday Times*, I did get my apology and a retraction – even if it was almost a year and a half later. On 3 April 2016, the *Sunday Times* admitted that it had 'reported incorrectly that Johann van Loggerenberg had written a "confession" letter to SARS commissioner Tom Moyane admitting that he had indeed run a "rogue unit". The document contains no such confession. It was, in fact, a denial ..."[24]

Throughout this period, none of those affected were allowed to publicly defend themselves against any of the *Sunday Times* articles, and our silence only helped to bolster the 'rogue-unit' myth. To my constant surprise, SARS also did nothing to counter it. In fact, on 13 October 2014, barely two weeks into his tenure as the new commissioner, Moyane distributed a newsletter to all SARS staff:

> You will all have seen and read the *Sunday Times* story about SARS yesterday, quite a bad picture and a negative exposé of what we are about. In fact, it has dented our image and reputation before our important stakeholder – the South African taxpayers. We have lost the moral high ground with these serious allegations ...
>
> I met with EXCO and GE's [group executives] earlier today to discuss these stories and the wider issues. I want to assure all of you that under my watch, I will not allow a culture of flouting laws and rogue activities in whatever form or shape. We must conduct our activities within the parameters of the laws of our country.
>
> There are several enquiries underway to look into the matter, and I do not want to pre-empt any of them. However, I have requested that the panel chaired by Advocate Muzi Sikhakhane SC provide me with a provisional report no later than the close of business on Friday. This will assist me in gaining a fuller understanding of the problem ...
>
> I made it very clear that we cannot and will not have any so-called 'rogue elements' at SARS. The SARS has an important role to play in combating illegal and illicit trade, but once again it must at all times be done within the law. Accountability and transparency must be our mantra. I will keep you updated as we go forward. Regards, Tom.[25]

I understand that Moyane had just arrived at SARS and wouldn't necessarily have known about the institution's inner workings. Nobody could have expected him to know everything about SARS in its absolute detail. SARS is a complex organisation with a myriad of units and a history of complicated matters.

But I had now started doubting Toby, who assured me that Moyane had been fully briefed about everything I had provided to him. Why would Moyane then take such a strong position at this early stage and simply assume that the *Sunday Times* articles about a 'rogue-unit' were accurate? Clearly, some things were slipping through the cracks, I thought.

15

The Sikhakhane Panel

By the end of 2014, the approaching storm had turned into a howling hurricane. The *Sunday Times* kept churning out more and more 'exposés'. It was during this period that a second panel came into being at SARS. To explain more about what this process entailed, we need to go back a few months before my suspension in November.

On 3 September 2014, Ivan, still acting SARS commissioner, issued a public statement explaining that, even though the Kanyane Panel had not proven any wrongdoing or breaches of the law on my part, he believed it paramount to further investigate the issues that were raised 'to safeguard the integrity of SARS'. He appointed a new, external committee 'to delve into the observations made by the previous panel of review regarding possible breaches of taxpayer confidentiality, of conflict of interest and of procedures of good governance'.[1]

So the Sikhakhane Panel was born. It was led by Advocate Muzi Sikhakhane SC, who was assisted by two other external advocates of his choice and an external attorney.

The back story to the creation of this panel is that Ivan was concerned that the comments made in the Kanyane report would reflect badly on SARS and he believed it was necessary to get absolute clarity on those matters. I respected Ivan immensely and hardly ever disagreed with him.

But my view on this panel was slightly different from his.

I felt I was being treated unfairly and I told him so. Why give these people another bite at the cherry? I said. I felt it was like being tried in court, a bad court at that, which doesn't even hear out the accused, and when it cannot find the accused guilty insists on a retrial.

Unfortunately, Ivan was away for most of August and things were moving quickly. I never really had a chance to take him through the many things I had uncovered about the tobacco industry, the Illicit-Tobacco Task Team and other related information. Ivan convinced me that the Sikhakhane Panel would be an improvement on Kanyane. 'Sikhakhane is a good man, a fair man and, I'm told, a good jurist,' he told me. 'Give the process a chance: do it for SARS,' he said.

It didn't sit well with me, but out of respect for Ivan and, in the spirit of the higher purpose, I agreed. I had harboured the hope that a properly constituted panel would consider my submission and evidence, and hear my side regarding the allegations made against me. The truth would ultimately surface, I thought. I was intent on exposing the allegations against me for the shams they were. I believed I could expose all the corruption, fraud, crimes against the state and the abuse of state power that I knew lay behind all of it. But that was not to be.

I appeared twice before the Sikhakhane Panel. In the first meeting, I found the panel to be professional, to the point, courteous, clear and unambiguous. It wasn't a very long meeting and they asked me only a few questions. They asked me to trace my history at SARS and to describe my role and function in the organisation at that point.

To avoid a repeat of the Kanyane Panel, my legal representatives and I wanted confirmation that I would be heard on any matter that was adverse to me before the panel reached its findings or concluded its report. After all, the principle of *audi alteram partem*, to hear the other side in a legal dispute, is a basic tenet of justice. This concept is so ingrained in our legal system that no legal practitioner would oversee such a fundamental principle, right? Wrong.

I was under the impression that I only had to answer the allegations made against me as they stood at that point and I undertook to do so by way of a sworn affidavit, complete with supporting evidence in substantiation. Besides Ivan, who provided two submissions in writing, nobody else who appeared before the panel testified under oath or provided written submissions, and certainly not by way of an affidavit. I was the only one prepared to do so.

It is important to note that at this stage there hadn't yet been mention of a 'rogue unit' in SARS or any allegations relating to it. This didn't feature in the Kanyane report and, consequently, it didn't feature in the scope and mandate of the Sikhakhane Panel.

However, after the Sikhakhane report was published, it turned out the panel had 'investigated' allegations of a 'rogue unit'. The report states in paragraphs 57 to 59 that 'shortly after the panel was appointed and commenced its work, the media reports escalated and alleged the existence of a covert unit that had been operating at SARS. By this time, we had already interviewed some SARS officials, including Mr Van Loggerenberg'.[2]

The panel acknowledges in its report that the existence of such a unit was not specifically part of its terms of reference. 'However,' it states, 'the terms of reference extend, in our view, to the consideration of the existence and operations of a covert unit, to the extent that had we not considered such issues once they became apparent, we would have failed in our obligation to fully respond to our mandate ...'[3]

The only snag is that the panel didn't bother to inform me of their 'extended' terms of reference or to interview me about the media reports because, according to them, I had already been interviewed. So, once again, I was not given the opportunity to state my case or respond to allegations made against me. And the panel didn't inform Ivan, as deputy commissioner, or any other person interviewed, of their intention to investigate the legality of the establishment and operations of the unit.

Paragraph 54 states: 'The existence of the NRG was not volunteered to the panel until it was revealed in the media.'[4] The panel was even more emphatic in paragraph 89.10: 'During the first session, Mr Van Loggerenberg, like others, never volunteered the existence of the NRG or the HRIU or any of its predecessors.'[5]

Not so. At my first appearance before the panel, I told them in no uncertain terms about the HRIU. I had nothing to hide about any of the five units I managed and not only named each one, but also gave a brief outline of their size, locations and mandates. The recordings of that day's submission to the panel will bear me out on this point.

Another slip in the Sikhakhane Panel speaks volumes. The report states that I first met Walter *alone* on 2 September 2013 at an informal meeting, which took place at my office at SARS, and which she attended as chairperson of the Fair-Trade Independent Tobacco Association. 'We point out that meeting a taxpayer or his representative alone is a contravention of SARS' Code of Conduct.'[6]

Had the panel presented me with this information and allowed me to formally respond to it, I would have been able to provide evidence to show that I was not alone that day. At that meeting I was accompanied by another SARS official, an executive manager who reported to me. Further proof of this can be found in an unrelated affidavit filed at the Registrar of the Gauteng South High Court in 2015, in the matter of *Martin Wingate-Pearse v The Commissioner for SARS and others*. In a supporting affidavit to Wingate-Pearse's application, Walter points out that I wasn't alone that day and that the Sikhakhane Panel erred in this finding.

The panel's report also states that, at our first meeting, Walter wore 'a concealed recording device provided to her by the SSA in order to record the meeting as there was a belief held within the SSA that Mr Van Loggerenberg was corrupt'.[7] Most interestingly, the panel didn't ask for this recording to check who had really attended the meeting.

They also didn't seem aware of, or disconcerted by, an apparent contradiction in their report. In an earlier paragraph,[8] the report states that Walter admitted to being an agent of the SSA until the end of 2012, after which she cut her ties with the agency. If this were the case, why would she act on their instruction and use their equipment more than nine months later at that first meeting with me and a colleague at SARS in 2013?

At my second appearance before the panel, on 17 October 2014, I detected a change in tone and what I believed to be an unwillingness on their part to meaningfully engage on the few issues they raised. I sensed an apparent rush to conclude our interaction. Questions were put to me in haste and I wasn't allowed to deal with the details in depth.

I believe paragraph 14 of their report is significant: 'While we were in the midst of our investigation, the President of the Republic of South Africa, Mr JG Zuma, appointed as new SARS Commissioner, Mr Tom Moyane ... The panel met with Commissioner Moyane in his Brooklyn office on 17 October 2014 and confirmed its terms of reference with him. Commissioner Moyane expressed and offered his full support to the panel and its work.'[9]

After the Sikhakhane report was handed to Moyane on 5 November 2014, Ivan sought legal advice on it and compiled a critique on the findings, which he presented to Moyane in early December.[10] In it he picks the report apart piece by piece, pointing to several inconsistencies, contradictions and illogical or meaningless findings. He states, for instance, that key witnesses had not been called and that the report attributes equal evidential value to all evidence placed before the panel regardless of whether it was from unnamed sources, unsworn statements, oral submissions or affidavits.

Furthermore, on certain points the report relied greatly on allegations that could easily be contested or disproved if properly examined, and that it made 'facile psychological commentary' that should have been avoided. As an example of the latter, Ivan points to how the panel refers to SARS as being 'hypnotized' by my perceived power and charm.[11]

Since I've never been afforded the right of a public reply to the findings of the Sikhakhane Panel, I would like to respond to some of its findings here, firstly with regard to my brief relationship with Walter and, secondly, to the 'rogue-unit' allegations – even though these weren't officially part of the panel's mandate.

In terms of my relationship with Walter, the panel found the following:

Finding: 'Although there is no SARS policy prohibiting a romantic relationship with a taxpayer under investigation or a representative of such taxpayer, Mr Van Loggerenberg's relationship with Walter showed poor judgment on his part as there was a conflict in his role as an investigator and that of Walter as a representative of FITA and Carnilinx. In particular, in his failure timeously to disclose the relationship, he failed in his duty as a senior manager to report a potential conflict as would be required of a manager at his level.'[12]

My reply: Firstly, I wasn't asked about this issue by the panel and their suggestion that I only reported the relationship to my employer in February 2014 is factually incorrect. Secondly, if I had been, I would have provided evidence in writing to show that I reported the relationship within days after it began and moved promptly to remove any possible perceived conflict. Thirdly, I provided the panel with a complete set of text exchanges from the first three weeks of this relationship, which clearly show how each time I came to discover any potential or perceived conflict of interests, I raised it with Walter and we discussed ways to deal with it.

In any event, not only did I disclose the relationship to my line manager and two other senior SARS officials, but Walter – in the letters she wrote to the *Sunday Times* on 5 and 7 February 2014 – also dispels any allegation that we were unaware of or disregarded the issue of conflicting interests. I referred to these letters in my submission to the panel and annexed copies of them, in substantiation of my version of events.

In one of these letters, she states: 'The possibility of a misunderstanding regarding my romantic relationship was discussed at length and thought through with my partner at its inception ... We went out of our way to precisely avoid any perceived prejudice to any third party, associated person, employer etc. We primarily did so particularly to protect the integrity of the institution for whom my partner works.'

Finding: 'Although his involvement with Walter was improper, there is no evidence that he entered the relationship with the sole purpose of obtaining incriminating information about her clients.'[13]

My reply: I wonder, given what subsequently transpired, whether the panel ever considered the possibility that exactly the opposite of this allegation may have occurred?

Finding: 'Although he [Van Loggerenberg] was indeed intimately involved in the functioning and later management of the NRG, there is no direct evidence linking him to any illegal interception of conversations of Walter or any other taxpayer.'[14]

My reply: Yes. Of course there wouldn't be any such evidence, because it didn't happen.

Finding: 'Mr Loggerenberg's role [sic] in the audit conducted on Walter while he was in a romantic relationship with her was in violation of the Code of Conduct and the principles of good governance.'[15]

My reply: Once again, I wasn't asked about this audit and, secondly, I played no role in it. Audits in SARS are prescribed by formulated policies and standard procedures, and each step of an audit is recorded on a case management system. If I had anything to do with any audit, it would have easily been detectable and evidenced. It is significant that no description is given as to exactly how I was supposed to have played a 'role' in the audit.

In terms of the unit, the panel found the following, among others:

Finding: 'In respect of the establishment of the Special projects Unit [sic], NRG and High Risk Investigations Unit, we find as follows: The establishment of the unit without having the requisite statutory authority was indeed unlawful.'[16]

My reply: Absolutely no legal or factual basis was provided in support of this finding, making it impossible for me to defend myself. Firstly, I wasn't involved in the establishment of the unit. Secondly, as I have explained at the start of this book, the unit was approved at the level of the Finance Minister, Deputy Finance Minister, Commissioner of SARS, SARS Head: Corporate Services and at general manager level. In the history of SARS, no other unit can claim such high levels of approval.

The unit's mandate – to act in support of other SARS enforcement units, investigate tax and customs crimes only and do so within the SARS legal and policy frameworks – was also shared with the media, certain MPs and the NIA in early 2010. If the NIA, police or MPs believed the unit was unlawfully and illegally established, why didn't they raise it with SARS back then?

On this point, Ivan stated in his critique that in light of the fact that the unit had been established in the period between 2006 and 2008, the relevant witnesses had not been called. The establishment of the unit, as Ivan explained, 'reaches back to previous Commissioners, Ministers and Deputy Ministers of Finance, and it would seem prudent and procedurally proper for the Panel to have called for representations from these parties. This was not done ...'[17]

According to Ivan, the most blatant omission was the failure by the panel to call Pete Richer, as he had been instrumental in conceiving the initial unit and he was involved in the consultations with SARS and the former NIA. Ivan also took issue with the panel's claim in paragraph 61 that 'the existence of the unit was not volunteered to us'. This is in direct contradiction with paragraph 43.4 of the report, which states that, in his first interview with them, Ivan explained that 'SARS, through its highest office, approved the creation of a group which was known by different names', referring to the unit.[18]

Then there is the panel's question in paragraph 45 as to 'whether SARS in its current form has the statutory power to investigate organised crime'. In other words, according to the panel, SARS had no legal power or obligation to investigate organised crime.

To this Ivan responds by saying: 'This statement betrays a lack of due diligence in reading the law on the part of the Panel and the question itself is absurd. It is an established principle in law/by statute and by judgements of the court, that where a tax and customs offence may have been committed it is a prerogative of the Commissioner [of SARS] to investigate the tax or customs crime.'[19]

Referring to the legally accepted definition of organised crime, Ivan said that whether 'a person may have acted in concert with another in committing a tax or customs offence [therefore organised crime] cannot by simple logic be precluded from an investigation simply by the fact that they have acted in concert'.[20]

Finding: 'There is *prima facie* evidence that the unit may have abused its power and resources by engaging in activities that reside in the other agencies of Government, and which it had no lawful authority to perform.'[21]

My reply: The panel doesn't provide evidence in support of what is claimed here. The 'power and resources' that the unit allegedly abused are not described, nor are the activities that it engaged in and that reside in other agencies. So how does one answer this? All I can say is: not under my watch.

Ivan was scathing in his response to the use of '*prima facie* evidence' by the panel. He pointed out that courts of law and tribunals that are called upon to investigate and report on allegations make 'findings of fact', based on evidence, and draw conclusions based on those factual findings and the law.[22] He said that a statement by a court or a fact-finding tribunal to the effect that certain evidence may exist is neither a finding of fact nor a final conclusion.

'*Prima facie* evidence,' he said, 'is generally accepted by courts and fact-finding tribunals to mean evidence which, in the absence of rebutting or contrary evidence, may reasonably justify a finding in favour of the party making an allegation. The existence of *prima facie* evidence to support an allegation is of little significance where there is rebutting or contrary evidence ...

'Insofar as the Sikhakhane panel reported that "*prima facie* evidence exists", without critically evaluating all the available evidence and assessing the weight and veracity which should be attached to the evidence, and failed to make findings of fact, it has failed to fulfil its mandate, and no reliance could or should properly be placed upon its report.'[23]

> **Finding:** 'There is *prima facie* evidence that the recruitment, funding and practices of the unit were in violation of SARS's own Human Resources policy.'[24]

> **My reply:** Again, no evidence is provided for this finding. I can unequivocally state that the unit was funded in a way that was no different from other units in SARS. The unit, including its finances and operational structures, was audited annually by a SARS internal audit and by the Auditor-General of South Africa, and no issues were ever raised.

> **Finding:** 'There is *prima facie* evidence suggesting that the activities of the Special Projects Unit may have included rogue behaviour that

had the potential to damage the reputation of SARS as an organ of state.'[25]

My reply: This issue was never put to me and, furthermore, no evidence in support of this finding is provided. *'May have'* included rogue behaviour? To my mind, this is just a throwaway statement. In this book I have described most of the projects the unit worked on and how they operated. As far as I am concerned, the unit did excellent work and helped our country combat crime with very few resources at its disposal and with absolute dedication. There was nothing rogue about this unit.

Finding: 'Finally, there appears to be serious concerns about whether settlements concluded with taxpayers who were the subject of investigation, were validly and properly concluded ... SARS should conduct a forensic investigation into all the settlements concluded with taxpayers that had been under investigation since 2005.'[26]

My reply: Firstly, I can't comment on matters that weren't put to me. Secondly, no evidence in support of this statement is provided. The panel doesn't list any settlements or taxpayers that they may have had in mind, nor do they explain why they came to this view. What I can say is that I have personally never concluded any settlement with any taxpayer that was a subject of an investigation. In SARS, settlements for tax debts are properly evaluated and considered by various tiers of committees. No single person could conclude a settlement with a taxpayer and, in any event, the unit was never involved in any tax settlements because this was never part of its mandate.

I don't know whether SARS ever followed the suggestion of the panel to 'conduct a forensic investigation into all the settlements' and I haven't been able to find anything in the public domain to show that SARS did that.

There were many reasons why I had to question the findings of the Sikhakhane report. The following finding was by far the worst for me, though: 'While SARS remains an efficient and effective organisation, the unlawful establishment of a unit that operated ostensibly in a covert manner, has created a climate of intrigue, fear and subterfuge within the organisation.'[27]

So, the Sikhakhane Panel wants to claim two contradictory things: that there was a covert 'rogue unit', which implies nobody knew of its existence. However, the panel also said that this unit created 'a climate of intrigue, fear and subterfuge' within SARS and, therefore, people must have known about its existence. So, which was it?

Shortly after my second appearance before the panel, I was called and asked to report to SARS on 12 November 2014. I was met by two officials and the Human Resources Executive, Luther Lebelo, who was now start-ing to act as SARS spokesperson. He handed me a notice of suspension. At that meeting, I predicted that my suspension notice would leak to the media. I was given all kinds of assurances that it wouldn't.

But of course it did. That week it found its way to the *Sunday Times*.

After I heard that the Sikhakhane report had been handed to Moyane on 5 November 2014, I asked for a copy. I was told that I wasn't 'legally entitled' to the report. This, despite the fact that the report had been shown to members of the SARS executive.

I asked my attorneys to write a letter to Moyane in December 2014 to formally request access to the report. The request remains unanswered. I asked verbally and in writing to meet with Moyane in November and December 2014 but every time I was told he didn't want to meet with me.

In the first week of December, Moyane suspended Ivan and Richer, because they were 'implicated' in the Sikhakhane report.[28] In a SARS media statement, Moyane quotes from the panel's report highlighting its findings that the unit was established illegally and operated covertly. As well as the two suspensions, he undertakes to 'disband the covert unit and conduct a forensic investigation to ensure that the alleged unit and its activities cease to exist in its entirety'.[29]

However, according to News24, Moyane's reasons for the suspensions were cast into doubt after Imraan Mohamed, the Sikhakhane Panel's attorney, told Eyewitness News that 'no findings were made against any third party'.[30]

Indeed, the report makes no finding against Ivan or Richer, nor were they 'implicated' in the report in any way. Ivan and Richer approached the Labour Court that week seeking to have their suspensions overturned. They succeeded. Ivan won his case and his suspension was overturned on 18 December 2014, when the court ruled it to have been 'unlawful'.[31]

SARS settled out of court with Richer before the matter could be heard and withdrew his suspension. Ivan proceeded to bring the matter before the Commission for Conciliation, Mediation and Arbitration (CCMA), and a hearing was set for 22 January 2015.[32] But, on the eve of the CCMA hearing, Ivan was suspended by SARS for a second time on rephrased allegations, this time because he had allegedly been 'instrumental in setting up a rogue unit within SARS'. Richer too was suspended, for unknown reasons.

Ivan's CCMA matter was postponed to 28 January 2015; in it he and SARS settled.[33] SARS said in a media release that the CCMA's resolution 'has no effect on Mr Pillay's [second] suspension'.[34]

In all instances, the two Labour Court cases and the CCMA case, SARS not only had to pay their own legal costs, but also those of Pillay and Richer.

In the second half of 2014, SARS was not the only state institution being battered by storms. Around this time a curious pattern was emerging in various other law-enforcement agencies where incriminating information would be leaked to the media that questioned the integrity of the heads of these institutions. These reports were then used as a pretext to launch an investigation into these officials. There were leaks from within the Hawks, the NPA, the Independent Police Investigative Directorate (IPID) and SARS.

These leaks had an impact on generals Anwa Dramat and Shadrack Sibiya from the Hawks, who were supposedly involved in the so-called Zimbabwe illegal renditions saga, and Robert McBride, head of the IPID, who allegedly altered a second investigative report into these alleged 'renditions' to exonerate Dramat and others. Another victim was General Johan Booysen, head of the Hawks in KwaZulu-Natal, and his team of investigators in the so-called Cato Manor death squad saga.

In May 2016 Dramat, McBride and Pillay released a joint statement in which they divulged more information about what they claimed was sustained political interference that threatened the independence of the country's public institutions, especially law-enforcement agencies. They explained how all the affected individuals were suspended pending the outcome of the probes into the allegations against them. The statement read:

> They are never called to answer to any allegations by the investigators, while any representation is usually ignored, distorted or rejected by the institution in question.
>
> They [Dramat, McBride and Pillay] said that during the 'investigations', affected officials are suspended and prevented from defending themselves publicly ... When an 'investigation' fails to reach a conclusion, the institutions enter into settlements with the officials. Later, based on the same allegations that preceded the settlement, officials are then criminally charged. It appears from this pattern that the intent is to hound officials out of institutions and destroy their credibility publicly.[35]

The findings of the internal probes into these cases were leaked to the same journalists even before the affected officials had been informed of the outcome or been afforded an opportunity to respond to the findings. Often, further 'inside information' would be leaked to the journalists by 'insiders', which the newspapers then used to 'vindicate' and 'corroborate' their reports. This pattern was most visible in the reporting on the 'rogue unit' at SARS.

In the instances of the Hawks, IPID and SARS, the new bosses almost immediately began restructuring the institution and moving those considered loyal to the 'old' leadership into other positions. At no stage would the new incumbent stand up to defend those affected or even the integrity of the institution. Dramat, McBride and Pillay said in their statement:

> In our view, attacks on individuals in these institutions are aimed at undermining the fight against corruption. A key part of all of our mandates was to investigate cases of corruption. In reviewing our individual experiences over recent weeks, we have discovered a convergence in the cases that we were working on.
>
> A common thread is that cases under investigation involved individuals or entities with questionable relationships to those in public office. Most of these cases involved state tenders of some kind that were awarded due to patronage with influential individuals in public office.[36]

Another incident is worth mentioning here, as it also relates to the *Sunday Times*. In May 2012, after various investigations into allegations pertaining to the police Crime Intelligence Division, a report compiled by Colonel Kobus Roelofse of the Anti-Corruption Task Team (a joint governmental task team on corruption known as the ACTT) was made public.[37]

The report covers investigations into infighting in the police's Crime Intelligence Division, but a particular section caught my eye. Paragraphs 85 and 86 state:

The investigating team have also been informed on 10 October 2011 by the member [of Crime Intelligence] that on the same evening he was taken to Major General Lazarus's house he heard them discussing the placement of a newspaper article relating to Lieutenant General Dramat and Major General Sibiya.

He stated that Major General Lazarus wanted to use *sources within the media (journalists paid by Crime Intelligence) to write a story in order to take the focus away from them.* This according to the member is is [sic] a strategy employed to cast suspicion on those they perceived to be a threat.[38]

As Roelofse explains, 'This newspaper article was published in the *Sunday Times* on 23 October 2011.'[39]

What Roelofse was alleging and placing on record to our country's highest anti-corruption body, the ACTT (which consists of the heads and representatives of all law-enforcement agencies), was that there were journalists on the payroll of the Crime Intelligence Division and that the media were used to plant false stories. I went in search of the *Sunday Times* article referred to in Roelofse's report and found it unattributed to any particular journalist. The by-line simply says 'Special report by investigating staff'.[40]

Unsurprisingly, the article concerns the alleged illegal renditions of Zimbabwean nationals, supposedly by Dramat and Sibiya.

At the time the *Sunday Times* vehemently denied the allegations and sought proof of the claims made, seemingly to no avail. Yusuf Abramjee, then Chairperson of the National Press Club, called for an urgent investigation. 'These allegations are very worrying and very serious. Authorities need to get to the bottom of them as a matter of urgency. We need to get the facts and if there were any payments made as alleged, criminal charges should follow,' he said.[41]

But the matter seemed to have died a quick and silent death.

16

Aftershocks

By January 2015, two things had become clear to me – I was no longer wanted at SARS and saw no evidence that the tax authority deemed it necessary to defend itself against the onslaught of *Sunday Times* articles. I had been served with the most bizarre internal charge sheet.

I had also lodged nine complaints with the Press Ombudsman against the *Sunday Times*. By then the 'rogue-unit' label seemed to have become standard currency and was commonly used by other media institutions.

In the meantime, my health was suffering and I had lost more than 10 kilograms. I could no longer afford to pay for the place where my mother was staying and had to find a smaller house for her. It also concerned me greatly that she developed a heart condition during that time.

I wanted to go public with all the information I had and decided to seek the advice of Toby, who had approached me in June 2014 on behalf of the SSA and tried to help me dispel the notion with senior government officials that there was a 'rogue-unit'. I explained to Toby how ludicrous the charges against me were. SARS had effectively accused me of not having disclosed precisely the criminal offences that implicated Walter and officials of the Illicit-Tobacco Task Team. These were the very offences I had pointed out long before, first to SARS, then to the Kanyane and Sikhakhane panels.

However, if I challenged the disciplinary allegations, it would force me to rely on the content of the data on the phones I had been given and on the data cloud, as well as the recordings and correspondence given to me by Walter. I told Toby that this would have the unintended consequence of also exposing other aspects concerning the state not relevant to my matter. He then advised me against doing so, warning of the possible harmful effects should this information be made public. The matter had already been attracting significant media attention and no doubt my disciplinary would too. Toby felt the country couldn't afford more scandals and further destabilisation of state institutions.

The only option left to me, therefore, was to leave SARS in an effort to bring matters to a close. I resigned from SARS on 4 February 2015. I wrote a confidential letter of resignation addressed only to Commissioner Tom Moyane. In it, I also offered to help SARS refute the *Sunday Times* articles and to help in any future legal cases where SARS may require my assistance.

Moyane wanted me to amend aspects of my resignation letter, which I complied with. Curiously, I was asked to retract my offer to help SARS refute the *Sunday Times* articles. Furthermore, a condition of my resignation was that I withdraw my Press Ombudsman complaints against the *Sunday Times*.

And then, just before my resignation, I finally got to meet Moyane – on four occasions, in fact.

I have been told he had sacrificed much of his life for our political freedom and had lived in exile in Mozambique. Moyane is well-spoken, charming and seemed quite willing to hear me out. I shall reserve my views of him because I never got to know him well or to work for him. At our last meeting, my last day as a SARS official, he asked someone to take a photo of the two of us together in his office, both smiling at the camera. We shook hands and I wished him well in his future endeavours as the head of SARS.

That very Sunday, details of my confidential separation agreement ended up in the hands of the media. Piet Rampedi of the *Sunday Times* would later claim victory on social media and when he addressed a forum of journalists at a meeting in Botswana, because I had withdrawn my complaints to the Press Ombudsman.

The truth is, although I believed my complaints had merit (and this would be confirmed by the Ombudsman later that year), by February 2015 I had reached breaking point. I didn't have the stomach for any more litigation and just wanted to move on with my life. I left SARS and I believed that would bring an end to the saga for all concerned, including Ivan Pillay and Pete Richer.

More resignations followed in quick succession after I had been suspended in November the previous year and after I resigned. The former SARS Chief Operating Officer, Barry Hore, served his notice in December 2014. It was reported that he was to face disciplinary charges for alleged racism.[1] Earlier that year, Hore had apparently asked a colleague, who happened to be black, to make coffee for the director general of another state department during a formal meeting.

Jerome Frey, head of modernisation and strategy, and Jacques Meyer, head of the case selection division, also resigned in December 2014.[2] ACAS head Clifford Collings left SARS in December 2014. For some reason, Lebelo told *City Press* that Collings had approached his employers about early retirement 'for personal reasons' and his application was approved.[3] At this stage Ivan and Richer were still suspended.

Adrian Lackay also resigned in February 2015. His resignation is still the subject of a CCMA constructive-dismissal case that has been dragging on ever since. Other resignations were to follow.

At the age of 46, I had to start my life all over again. After my resignation, I started looking for work. Soon after, I received confirmation from the attorneys for SARS that all actions against me had been withdrawn. I thought that would be the end of this chapter in my life. One of the options I had considered was to start work as an article clerk, in the hope of eventually qualifying as an attorney, and to build my professional career from scratch again. A number of law firms were interested, but they all told me more or less that until the dust had settled around me on the SARS matters, they would not be able to take me on.

The problem was, the dust didn't want to settle.

In fact, two matters kicked up even more dust just after I resigned. Towards the end of February, M-Net's flagship investigative programme, *Carte Blanche*, aired an insert that featured three characters we've met before – Walter, Peega and Niemann.

In the insert, Walter made further outlandish allegations against me, now claiming that 'the unit was used to target perceived enemies'. I had allegedly also told her that SARS was 'looking at ... politicians', and that 'SARS was doing an audit of a particular political party and that they [presumably SARS] were going to swing an election if they had to'.4 At this point her claims seemed to mirror some of the allegations made in the old Peega dossier of 2009.

All of a sudden she recalled how I had told her that SARS had acquired a so-called grabber, which is a sophisticated piece of equipment used to intercept communications. Strangely, none of these new allegations were previously ever put to SARS, or the Kanyane or the Sikhakhane panels. Neither do they appear in any of her court papers in the various matters she filed over the years. They most certainly didn't feature in the original complaint that started the fracas at SARS.

She also repeated her allegations about Wachizungu, the fundraiser I was part of, trying to link it with the 'rogue unit' and SARS. Walter also claimed that 'high-profile taxpayers who had been in trouble, including attorneys and advocates who had represented them, previous spin doctors in the industry who get you tax settlements for kickbacks' had made donations to Wachizungu, which she believed was a SARS charity.5 None of these claims are true.

Peega then went on to tell the nation how he had supposedly infiltrated a rhino-poaching syndicate on instruction from SARS as a member of the

NRG and had been wrongfully apprehended by the police. He went on to claim how SARS, by denying that he had been tasked to infiltrate the syndicate, had left him in the lurch and curtailed his distinguished, and apparently unblemished career in the revenue service.

A tearful Peega spoke about the alleged ill-treatment he had received while he was employed by SARS as an NRG investigator. He said that the NRG was 'unknown and secret' to fellow SARS employees.[6] Walter came out in support of Peega, saying that SARS had 'abandoned him because obviously what they were doing was illegal'.

Then Niemann was featured, giving his two cents' worth about how SARS should or should not investigate crime.

I was horrified by the lack of research and critical thinking in this insert. It was clear that the team from *Carte Blanche* had never read the book *Killing for Profit* and had not looked into Peega's confession to the police or the records released by SARS in 2010, or even media reports at the time. If they had done so, they would have known that, after his arrest, Peega had gone with the police to point out places where poaching took place. They could also have consulted Peega's disciplinary records, which had been released in February 2010 by SARS. This would have shown them that Peega never claimed to have been instructed to infiltrate a rhino-poaching syndicate when arguing his defence at the disciplinary hearing, nor did he do so during his subsequent appeal.

There are other, even more basic questions that could and should have been posed to Peega, such as which manager at SARS had tasked him to infiltrate the syndicate? And if indeed he was given this task, who at the NPA, and which judge, had authorised him in terms of Section 252 A of the Criminal Procedure Act 51 of 1977[7] to infiltrate the syndicate? How did he report back to SARS? And so on.

But perhaps the simplest and most important question that *Carte Blanche* should have asked was whether the SPU or the NRG ever investigated rhino poaching? The answer would have been a definitive no.

The *Carte Blanche* team also knew very well that I wasn't allowed to publicly comment on most of these matters for a period of six months because of my separation agreement with SARS, which I had concluded earlier that month. Still they raised none of the issues touched on by Niemann and Peega, but limited their questions to the Wachizungu matter.

Given this catalogue of shortcomings, I decided to take *Carte Blanche* on and laid a complaint with the Broadcasting Complaints Commission of South Africa. My main issues were with how they had slandered the fundraiser that I had been part of, had failed to draw from critical information, which was readily obtainable on the Internet, and that they hadn't referred to key information I'd given them to consult before the broadcast.

My case was heard three months later. We were in the boardroom of the Broadcasting Complaints Commission. I was on one side by myself (I couldn't afford legal representation), feeling rather alone and intimidated. On the other side were the journalist and the producer with a phalanx of the best media lawyers money could buy.

Apparently, it is standard protocol for the presiding commissioner to begin proceedings by asking whether there was any possibility of a settlement. The executive director of *Carte Blanche* indicated that he wanted to have a private talk with me. He asked if I would agree to a statement of fact. We went outside and agreed that they would give me 40 seconds of prime-time television during their next broadcast to correct the claims they had made in the documentary.

The matter was settled with virtually no resistance from *Carte Blanche*, which astonished me. They also wanted me to waive any civil proceedings as part of the settlement. Since I didn't have the money to take them to court anyway, I agreed to this.

The *Carte Blanche* programme led me to believe that perhaps Peega wasn't too far off when he originally bragged to us about his ability to infiltrate terrorist cells. If he could fool the experienced television journalists and producers of *Carte Blanche* so easily, he could've fooled anyone.

Within days after the programme was aired, news reports stated that

Peega had disappeared and wasn't answering his phone.[8] When I tried to establish what subsequently became of his rhino-poaching case, I could only find a report from 2011, which stated that the police dockets and evidence had apparently vanished. In August 2011 *The Star* reported that the NPA had started 'an urgent investigation' into the disappearance of the dockets 'while the man at the centre of the charges – Michael Peega – continues with his life in Mpumalanga'.[9]

In December 2014 the Sikhakhane report was handed to the Finance Minister, Nhlanhla Nene, and it was also to be submitted to Parliament's Standing Committee on Finance (SCOF) in the new year.[10] On 25 February 2015, Nene announced the appointment of an advisory board that would be chaired by retired judge Frank Kroon to look into the matter.[11]

According to Nene's statement, the advisory board's primary task would be 'to guide the direction of long-term strategy at SARS by ensuring that decisions about the revenue and customs authority's operations, personnel, budget and technology support its long-term strategy and plans'.[12] However, the board would also 'review the events that have been reported on by the media in recent months and advise the Minister and the Commissioner about the best way to prevent such from occurring [again]. On this issue, I would like to inform South Africans that there are processes underway to bring about closure on this matter as soon and as amicably as possible,' Nene said.[13]

After I read about the appointment of the Kroon Advisory Board in the media, I wrote to Moyane and the board, asking for an opportunity to address the board. I received no reply – not even an acknowledgement of receipt. In March I also read that Moyane was to appear before the Standing Committee on Finance in Parliament to answer questions from the committee on the 'rogue-unit' allegations.

I resolved to write to Parliament and asked my attorneys to help me draft the letter. I approached Adrian for advice, as he had years of experience in dealing with parliamentary committees. However, my lawyers then advised me that my resignation agreement with SARS placed certain limitations on me for a period of six months, and that scuppered my intention to address Parliament.

Adrian, who by then had also left SARS, wasn't under any such restraints and took it upon himself to address Parliament. He told me he wanted the truth to be heard by those who are mandated by our Constitution with an oversight responsibility for state institutions and the government. Adrian was also concerned about how critical facts concerning the 'rogue-unit' narrative were either being ignored or suppressed – specifically the information relating to alleged espionage, corruption, money laundering and the abuse of powers within intelligence and law-enforcement agencies.

Parliament is the highest body of governance in our country, so – surely, we felt – they would be concerned about the events at SARS and other state institutions. At least they should be apprised of these matters.

On 24 March 2015, Adrian sent a letter to the chairpersons of two committees in Parliament – the SCOF and the Joint Standing Committee on Intelligence. In it, Adrian pointed out the most relevant facts and the sequence of events at SARS concerning the 'rogue-unit' story. He asked Parliament to consider contacting Ivan Pillay, Pete Richer, Yolisa Pikie and me if they wished to find out more. He received no meaningful reply from either committee.

Without asking for permission, a Member of Parliament from the Democratic Alliance (DA), Dr Dion George, then published the letter on the Internet. This had three significant consequences.

First, the letter caused SARS to go on the offensive in the media. Through their now de facto spokesperson, Lebelo, they dismissed the letter outright – without engaging with any of the content.

Secondly, SARS and Moyane instituted a civil claim against Adrian, in which they are suing him for R12 million for alleged defamation of SARS and Moyane. Neither George, nor the party he represents, the Democratic Alliance, or the website Politicsweb, which published the report, or any of the media houses that then reported on its content were sued. The fact that, by law, state institutions or public figures in South Africa cannot be defamed did not seem to matter.

Lastly, and this still amazes me to this day, even though Adrian had put evidence of significant crimes to Parliament, some of which could even qualify as crimes against the state, to date no law-enforcement agency has bothered to contact Adrian, or any of us for that matter, to obtain this evidence.

It was an extremely tumultuous time for me after my resignation. But it wasn't all doom and gloom, though. On 28 March 2015 I got married.

I had met Nicole 11 years before at a party. At some stage during the evening, a tall, very beautiful, long-haired woman came up to me from nowhere and started talking to me. Nicole was young and fearless, and turned out to be very interesting.

We ended up in a relationship for the next five years until 2010. By then, Nicole had passed the gruelling Bar Council examinations and had started what would later become a successful law practice. However, our relationship floundered and I made the terrible mistake of placing her, and our relationship, below my work and the higher purpose I believed I was pursuing at SARS.

One consequence of the events that unfolded at SARS, and the way in which I'd been laid bare to public scrutiny, was that it forced me to seriously take stock of myself as a person and my life in general. Who I was, what defined me and where I wished to go in life now became more important to me. Today, after much introspection, I feel I have a better hold on things and that I have a far more solid grounding than before.

Fortunately, Nicole and I would meet again. In August 2014 we held the memorial service for my dad. It was a few days before the *Sunday Times* let loose the dogs of war on me and SARS. I was alone in the hall next to where the memorial service was to be held, among the flower arrangements and the cakes, feeling overwhelmed and dismayed. I didn't know what to do.

When I looked up, silhouetted against the doorway was Nicole. She always had a special bond with my dad, so she had come to the memorial. She looked me in the eyes, walked towards me and took me in her arms. She just knew and understood. When the service was over, she bundled me into her car and took me to a spot in nearby Melville, Johannesburg, where we had a drink on my dad.

From that point on, Nicole and her family were to become my pillar of strength in the dark days that lay ahead. She is the most magical of beings I have ever met – a blend of the dramatic, a lover of arts, a trained opera singer, a hard worker, a true free spirit and someone who is complex in her thinking of how life works.

By December 2014, when I had been suspended and humiliated publicly in article after article in the *Sunday Times* without being able to defend myself, I found myself at breaking point. Nicole dragged me off to Thailand for a break. We had a blissful time and that holiday saved my life.

It was then that I proposed. Somewhere in the jungle in Thailand, riding on the back of an elephant, with butterflies flitting all around us (as well as in my stomach), and amid the rumbling of the elephant and the chattering of monkeys, I turned to Nicole, looked her in the eye and asked her to be my wife.

During our time in Thailand, there was one unsettling incident, however. The Sikhakhane report was leaked to the media, first to the *Sunday Times*, of course. As I was checking my emails one day, I found a request from the *Sunday Times*'s lawyer for me to comment on the report – a report that I wasn't allowed to see, yet the *Sunday Times* had a copy.

I sent an email to Lebelo and copied Moyane. I told them I wished to invoke my basic human right to defend myself in a reply. Neither responded. In quick succession, other newspapers also sent questions, although it appeared that they didn't have the full report, as the *Sunday Times* did.

I penned a rather bland response to the *Sunday Times*'s queries.

Essentially, I explained that I had not seen the report, had not been afforded a right of reply to the report and denied any wrongdoing on my part.

I copied Lebelo and Moyane out of courtesy. Within minutes, Lebelo sent me an email or, more precisely, an instruction. Withdraw your statement or face immediate and summary dismissal. One of my conditions of suspension was that I wasn't allowed to talk to the media, and I was now potentially in breach of this. I had no choice but to email all the journalists and withdraw my statement.

As I have mentioned, Adrian's letter to Parliament was made public by a member of the DA and was published on the website Politicsweb on 23 April 2015. Five days later, the Kroon Board called a media briefing and issued a statement, which I believe was an attempt to counter the public outcry following Adrian's letter.

The statement describes how the board – after it had 'studied and discussed' the Sikhakhane report – had 'satisfied itself' that 'a secret unit was established within SARS in 2007 which among others had the purpose of the covert collection of intelligence' and that 'the establishment of such a unit was unlawful'.[14]

It is important to understand that the Kroon Board conducted no investigation and did not interview a single witness or any of the accused. It did not in any way represent an independent probe. It simply took the Sikhakhane report and endorsed it. At the same time, it advised SARS to publish the report because it was in the public interest to do so. SARS made the report public and, that day, like the rest of the world, I got to see the complete Sikhakhane report for the very first time.[15]

I have already discussed the shortcomings of the Sikhakhane report. It is fundamentally flawed. It is not even reviewable in a court of law, as I came to discover later, when I sought to challenge it legally. In 2016 two respectable and experienced advocates gave exactly the same legal opinion on the report independently of each other. The report – and its endorsement by the Kroon Advisory Board – has no legal standing.

After I read the Sikhakhane report, I realised that Pete Richer, one of the founding members of the unit, wasn't even interviewed. Another interesting aspect concerning the publication of the report was that although it refers to annexures, these were never published. It also refers to submissions made in writing by Pillay and me but neither of our submissions were published either.

What the Sikhakhane Panel was saying was that the public had to make do with the report itself and take its findings at face value. Once again, the voices of those affected by the allegations were silenced.

17

Scope creep

What none of us had realised initially, but would start to understand as things unfolded over time, was that the campaign against us was apparently also aimed at Pravin Gordhan, or PG, as some liked to call him. After the 2014 general election, Gordhan was replaced by Nene as Finance Minister and appointed as Minister of Cooperative Governance and Traditional Affairs.

With hindsight, the first indications that PG was also being targeted became evident in media reports from around November 2014. Whereas the *Sunday Times* articles had initially published photos only of me, and later of Ivan and Richer, from this point onwards they also started including photos of Gordhan and, in some instances, Trevor Manuel. These articles about the 'rogue unit' seldom referred to them directly, except to portray them as part of the hierarchy of the management structure at SARS or the Treasury.

The first direct allegation against Gordhan, however, came on 2 February 2015 – the month I resigned – during an interview with SARS spokesperson Luther Lebelo by 702 Radio talk-show host John Robbie. Walter called the station and went live on air. She alleged that the unit 'was a very small element within SARS and it was hidden within SARS; they didn't operate within SARS offices and 90% of SARS employees weren't aware of it …

I cannot speak about Trevor Manuel; in documents I have seen Pravin Gordhan was definitely aware of it.[1]

To this, Robbie responded by asking her, 'And this unit was definitely illegal? And he would have known it was illegal?'

'Yes,' she answered.[2]

Precisely what documents she had seen, who had shown them to her, and why she sought to implicate Gordhan and mention Manuel in relation to the unit are open to speculation.

In May 2015, Gordhan deemed it necessary to issue a media release 'to set the record straight' because, the statement said,

> some have seen it necessary to cast unwarranted aspersions on my integrity and record of public service. This is unacceptable and must not go unchallenged. At the outset let me state that I have never approved, as Commissioner of SARS, of any illegal activities. The establishment of an additional unit within the Enforcement Division was entirely legal. Any suggestion to the contrary is rejected emphatically. It is, in fact, during my stint at SARS that a whole range of institutional checks and balances were set up to ensure that no individual had unfettered powers and discretion in applying the law.[3]

By May 2015 most of the top management of SARS, who had served the institution for many years, were gone. The previous month, Ivan's special adviser, Yolisa Pikie, resigned and shortly afterwards the deputy SARS spokesperson, Marika Muller, followed.

It was suggested that my manager, Gene Ravele, the Chief Officer: Tax and Customs Enforcement, had also handed in a resignation letter in April 2015 but he was purportedly persuaded by Moyane not to resign.[4] In the end, Ravele, a chief HR officer, Elizabeth Khumalo, the Group Executive: Tax and Customs Enforcement, Godfrey Baloyi, and Brian Kgomo, Group

Executive: Internal Audit, who served on the first Kanyane Panel, would leave SARS during the year.

They were part of the group of 55 senior officials who ultimately left the institution over a period of 19 months following Moyane's appointment in October 2014.

Pillay and Richer resigned with immediate effect at the beginning of May 'after a protracted and acrimonious disciplinary process', according to *City Press*.[5] Shortly before his resignation, nine more charges were added to Pillay's disciplinary-hearing charge sheet. In light of the claims that the unit had acquired and used all sorts of sophisticated spyware, I found it ironic that Ivan was also being charged for not providing the unit with sufficient resources, such as laptops and mobile phones.[6]

His hearing was set to start later that month. Lebelo is quoted as saying that the parting of ways were 'amicable' and that 'all charges and related investigations' against Pillay and Richer had been withdrawn.[7]

But, just days afterwards, the *Sunday Times* then ran a story with the headline 'Pillay faces criminal charges after SARS spies explosive confession'.[8] The article relates to events that allegedly took place in 2007 and were referred to as Project Sunday Evenings. Significantly, the *Sunday Times* claimed to have seen two affidavits by SARS officials supposedly dated 14 May 2015, three days before the story was published.

I can prove that no such affidavits existed then. I can only wonder what exactly it is that they saw, who showed them these 'affidavits' and how they determined their authenticity. Without unpacking this particular *Sunday Times* article, I can only conclude that there were still forces out there who were determined to completely discredit us.

Almost a year later *City Press* revealed that, just days after Pillay and Richer had left SARS, Moyane had registered a case with the police against Pillay, Gordhan and other former SARS officials.[9] Apparently, Moyane had told the police that the alleged crime was committed at SARS's Nieuw Muckleneuk headquarters after 4 May 2007.[10]

So much for an 'amicable' parting of ways …

The KPMG investigation

In December 2014, after SARS had been given the Sikhakhane Panel's report, it acquired the services of auditing firm KPMG 'to look further into the full detail surrounding the establishment of the unit'.[11] I wasn't privy to the precise details of KPMG's brief.

It was around this time that Toby contacted me to say that I had to go to the SARS head office urgently to meet a senior official there. Certain files were kept in the safe in my old office and I had to hand them over to this official. Basically, I was told we had to ensure that files concerning matters of national importance were safeguarded.

Since this matter may become a subject of court action, I can't divulge much more, except to say that I believe this may also have contributed to the harm that came our way. When I got to my office, I was shocked. Clearly, people had been going through my office in my absence.

I made very sure I had sufficient evidence to prove that I went to the SARS offices that day and met certain people. I wanted to avoid a situation where someone later could claim some of the files had 'disappeared' and blame me.

Since the day I left SARS I had also sent several messages to Lebelo to arrange for a formal handover of everything in my old office at SARS and to remove personal belongings. He never replied to my requests.

However, some months later, towards the middle of 2015, I received a call from Lebelo late one Friday afternoon. He insisted that I come to the SARS head office immediately and open the safe in my old office. The time wasn't convenient for me, so I asked whether it couldn't wait until the Monday. He then threatened to break open the safe, which was state property and rather expensive. To avoid such a waste of state resources I decided to go there and then.

At SARS I was met by Lebelo and his bodyguard. I was then introduced to several KPMG employees, led by forensic auditor Johan van der Walt, who had been a witness for the state in the Schabir Shaik trial. There were few formalities – I was simply told to open my safe and informed that the

KPMG employees were going to go through the documents. The safe was in quite a mess, so I asked Van der Walt to put it on record that I had been asked before to remove certain files on high-risk investigations from my safe and hand them over to a certain senior official.

I believed this to be important for a number of reasons. Firstly, by now I wouldn't have put it past some people to plant information that would have implicated us in some kind of wrongdoing and, secondly, they could also claim that certain documents did not exist. Thirdly, I realised that if matters ever went to court, I'd want to be able to maintain the so-called chain of evidence. In other words, I would need to be able to say that after I had left that office in June 2014 the locks had been changed and I never had access to it again, except on the two occasions I have described.

I also told Van der Walt that even though some files had already been removed, there were others I believed were extremely sensitive and that they should not fall into the wrong hands. I suggested that they should be handed to Moyane in a sealed box – I felt it should be up to him to decide how to deal with the files in question, and not left to the KPMG investigators. We agreed to this.

We went through the safe document by document. I gave a description of each item. There were also multimedia devices and memory sticks, which we sealed, to be dealt with on another day.

This was the last time I set eyes on my office. I asked for my personal belongings again, which I finally collected a short while later from the KPMG team.

It gave me hope that KPMG and someone of Van der Walt's calibre were involved. I had never dealt with him before but was aware of his reputation as a meticulous forensic auditor. Sometime later, I met with him and his team at their offices in Johannesburg. I was asked to explain the details of all the files and data taken from my office.

Together with the team, I went through recordings, memory sticks and other multimedia devices that they had taken from my office. No allegations were put to me to answer or respond to.

However, as I went through all the items, giving them a description or explaining their origins, I couldn't help thinking that Van der Walt would get to the bottom of everything. He and his team were courteous and professional, and I had no reason to doubt their independence. This time, I thought, the truth will come out. Wait until he goes through my submission and evidence submitted to the Sikhakhane Panel, I thought.

In October 2015, in their usual, day-before-the-Sunday-publication hurried manner, I got a text message from Stephan Hofstatter of the *Sunday Times* asking me to comment on the KPMG report.

I said that I hadn't seen it. In fact, I wasn't even aware the report had been completed. Parliament, who had also asked to see the report, had definitely not been given a copy by SARS. Yet, somehow, once again, the *Sunday Times* had managed to get hold of a copy.

Their front page on 4 October 2015 boldly claimed: 'Call to probe Pravin over SARS spy saga – KPMG report confirms our story, piles pressure on ex-finance minister'.[12]

The story starts by saying that an 'explosive KPMG' report has been submitted to Moyane that recommends, among other things, that it should be investigated whether Gordhan knew about the existence of the 'rogue unit' in SARS. With this, Gordhan had now been firmly drawn into the 'rogue-unit' saga.

The journalists used the 'findings' of the report to claim that the *Sunday Times* had all along been correct in their reporting on the so-called rogue unit. 'It confirms *Sunday Times* reports that the unit was "engaged in unlawful interception of communications",' they wrote. 'The report, seen by *Sunday Times* reporters, reveals that SARS blew more than R106-million in taxpayers' money running "a covert and rogue intelligence unit" that spied on South Africans, and then repeatedly lied about its existence to the public … The report says Pillay established the rogue unit at the time Gordhan was commissioner of SARS.'[13]

The *Sunday Times* story also repeats the claim that Gordhan had acted in an irregular manner by approving an extended contract for Pillay after his retirement.

There were other related articles in the same edition. Under the headline 'Taxmen's braai with prostitutes – "not a brothel"', Stephan Hofstatter, Piet Rampedi and Mzilikazi wa Afrika reported that their original source for the brothel story had recanted the earlier claim that 'Taxman's rogue unit ran brothel'. Now the source stated that he had merely gone to a braai that was 'attended by prostitutes' at a Chinese informant's house.[14] This was a reference to Stoffel's lewd house party. I saw this as their way of begrudgingly dealing with the embarrassment that their wild, headline-grabbing claims had proved to be untrue.

Then there was an editorial that makes it clear that the newspaper uncritically accepted the 'findings' of the Sikhakhane report, the Kroon Advisory Board and the KPMG report: 'All three have been unequivocal about their findings – that former deputy commissioner Ivan Pillay should be held accountable for establishing an unlawful unit that operated with intelligence functions,' it reads. 'The KPMG report – on which we report today – asks that Pravin Gordhan explain how he could not have known what was happening under his watch, first as SARS commissioner and then as minister of finance.'[15]

The die was cast – war had been declared on Gordhan.

When we saw the *Sunday Times*'s lead article, 'Call to probe Pravin over SARS spy saga', Ivan and I decided to take the newspaper to the Press Ombudsman. By then, we were no longer subject to conditions in our settlement agreements that precluded us from defending ourselves publicly. Pillay and I appeared before the Press Ombudsman on 1 December 2015.

Independently of us, Gordhan had also complained to the Press Ombudsman, who considered his complaint separately. In his case, the Ombudsman ruled that the *Sunday Times* had committed a serious violation of the Press Code. The newspaper was instructed to unconditionally retract all the texts that were in dispute (the stories as well as the editorial), and to apologise to Gordhan for not having provided him with a copy of the summary of the KPMG report despite asking for his views on that document, for not having given him reasonable time to respond, for not having asked for and published his views on comments made to the newspaper by Oupa Magashula, former SARS commissioner, and for failing to exercise care and consideration regarding his dignity and reputation.

The *Sunday Times* was directed to publish prominently, on page 1, above the fold, a kicker with the words 'apology' or 'apologises', together with Gordhan's name, with a reference to the full apology in the text, to be published on page 2. This text was to include references to all the allegations made in the texts that were in dispute.[16]

In our complaint over the newspaper's argument in the editorial piece, Ivan and I invoked all the previous articles in which the *Sunday Times* had written about the 'rogue unit'.

The boardroom where the Ombudsman's hearing was held was packed. There were journalists from other media houses. Richer, Pikie and Adrian were present in support, as was retired Judge Johann Kriegler and a number of other people. Rampedi arrived late at the hearing; Hofstatter and Wa Afrika did not even show up to argue their case before the Press Ombudsman, Johan Retief, and his panel of assessors.

During the proceedings, Ivan attached as an annexure an affidavit by former *Sunday Times* journalist Pearlie Joubert, which caused a bit of a fracas. Joubert was once part of the *Sunday Times* investigative team. She left in protest on the grounds, she stated, of what she believed to have been unethical conduct on the part of the newspaper with respect to the stories about the 'rogue unit'.

Ivan also disclosed a letter Joubert had written to the Minister of Finance earlier that year. In these documents she stated that a long-time friend of hers, Rudolf Mastenbroek, a former SARS official who left the tax authority in 2013 and later became an advocate of the Johannesburg Bar Council, had approached her and the *Sunday Times* as a source with a request to publish negative allegations about Ivan, me and SARS.

This apparently happened in 2013 and Mastenbroek approached the paper again in 2014, when he also suggested that the *Sunday Times* should engage Magashula because he was 'ready to talk'. Mastenbroek happened to be the ex-husband of Phylicia Oppelt, at the time editor of the *Sunday Times*. He was also appointed by Nene to serve on the Kroon Advisory Board, which passed judgment on the 'rogue-unit' allegations, and specifically on Pillay and me.

I had met Mastenbroek during my early years at SARS when he was part of the newly established Asset Forfeiture Unit in the NPA. He impressed me greatly. He's clever, assertive and has a natural air of authority. I would meet him again later when Ivan appointed him at SARS. Mastenbroek was later temporarily seconded to the NPA at their request. On his return to SARS, he became the national head of the Criminal Investigations Division.

He left SARS in 2013 to become a practising advocate. We had our differences and privately disagreed on how he believed SARS should have 'helped' the NPA with certain politically laden cases in earlier years. But I always respected him and believed we had a fair and professional relationship, which probably shows my naivety when it comes to personal relationships.

According to Joubert, Mastenbroek wanted the *Sunday Times* to report that Ivan and I had, among other things, been protecting certain ANC councillors and a former police deputy commissioner. He apparently claimed that I was a 'former security branch policeman' and an 'apartheid spy' who was 'close to [former police commissioner Jackie] Selebi' and that I 'liked former Bantustan policemen'.[17] He apparently also claimed that Ivan would call for the case files of taxpayers and make them disappear, and in this regard referred to the settlements between SARS and politician Julius Malema and well-known businesswoman Shauwn Mpisane.

Joubert and Mastenbroek were friends since university days and it must have taken immense courage and conviction for her to publicly disclose how Mastenbroek had tried to get her to publish stories in the *Sunday Times* seeking to discredit SARS, Gordhan, Pillay and me. In doing so, she effectively also committed the ultimate 'sin' for a journalist – exposing a confidential source.

I think the media would do well with more people of her calibre.

When these revelations surfaced, much was made by the *Sunday Times* about a supposed 'relationship' between Joubert and me. There was no relationship – I hardly knew her; I had interacted with her two or three times in my entire career at SARS.

On 16 December 2015, the Press Ombudsman ruled in our favour – three times. In his ruling, Retief made scathing remarks about the articles. He ruled that the KPMG report was not a final report, as the *Sunday Times* had stated, and that it was wrong of the newspaper to have presented it as such. The office of the Ombudsman did a cursory check and established from KPMG that as many as six draft reports were submitted to SARS and that the final report wasn't yet out when the *Sunday Times* reported on it in October 2015.

Retief also found that the *Sunday Times* had committed a serious breach of the Press Code and ordered it to unconditionally retract all the texts that were in dispute (the news reports as well as the editorial). The newspaper had to apologise to us for not having provided us with a copy of the summary of the KPMG report they relied on, and for unnecessarily tarnishing our dignity and reputation.

The *Sunday Times* received the same instructions as in the case of Gordhan regarding the wording and layout of the apology.[18]

At the hearing I ran into Rampedi. I asked him why he didn't seem to care about our version of events and whether he would consider hearing me out now. He simply wasn't interested. Not even by then. During this encounter, he attributed his information to SARS officials, past and present, and, yes, 'intelligence officials'.

Looking back, in May 2014, when the complaint against me was first laid, the matter concerned only me – how I was unfit for office, how I had supposedly unlawfully revealed taxpayer and SARS information to an ex-girlfriend and illegally intercepted communications. By July 2014 the complaint included claims that a fundraiser I was involved with had supposedly improperly received donations and that the relationship with Walter presented a conflict of interests. The scope creep had begun ...

By October 2014, the *Sunday Times* had started claiming that a 'rogue unit' existed in SARS, which had broken into homes and bugged Zuma. By November 2014 the 'rogue unit' had sophisticated 'spy equipment' worth millions, had acquired new homes and cars for themselves, had access to slush funds, front companies, ran a brothel and spied on top cops, politicians and taxpayers.

The scope creep continued. Ivan and Richer were then dragged into the mess, supposedly because they had established this unit unlawfully. By February 2015, it was claimed we had been involved in plotting to 'swing elections' and, allegedly, there were documents that demonstrated that Gordhan had known that the unit was illegal.

By April 2015, the Kroon Advisory Board had 'confirmed' the unlawful establishment of the unit even though they didn't investigate the matter and relied on only one report.

By October 2015, the *Sunday Times* had dragged in former intelligence minister Ronnie Kasrils, in what they claimed were 'findings' by KPMG about preferential tax treatment he had supposedly received from Pillay. The newspaper also reported that, apparently, it was not clear whether Gordhan, while he was SARS Commissioner, knew anything about the 'rogue unit' and should therefore be 'probed'.

Over about a year and a half, the original complaint against me had not only morphed, but a whole host of other people and at least one serving minister and a retired minister had also been dragged into the mess.

What happened to the KPMG report?

At the end of August 2015 during a presentation to Parliament's Standing Committee on Finance, Moyane revealed that the KPMG report into the 'rogue unit' had been finalised and was in the possession of the Finance Minister.[19]

According to an article published in the *Daily Maverick*, a legal firm that acts for SARS sent a letter to the KPMG director, Van der Walt, 'recommending that specific findings be made in their [KPMG's] report', including the recommendation that Gordhan, Ivan, I and others should also be investigated. So, in what is supposedly an independent process, a law firm representing SARS instructs an auditing firm that certain findings should be reflected in its report.

And then KMPG apparently does exactly that. Typos and all.

A copy of the legal firm's letter was published by the *Daily Maverick*. In it, the firm recommends that KPMG make the following findings, among others:

> On instructions of Mr. Pillay, the unit unlawfully monitored, intercepted communication [*sic*], recorded and transcribed recordings at the NPA offices [in 2007]. The SARS intelligence gathering exercise at the NPA was known as 'Project Sunday Evenings' and was aimed at gathering intelligence in [*sic*] the criminal investigation of Jackie Selebi ...
>
> The members of the unit were permitted to use technical surveillance.
>
> SARS unlawfully engaged in the procurement of intelligence gathering equipment with the necessary interception capability ...
>
> The relationship between Mr Van Loggerenberg and Belinda Walter caused conflict of interest [*sic*].
>
> Mr Van Loggerenberg unlawfully interfered in the tax audit of Belinda Walter.[20]

All the old complaints against me and Ivan were repeated in the KPMG report. However, the *Daily Maverick* also reported that KPMG added a strange disclaimer to their report – that the document was not to be used 'for the resolution or disposition of any disputes or controversies thereto and is not to be disclosed, quoted or referenced, in whole or in part'.[21] This effectively rendered the report useless for any purpose.

Then the *Sunday Times* published what they claim to be a summary of the actual KPMG report on their website on 5 December 2015.[22]

In January 2016, KPMG issued a public statement after the 'considerable exposure' its report had received, which, according to KPMG, should not have happened 'as the work was being conducted under strict rules of confidentiality which were clearly articulated in our letter of engagement as well as in our findings'.[23] According to the statement, KPMG submitted a number of drafts to SARS on which they received feedback and their last report was submitted to SARS on 4 December 2015.[24]

'Our mandate was to undertake a documentary review *and did not include interviewing individuals named in the report, nor were they given sight of our findings by us.*'[25]

The KPMG report, which had cost the state R23 million, was therefore not a comprehensive forensic investigation but merely a 'documentary review'.

I also wonder how they could claim they didn't interview anyone named in the report, when I met with the KPMG team on two occasions, at their request.

The report contains sweeping statements, is factually incorrect and there is little or no substantiating evidence in too many instances to mention here. The following examples should give the reader an idea, though, of how taxpayers' money was spent on a KPMG 'investigation'.

Take, for instance, the following finding: 'We found no evidence indicating that the Minister of Finance, at the time, new about the existence of the Unit in SARS.'[26]

Firstly, the word 'new' means something entirely different from the word 'knew'. Secondly, since that 'unit' was established there have been three ministers of finance and three deputy ministers and two SARS commissioners and deputy commissioners. Which particular minister was being referred to here, and why leave out the deputy ministers and commissioners?

A real red herring was the finding on equipment: 'The Unit unlawfully engaged in the procurement of intelligence gathering equipment with the necessary interception capability.' A list of very complex descriptions of equipment is then provided.

This is absolutely not true. The listed equipment was acquired by an entirely different unit in SARS, the Anti-Corruption and Security Division, under Clifford Collings. As a cost-centre manager, I was not aware of the acquisition of any equipment of the kind that KPMG refers to. There will be no evidence that the unit acquired any of the equipment mentioned simply because it never happened. Nor did the unit ever use the equipment that was acquired by ACAS.

Furthermore, you can buy any of these items over a counter. And none have 'interception capability'.

It gets even more ludicrous. The reports states that during the period 2006 to 2014, the unit 'acquired and or attempted to acquire, offered intelligence gathering equipment such as ...' Here the report mentions equipment such as audio recorders, video recorders and a 'pinhole covert camera'.

The finding is nonsensical. Either the unit acquired the equipment, or it didn't. Offered equipment? To whom? But, as I said, the unit never acquired or used any of the listed equipment in the first place anyway.

Probably the most laughable of the findings is the following: 'There is no evidence that SARS owed [sic] a brothel but it seems that some members of the Unit engaged services of prostitutes during their leisure time.'

I should really hope SARS never 'owed' a brothel any money. We know SARS never *owned* one either, as the *Sunday Times* seemed to believe once, and tried to make the nation believe. As for the guys and their 'leisure time' – different strokes for different folks. But why exactly is this any of KPMG's business to start with?

It is most interesting that the allegations that the unit bugged Zuma, got new homes and cars, spied on top cops and infiltrated politicians have now completely disappeared.

One other small example. Back in 2010, I met with people in the tobacco industry who had asked to meet with the team members of the unit. I recorded the conversation, which was later transcribed. They warned us about the existence of a 'project' to discredit SARS officials involved in the tobacco industry investigations for which R600 000 had been made available. We were told how certain individuals had been infiltrating state intelligence, the Hawks and the NPA, and were going to use these institutions to discredit us.

I know that KPMG had access to this recording, as well as a document that was ultimately going to become an affidavit that proves the aforesaid. They had the 'Project Broken Arrow' reports and the warnings we received of people who were trying to discredit us. But not a word of any of this appears in KPMG's 'findings'. Why was this information not considered relevant to their 'documentary review'?

18

PG

December 2015 brought us Nenegate. Inexplicably, Zuma replaced Finance Minister Nene with a relatively unknown parliamentary backbencher, Des van Rooyen. Overnight, the rand depreciated to record lows against global currencies. It was estimated at the time that the capital losses sustained by South African bonds and directly affected equities amounted to R506 billion as a result.[1] Van Rooyen spent less than a week in office before Gordhan replaced him.

The country breathed a sigh of relief when Gordhan was back in his old post. But it wasn't long before trouble surrounding the SARS 'rogue unit' started brewing again.

On 18 February 2016, Gordhan received a letter from the Hawks instructing him that he had to answer three pages containing 27 questions, that he had to 'keep the letter confidential and not interfere with "state witnesses", without indicating who such witnesses are'.[2] He was instructed to answer it within ten days.

The document was sent to Gordhan by Hawks boss Major-General Berning Ntlemeza, who had replaced Dramat.[3] This letter arrived six days before Gordhan had to present his 2016 budget to Parliament and was conveniently leaked to the media. Watching the 'Hawks 27 questions' saga play out from afar, it all looked very familiar to me.

I am quite sure that the minister was livid. Given the economic turmoil our country is facing, the 2016 budget speech was probably his most difficult ever. With a stagnant economy and muted growth, the prospect of a downgrade by ratings agencies, the political uncertainty and market turmoil following Zuma's unceremonious removal of Nhlanhla Nene as Minister of Finance, the letter from the Hawks must have caused him to question its timing. In his reaction, Gordhan didn't hold back. In a statement two days after the budget, he wrote:

> Immediately after the Budget was tabled, the Hawks letter and questions were maliciously leaked to the media, together with misinformation about what might or might not have transpired at discussions that followed receipt of the letter, including the ANC caucus meeting in Parliament yesterday.
>
> I am therefore compelled to clarify the following issues: The letter from the Hawks is an attempt by some individuals who have no interest in South Africa, its future, its economic prospects and the welfare of its people. If necessary, I will take appropriate legal action to protect myself and the National Treasury from whatever elements [are] seeking to discredit me, the institution and its integrity ... I can categorically state that the Hawks have no reason to 'investigate' me.[4]

Some of the questions in the document were as ambiguous as they come. Like this one, listed as question 14: 'Were there things at Sars [when you were the commissioner] that would have happened without your knowledge?'[5]

In an institution of 15 000 people? As Sam Sole commented in the *Mail & Guardian*, 'Erm ... Ya think? And does that include unknown unknowns?'[6]

I felt deep empathy for Gordhan. I knew from experience that your answers don't matter, you'll be damned if you do (answer) and damned if you don't. In the court of public opinion, popular sentiment was divided on the Hawks questions. Some suggested that Gordhan should answer the questions if he had nothing to hide. His failure to do so would imply that he had something to hide, some argued.

Others felt that he shouldn't need to respond, given that the Hawks didn't want to say whether he was a suspect or witness in a criminal investigation.[7] Gordhan apparently sought clarification from the Hawks on this but to no avail.[8]

Constitutional law expert Pierre de Vos publicly questioned the legal basis of the Hawks investigation: 'In the absence of a credible explanation … serious questions arise about the credibility as well as about the legality of the Hawks investigation. It is unclear what the legal basis is for the Hawks investigation relating to the establishment of a so-called "rogue spy unit" by Sars, as the relevant legislation does not create any criminal offences that the Hawks would be entitled to investigate,' De Vos said.[9]

De Vos also explained that the Hawks, by posing these questions, 'did not refer to the specific crimes being investigated, nor to the specific sections of the relevant legislation, which supposedly created criminal offences allegedly breached by Sars officials when it created the so-called "rogue spy unit".'[10]

One thing was clear: the Hawks weren't too concerned about the pressing nature of the minister's budget speech. This was one of our fledging democracy's most difficult financial years. Gordhan had an exceptionally demanding schedule following the tabling of the 2016 budget. He was due to attend a series of meetings with investors and ratings agencies during an international roadshow covering London, New York and Boston. Alongside his team at the National Treasury, business leaders and trade union federation leaders, Gordhan somehow had to convince these influential audiences that South Africa's macroeconomic fundamentals were sound and that the budget's fiscal framework was credible. All the Hawks seemed to care about was playing a game of 21 (or 27) questions.

Writing for the *Daily Maverick*, Marianne Thamm said the questions read like 'an amateurish fishing expedition' and described the investigation as a 'witch hunt':

> Considering copious and detailed documentation available to Hawks investigators – including minutes of meetings with State Security Agency officials, various signed agreements as well as statements by key players – which were all submitted to the Kanyane and Sikhakhane panels, as well as an inquiry headed by Judge Kroon, the charges would have been drawn up by now if a criminal case was to be made.
>
> Particularly considering this is a matter of national and international importance and involves the country's revenue collection service and its Minister of Finance. And even more so considering an apparent 'war' brewing between opposing factions within the ruling party.[11]

Once again, the rand took a dive.

During that time there were numerous media reports about tension between Gordhan and Moyane. Thamm writes that after Gordhan's reappointment, he was 'quick to establish his authority, popping in to make a surprise visit to Moyane at SARS head office in Cape Town just before the [December] holiday break. The men apparently met three times afterwards in what seemed to be tense interactions.'[12]

This appears to have come after Gordhan, shortly after his appointment as finance minister, asked Moyane to halt a restructuring process that had been started at SARS until he had time to assess its effect. Moyane seemingly refused, apparently stating that he had got approval from Nene.[13]

According to *Business Day*, the 'far-reaching' restructuring project for the tax authority was one of the first initiatives undertaken by Moyane following his appointment as commissioner in October 2014. The same report claims Gordhan and Moyane's relationship got off to a rocky start because Gordhan was 'perturbed by Mr Moyane's allegations about a controversial "rogue" investigating unit that was set up within SARS while Mr Gordhan was the commissioner, and by Mr Moyane's purging of top SARS executives allegedly implicated in it'.[14]

About a week after the Hawks sent their questions, Zuma responded by saying that Gordhan's position as finance minister was not in jeopardy even though he would not stop the Hawks investigation.[15]

On 3 March 2016, about a week after the drama caused by the Hawks questions, the ministers for police and state security called a media briefing to address the nation on the allegations of a SARS 'rogue unit'. This followed a media statement issued by SARS two days before. After all the resignations, the salacious stories, all the *Sunday Times* allegations, for these ministers, the whole 'rogue unit' narrative had now been reduced to a mere three issues.

Firstly, said the ministers, the unit may have been established unlawfully and/or illegally. Precisely what law had been broken was yet to be determined. Secondly, the unit was involved in 'Project Sunday Evenings' and, lastly, the unit had allegedly acquired spy equipment that was considered potentially unlawful and/or illegal. These were the matters that were now being investigated by the Hawks. However, as I have already explained, the unit never acquired or used any such equipment, so whoever briefed the ministers on this didn't do it properly.

Something very curious occurred at this briefing. An incorrect date was repeated by the ministers – and it was exactly the same wrong date that was contained in the SARS media statement issued two days before.[16] The ministers said: 'Following a media coverage of the alleged "Rogue Unit" on 11 June 2014, the then Acting Commissioner of SARS, Mr Ivan Pillay instituted an investigation led by an Attorney, Mr Moeti Kanyane. Mr Kanyane, in his findings, recommended a further investigation, given the limited scope of his mandate.'[17]

The reason this incorrect date is significant is because it creates the impression that Ivan, and not Moyane, had first started the investigation into a 'rogue unit' and would therefore, according to a certain logic, be to blame for everything that has since followed. As I have explained, when the Kanyane and Sikhakhane panels came into being there was no reference in their mandates to any unit in SARS whatsoever and both were intended to investigate Walter's allegations only. The allegations around a 'rogue unit' at SARS first featured much later in the *Sunday Times*. As the Sikhakhane Panel explained in their report, they took it upon themselves to add the media reports to the scope of their investigation only after it had featured in the media in October 2014.

On 30 March 2016, Gordhan answered the Hawks questions and issued a statement.[18] He said he wanted to inform the country of certain matters. These included that his legal advice confirmed he was not obliged under any law to answer the questions sent to him by the Hawks, but that he believed it to be in the public interest to provide the Hawks with the information they sought.

He said that his legal advice concluded that the establishment of the unit was lawful. He went on to say that his legal advisers believed that a finding of the Sikhakhane Panel, namely that the establishment of the unit contravened the National Strategic Intelligence Act, 'was wrong and based on a superficial and clearly mistaken reading of the aforementioned Act'.[19]

Gordhan confirmed that the unit 'was part of the broader enforcement division of SARS – similar to the enforcement capabilities required in any tax and customs administration in the world'. He stated that, to his knowledge, the unit performed its functions lawfully and that the funding of the unit was done through normal budgetary processes applicable to SARS. He also said that he had no knowledge of the operation codenamed Sunday Evenings.[20]

He also pointed out that the Hawks had declined to answer his questions in which he sought clarity on what offence specifically they were investigating and by what authority they were acting.[21]

The *Sunday Times* recants

After nearly two years, a degree of sanity somehow finally became installed at the *Sunday Times*. In March 2016, following discussions between the Times Media Group, the *Sunday Times* and a number of former SARS colleagues, we managed to properly engage with the newspaper to see if we could avoid protracted and costly litigation. I initiated discussions with their editorial executives after sending letters to the Times Media Group board.

In my letters I pointed out that, as a listed company with a board of directors and with responsibilities to its shareholders, the organisation had a duty to reflect on the harm it had caused us. To their credit, the Times Media Group immediately responded and gave me an undertaking to consider what I had put to them. For the first time in almost two years, I found people in senior positions at the newspaper who were responsive, prepared to have an open mind and listen to those of us who had been affected by their articles.

In January 2016 Bongani Siqoko had taken over from Oppelt as the new editor of the *Sunday Times*. Between Siqoko's team and us there were three interactions. Contrary to what one journalist would later claim, Gordhan wasn't involved in any of these discussions. It is my understanding that Siqoko and other senior journalists in his newsroom painstakingly reviewed the editorial processes around more than 30 articles regarding SARS that had been published since August 2014.

They were not comfortable with how the SARS 'rogue-unit' saga had been portrayed and we came to an amicable agreement. Like the *Carte Blanche* management, they also wanted me to waive my intended civil suit against the *Sunday Times* and the Times Media Group, and asked me to put that in writing. Finally, our voices had been heard.

On 3 April 2016, the *Sunday Times*, in unprecedented fashion, published a full-page article, effectively retracting their claims of having published certain 'facts' about me, Ivan and the 'rogue unit'. In an accompanying editorial, Siqoko wrote:

Did we get everything right with our SARS story? No. Did we get everything wrong? Again the answer is no.

Today we admit to you that we got some things wrong.

It is clear that SARS received approval to set up the National Research Group within the National Intelligence Agency from then finance minister Trevor Manuel. The unit was not in the end set up within the NIA but became a unit within SARS.

In particular, we stated some allegations as fact, and gave incomplete information in some cases. In trying to inform you about SARS, we should have provided you with all the dimensions of the story and not overly relied on our sources. Granted, it is our responsibility to build, sustain and protect a relationship with our sources, but we should have allowed you to make your own judgment based on all sides of the story.

In a front-page story headlined 'SARS bugged Zuma', published on October 12 2014, we stated that a former SARS official, known as Skollie, blackmailed SARS into paying him R3-million to keep quiet about how members of the unit broke into Zuma's house and planted listening devices. The story and headline stated as fact that members of the unit broke into Zuma's home and planted listening devices there. It should have been made clear, both in the headline and in the story, that this was an allegation, not a fact. The allegation was also not properly attributed.

Our sources did not give us an exact date, although they were adamant the bugging was done by the unit. One source with direct knowledge said it was some time after Zuma was acquitted of rape (in May 2006) and before the ANC's Polokwane conference when he was elected ANC president (in December 2007). The story could have given readers the impression that this could have been around 2005 or 2006, whereas the SARS unit, according to documents in our possession at the time of writing, made it clear that the unit was set up only in February 2007.

Former SARS deputy commissioner Ivan Pillay, in his right of reply, which we publish today, claims we refused to publish a statement by a former SARS official denying he ever told us he was bribed to leave SARS and stay silent about an alleged bugging of Zuma's home. It is true that the official sent an e-mail to our reporter denying ever making the claim. This is the e-mail that he then sent to SARS. But Pillay is not aware that the official later sent us another e-mail confirming our off-the-record interaction.

In another front-page lead, 'Taxman's rogue unit ran brothel', on November 9 2014, we again wrongly stated as fact in the headline and in some parts of the story that the unit had set up its own brothel. In fact, this was an allegation from a former member of the unit. The member had claimed that one of his colleagues had set up a brothel. This was not strong enough to report the allegation as fact.

In another article in the same edition, we reported incorrectly that Johann van Loggerenberg had written a 'confession' letter to SARS commissioner Tom Moyane admitting that he had indeed run a 'rogue unit'. The document contains no such confession. It was, in fact, a denial.

More errors were repeated in other reports, such as 'the infiltration of politicians as bodyguards', 'breaking into homes and conducting house infiltrations', 'running front companies' with secret funds of over R500-million, and 'spying on taxpayers and top cops'.

The SARS story has given us an opportunity to take a closer look at our news-gathering and production processes. We have found some serious gaps.

Efforts are being made to close those. Our news desk – made up of a team of section editors – is being restructured.[22]

In addition to this admission of editorial and procedural errors by the newspaper, Pillay and I were given an opportunity to each write an

800-word, unedited response. Strangely, or perhaps not so, despite the *Sunday Times*'s climbdown, there was no response from SARS.

The 'rogue-unit' narrative was a sham.

As I've mentioned, SARS had lost over 55 senior officials since Moyane's appointment. Directly or indirectly, the 'rogue-unit' saga also left a list of casualties in the media. Journalist Malcolm Rees, who wrote the very first front-page lead for the *Sunday Times*'s sea of articles about SARS, 'Love affair rocks SARS', appears to have been the first, when he left the newspaper in late 2014. Veteran investigative journalist Pearlie Joubert soon followed in February 2015, stating she was no longer 'willing to be party to practices at the *Sunday Times* which [she] verily believed to have been unethical and immoral'.[23]

In January 2016, another editor in the Times Media Group stable, Songezo Zibi, also resigned.[24] I understand Zibi was told in no uncertain terms that as editor of *Business Day*, he was taking 'editorial independence too seriously'.[25] In their reporting, *Business Day* had started to question the veracity of the SARS 'rogue-unit' stories published by the *Sunday Times*. I'm sure this must have caused tension within the Times Media Group.

Sunday Times editor Oppelt was moved to another business area in the group.[26] Rob Rose left Business Times and joined the *Financial Mail* and later became its editor.[27] Rose apparently left following a heated clash with Oppelt.[28] Another Business Times journalist, Loni Prinsloo, moved to Bloomberg, the international financial news agency.

Journalist Piet Rampedi seems to have left the *Sunday Times* in April 2016 after the newspaper published its retraction.

At the end of March 2016, in a rare public display of unity, Gordhan and Moyane announced that SARS had achieved its revenue target and collected over R1 trillion for the 2015/16 fiscal year. This was a new record for SARS.[29]

It was good news for South Africa and, for a change, good news for

SARS. The 15 000 SARS employees had done it again – as they had been doing, virtually without fail, year after year. They not only met their revenue target, but exceeded it. It matters not that the target was revised downwards twice that year. The world is in a financial turmoil and South Africa is facing its own unique financial and economic challenges, so that achievement deserves recognition.

In the meantime, those of us who had to leave the tax authority were trying to stay afloat. We did odd jobs here and there. Some of us were approached by people who had been under investigation by SARS and wanted us to help them – another unintended consequence of the 'rogue-unit' narrative. I was approached by individuals who wanted to use the 'rogue-unit' saga to their advantage. In legal circles it had become known as the 'rogue-unit defence'.

The thing is that people who were under scrutiny at SARS had realised the fault lines in the 'rogue-unit' story and that the new SARS management didn't want to publicly contradict this narrative. So, they brought all sorts of actions trying to force SARS's hand. I tried to contact SARS and offered to assist them in such cases, but when I got no response, I gave up. By the end of 2015, Julius Malema claimed in court papers to have been a 'victim' of the 'SARS rogue unit', and Martin Wingate-Pearse and Gary Porrit did the same.[30]

In Porrit's case, it was reported that 'the spectre of the South African Revenue Service (SARS) "rogue unit" had hung over the hearing, with Mr Porritt … claiming that a report done by auditing firm KPMG into the unit included evidence suggesting SARS had been biased against it. The KPMG report apparently cites an alleged meeting in 2001 between a one-time business associate of Mr Porritt … and former SARS officials Ivan Pillay and Johann van Loggerenberg.'[31]

I had to laugh at the idea of the 'spectre' of a phenomenon that never existed!

In early 2016 I met with someone with close ties to the intelligence community. He had asked for the meeting. He wanted me to provide a complete account in writing of my interactions with Toby for a certain faction within state intelligence. I wasn't prepared to do this, and certainly not in the manner it was asked of me.

A throwaway comment during that conversation lingered in my mind, though. This person told me that there had been an entire 'team' assigned to 'work' on me, and that he'd even had a discussion with the 'lead analyst' on my matter. I don't know if this is true or not, but the man had no reason to lie to me and had never deceived me before. My assessment was that what he suggested was actually quite feasible.

For a brief while, all was quiet. Until 15 May 2016, when the *Sunday Times* reported that Gordhan was facing imminent arrest.[32] The report stated that the Hawks wanted Gordhan and eight others to be charged for 'alleged illicit intelligence gathering and spying on taxpayers during his time there. The unit was allegedly responsible for this. The Hawks and the National Prosecuting Authority were reportedly waiting for "political go-ahead" before arresting him, the paper reported ...'[33]

This was followed by denials and clarifications by both the Hawks and the NPA. But the damage had been done. And the hurricane has still not died down. At the time of writing, reports and articles in the media suggesting that the Hawks and the NPA were continuing an 'investigation' into the SARS 'rogue unit' have not subsided. It seems there may very well be more to come of this 'rogue-unit' narrative in the future. Conflicting stories abound.

Another report, this time from 30 May 2016, stated that this investigation was continuing:

> The investigation into the 'rogue unit' at SA's tax agency is ticking along, with officials previously associated with Finance Minister Pravin Gordhan set to be interviewed by the Directorate for Priority Crime Investigation (Hawks) this week. The officials to be quizzed

worked closely with Gordhan during his tenure as commissioner of the South African Revenue Service (SARS). The move – officially denied by the Hawks – comes despite regular public declarations by the elite police unit that it is not targeting the minister ...[34]

In May, *City Press* reported that there was new activity regarding the criminal case registered by Moyane in May 2014: '[T]he docket history listed in the police's own case management system reveals that the case was closed in December 2015, but was suddenly reopened this week [May 2016].'[35]

On 23 August 2016 – as we were finalising the manuscript – Gordhan, Ivan, and I were 'summonsed' by the Hawks to present ourselves at the offices of their Crimes Against the State Unit (CATS) in Pretoria to be given warning statements. Why the CATS unit was dealing with this matter is anybody's guess, because the allegations do not remotely suggest any crime against the state.

Given the likelihood that things are heading for a final showdown, most probably in a criminal court, it would be unwise of me to elaborate further. What I can say, though, is that the letter addressed to me – and some of the others I've seen – was crafted in an atrociously poor manner. I can honestly say that such a letter would never have passed my desk during the time I worked at SARS, never mind be sent to someone we were investigating in the knowledge that it might become part of court papers.

Curiously, the letter addressed to me was hand-delivered by a major general of the Hawks on a Monday morning – it had been signed off the day before. Considering the apparent haste in which these letters were compiled, someone clearly had got their knickers in a knot that weekend.

In June 2016, I attended an event called The Gathering, organised by the *Daily Maverick*. Two occurrences at this event will stay with me for a long time. I happened to notice among the attendees Stephan Hofstatter from the *Sunday Times*. As most of the 30-plus articles advancing the 'rogue-unit' story featured him as co-author, you could say we kind of 'knew' each other. Out of courtesy, I greeted him, shaking his hand. He asked how I was. I said that it was tough times and that I was taking things day by day. I said that I had heard that the *Sunday Times* was under new management and asked him how he was doing.

Hofstatter said he too was taking things day by day. There was no apology. No acknowledgement of error, no mention of any of the articles under his by-line. Nothing. I greeted him and walked away.

Later that afternoon, journalist Ranjeni Munusamy interviewed Gordhan. At one point, she asked him about the recent news events and the effects these had had on him and his family. Gordhan did not answer immediately. On the big screens in the hall it was clear that he was taking a moment to compose himself. Tears welled up in his eyes and his voice began to crack – you could hear a pin drop.

He simply said that neither he nor any of the accused officials had ever stolen a cent of public money.

I looked around and saw quite a few other people with tears in their eyes. I was also overcome. After the interview, which was broadcast live on the Internet to a much bigger audience, Adrian went over to Munusamy, who herself was in tears. This saga has caused our country, our government, SARS, ordinary citizens and all of those who were dragged into it enormous harm.

When Gordhan left the stage, he received a standing ovation from the audience – people who represented the diversity of South African society. It was clear to me that, deep down, all of us really hoped and wished for the same thing. When you take away people's differences, we all want our country to succeed and become a better place for all its citizens.

We all appreciate the need for the higher purpose that people like Manuel and Gordhan advanced, the purpose that drove us at SARS, and reminded us that political freedom was but a part of our country's gains, and that economic freedom was still to be achieved.

Much of the heavy burden of taking our country forward in terms of its economic development rests squarely on the shoulders of a humble individual, known to some of us only as PG.

Epilogue

How do I finish my tale? How does one end a story that doesn't yet seem to have reached its conclusion?

Essentially, I wanted to tell the story of this SARS unit as best as I could. I promised the members of the unit that, even if it's the last thing I do in my life, I will ensure that their names are cleared and that their story is told.

The Kanyane and Sikhakhane panels, the Kroon Advisory Board, the team from KPMG, the Inspector General of Intelligence – none ever stopped to consider exactly what this unit did over the years. Despite my constant pleading and offers to do so, I was never invited by any of them to tell the story you have just read. I felt obliged to counter all the blatant lies, half-truths and twisted facts that were leaked to the media by 'former and current SARS officials' and 'intelligence officials' and expose the crimes that none of the panels seemed to care anything about. This, above all, is what drove me to tell this story. The public has a right to know the true facts, and it is in the interest of justice that the truth be told.

For all of us who were drawn into the 'rogue-unit' saga, the future is uncertain. We have had to start from scratch again. Although we have received tremendous support from people within SARS, civil society, business, state officials and former and current political activists, for many of us life isn't easy.

More civil litigation lies ahead. My co-author, Adrian, is facing the lawsuit SARS brought against him, as well as a constructive-dismissal labour case, and I am taking on a lawsuit that Walter brought against SARS and me in my official capacity.[1] This takes time, is expensive, and it keeps reminding us of the past. The criminal case being pursued by the Hawks at the time of going to print suggests some of us may be brought before court on some or other criminal charge.

Should we be prosecuted, the fact that we acted within the course and scope of our duties will probably be considered and we will have to go into a protracted cycle of arguments and postponements about legal fees. I have no doubt the publication of this book will cause some sort of backlash against us. But perhaps the opportunity may very well be the ideal one to surface the truth behind what had been going on over this period. Only time will tell.

Rumours about us also pop up every so often. It's difficult to move on when certain people don't want you to. The number and extent of the stories about some of us, which are still floating around, are truly astounding. I've been accused of being behind all kinds of schemes and media articles. According to the Sikhakhane Panel, I even had the ability to hypnotise people. We were turned into bogey men by this affair. If only they knew how normal I am and how I dearly just wish to get on with my life if only I could be allowed to do so.

In telling this story, I have elaborated on how the events of the past two to three years have affected me in a personal way. I found this incredibly difficult. I believe many of us – myself and other former members of the HRIU and others (some who left SARS and some who are still there) – have been significantly traumatised. But it is the unseen and unheard of who have suffered the most – our families, mothers, fathers, husbands, wives, brothers, sisters and children.

I continue to largely suppress my feelings about the matter. That is an old habit of mine, one that goes back to childhood days. By adulthood, it had become the norm. After spending my 20s working in very unnatural circumstances, I became unable to identify even basic emotions, such as anxiety and fear. Something had to give, and it did.

In 2000 I decided to seek treatment from a psychologist and a psychiatrist and, to a great extent, they helped me normalise my life. I started getting panic attacks but, with professional help, I managed to understand this phenomenon, tried to deal with it and eventually the attacks disappeared. Then, around 2013, owing to the pressure I was placing on myself at work, my lack of a work–life balance and because my stable relationship with Nicole had ended in 2010, the attacks started to reappear.

Experts will tell you that anxiety and panic attacks manifest differently from person to person. In my case, they took two forms. Firstly, I would suddenly wake up at night struggling to breathe, with the most terrible thoughts of dread and doom, and my heart palpitating. These attacks usually dissipated fairly quickly and didn't bother me too much. Then they would also occur when I had to speak in public or to groups of people. I would panic, struggle to breathe, become incoherent and unable to focus. I can assure you, it's a terrible malady to suffer from.

The normal kind of fear we all experience when we feel exposed to some degree was tremendously pronounced within my psyche. So, you can imagine how the very public exposure caused by the 'rogue-unit' saga affected me.

For instance, a day or two after Walter's 'complaint' against me landed at SARS, I arranged for the forensic laboratory to meet me at my office, along with Clifford Collings, and asked them to make complete mirror images of my laptop and mobile phone. I wanted to use information on my laptop in my defence, but at the same time it was deeply embarrassing.[2] People would now not only be able to read my official emails and memoranda, but also my private conversations in the form of emails, text messages, and so forth. I felt like a deer caught in the headlights.

Then there was the Kanyane Panel process, which I found demeaning and humiliating. I later managed to obtain recordings of the interviews they conducted. Some of the lies and twisted stories presented to the panel were not only shocking, but an absolute invasion of my privacy.

Once the *Sunday Times* articles appeared, my private and work life were suddenly on display in the public domain, out there for all to see. The reference to the fundraiser club I was part of, and the suggestion that this was somehow something vile and irregular, made matters worse for me. This was a labour of love that many people participated in, an organisation that truly changed lives. Yet in a front-page article published by one of our largest newspapers, it was being defiled.

It was also during this time that my father passed away and, as the oldest son in the family, I had to deal with the funeral arrangements. What added to my emotional state was that many people with whom I thought I was on friendly terms at SARS began to avoid me. I then started to deliberately avoid even former colleagues and friends who did reach out to me, because I feared any association with me might cause them harm. I felt isolated, defenceless and forlorn.

Then came the Sikhakhane Panel. Here were four people who were again going through my life with a fine-tooth comb. Once again, my private life would become of interest to people I didn't even know and, once again, I wasn't to be heard on matters that they considered implicated me.

I found the leaks from the KPMG report equally traumatising. Through all these processes, I was condemned without being given half a chance to put my case. Four times, the most basic tenet of natural justice, the right to be heard, was denied to me.

Then there were the letter exchanges with experienced, and expensive, lawyers – one stated that I was a 'person steeped in deceit' who was not to be believed. This simply because, many years previously, I happened to work undercover for the police.

Throughout this period, contrary to a formal agreement we had entered into in mid-2014, Walter went ahead and indiscriminately released several statements to the media, gave interviews on radio, television and to media houses, continually adding to her allegations and making the most outlandish allegations against me and, later, against others. In some cases, she made the most far-fetched allegations against people she came to know through me – my friends, people who wouldn't hurt a fly, who invited her into their lives unconditionally and accepted her just as she was. Later she would extend her allegations to include some SARS officials – people she didn't even know, people who had worked hard to serve the higher purpose, names she merely happened to hear when I took phone calls from them or talked to others at work about them. I felt ashamed for inadvertently exposing them to this mess.

The continued attacks on me in public by Walter, who knew full well that I wasn't able to publicly defend myself, were incredibly degrading and debasing.

Before writing this book, my evidence provided to the Kanyane and Sikhakhane panels failed dismally to expose the truth. In fact, the exact opposite seems to have occurred. Even less can be said about the Kroon Board and KPMG. Later, I also provided evidence to the police and offered it to the Hawks, hoping that good will triumph over evil but, given the signs, I'm not holding my breath that much will come of this. My appearances before the Broadcasting Complaints Commission and the Press Ombudsman presented the only real opportunities I had to make some of the truth known, and even then very little of my side of the story seemed to have seen the light of day.

As for the treatment I received at the hands of the Fourth Estate ... I usually got a call from the *Sunday Times* late on a Friday or a Saturday morning. The journalists would ask me a few ambiguous questions, just so the reporters would be able to say I'd been given an opportunity to comment. Later this occurred even though they knew full well that I wasn't allowed to publicly respond to them. I began to dread Fridays and Saturdays.

In some instances, I was quoted completely out of context and facts were blatantly twisted. In others, matters were raised that I wasn't even asked to comment on. And with virtually every single article the *Sunday Times* published, a large photo of me was used for the world to see – all over the front page. Then came the *Carte Blanche* 'exposé' and, again, I was not in a position to go on camera to tell my side of the story.

There were times when I felt incredibly angry about the miscarriage of justice and how the truth was being deliberately concealed. At other times, I felt like a victim because I wasn't able to publicly defend myself and I grew despondent about how administrative powers were being abused and manipulated. I felt a growing feeling of hopelessness, knowing that forces far more powerful than me were at play.

Fortunately, as time progressed and as more and more journalists and media houses began to dig deeper, aspects of the truth started surfacing from their investigative journalism. But it took a long time and much damage had already been done.

There are credible arguments why journalists have to rely, to an extent, on the information anonymous sources provide them. Whistle-blowers and anonymous sources are the lifeblood of the media. Without them, the press would struggle to uncover corruption. At the same time, what this experience has shown is that greater care should be taken to ensure media houses are not being used for nefarious purposes.

Article 11 of the South African Press Code deals with confidential and anonymous sources, setting out the provision that the media must protect such sources. It also says that the media should avoid the use of anonymous sources unless there is no other way to uncover a story. Care should be taken to corroborate the information, and the media should not publish information that constitutes a breach of confidence, *unless the public interest dictates otherwise* (my emphasis).

I believe this story serves as a serious warning to one of the bastions of our democracy. As solid as the Press Code and Press Ombudsman are as mechanisms for guiding the self-regulated media in our country, they shouldn't be the only means to ensure objective and factually correct reporting. Independent news organisations must ensure that due ethical processes of evaluation and internal checks on news gathering and how news is sourced are followed to avoid the kind of reputational damage several people suffered in our experience.

To me, nothing better demonstrates the real damage caused by the 'rogue-unit' saga than the look of shock and horror on the face of Johnny and Sandy's little boy that Sunday morning when the story broke about the alleged brothel. Or when one of the unit members called to tell me his wife had started divorce proceedings against him on the strength of the *Sunday Times* articles.

In July 2016, the wife of one of the former unit members, who also happens to work at a state institution, was discriminated against when she was denied a transfer by her bosses because her husband was implicated in the 'rogue-unit' affair.

Nothing can make up for the loss of livelihood and reputations of people who had devoted their entire adult working lives to the freedom of our country. A meeting between the 'new' SARS management and the former 'rogue unit' members who were still working at SARS in 2015 illustrates the incredible vindictiveness of these events. A senior SARS manager referred to those employees as 'vomit that had to be wiped from the floor'.

I have deliberately avoided speculating about the bigger political events unfolding around the same period as the 'rogue-unit' narrative or the possible links to these. In addition to legal limitations imposed on me, this is because I cannot claim to understand them all and I lack sufficient information to develop an informed view.

What I can say is that a number of conditions lined up over the years and, from 28 May 2014, when the 'complaint' by Walter landed at SARS, various agendas and events came together, leading to what ultimately unfolded. I believe the primary protagionsists initially comprised mainly of people in the tobacco industry and some of the officials in the Illicit-Tobacco Task Team. The 'complaint' against me then opened a door for others.

I suspect that some people saw this as an opportunity and whispered into powerful ears to advance the 'rogue-unit' narrative forcefully. I have no doubt that they made their stories sound very plausible and had a lot of help from different quarters. I think, at first, some of those powerful people perhaps believed these stories. I also believe at some point some of them found themselves in a bit of a quandary when the evidence didn't prove that we had bugged people, conducted house infiltrations, used millions in slush funds or spied on politicians. The next best thing was to just keep on sifting and digging, searching for anything that would remotely stick to us.

The rest was probably explained away by our detractors, with suggestions that the 'rogues' were so clever that one should expect to find no evidence of wrongdoing on their part. As the 'rogue-unit' narrative became entrenched, the absence of evidence turned into actual evidence. And, by then, our reputations had been so tarnished, and the negative accusations so ingrained in the public's mind, with the press publishing story after story, that no one was going to believe us anyway. It didn't really matter what we said. There will forever be those who believe that a 'rogue unit' did exist at SARS.

I have no doubt that the enemies we made along the way, together with some we had over the barrel because of their criminal activities, saw these events as a great opportunity to pounce upon us. And many of them did, often in collaboration with each other. The oddest of bedfellows joined up to advance the narrative. At least, when we end up in civil and criminal courts, the details of and the complete truth behind this whole affair, who the protagonists are and why they did what they did, will hopefully be exposed. Only time will tell whether we will get this opportunity.

With the benefit of hindsight, I also believe that Tom Moyane wasn't as fully briefed on the true state of affairs at SARS as he should have been when he was appointed as commissioner. I believe that whoever did brief him, failed him, along with SARS and the country as a whole. I have no doubt that whatever Moyane had been told when he took over was a one-sided, jaundiced view. Perhaps, one day, if our paths were to cross again, we might be afforded an opportunity to reflect on what happened during these times. After what has happened to me, I believe anything is possible.

In the end, what seemed to be such a sensational scoop for the *Sunday Times*, which provided it with numerous articles over two years (many on the front page above the fold line), screaming headlines and posters, actually ended up being merely about how a tiny unit was established within SARS, how some staff members were appointed, Ivan's pension, a fund-raiser in which I was but one of many involved, something three people allegedly did or didn't do on Sunday evenings way back in 2007 and a list of equipment (or rather equipment for an entirely different unit altogether) – nothing more.

Having said all of this, I am still grateful that I was able to be part of an organisation such as SARS, and serve government and South African society to the best of my ability. In the process, I've sacrificed the best years of my adult life and the prospect of living a balanced life. But I have no regrets about that. I have made peace with the fact that my (and others') time to do my bit has come and gone. It is time for the new generation to take the higher purpose further, and I wish them all the best.

I consider myself extremely fortunate to have been a participant in advancing the struggle for economic freedom (as Manuel and Gordhan had put it). I was not alone in this. This spirit of participation applies to all of those who have been affected by the 'rogue-unit' story and the events that transpired – even more so their families, who not only sacrificed much during the time we all worked for SARS, but also stood by each other when these events unfolded.

If I had a magic wand, I would simply make the years 2013 to 2015 disappear, but I can't. There was no 'rogue unit'; Gordhan, Pillay and Richer didn't do the things they have been accused of. Neither did the personnel in the unit.

If I could have things my way, I would hope that Moyane and his new management team will reflect on this story and realise that the kind of unit that we had in SARS can really make a difference in combating crime, specifically economic crime and organised crime syndicates, which threaten the fiscal prospects of our country and the security of our people. If he and his team don't want the unit in SARS, then place it elsewhere.

I would also wish for the heads of all law-enforcement agencies to take their cue from this story, and realise that, even through small groups, the state can make a measurable difference to function more effectively. Law-enforcement officials in our state agencies should realise that they are one team and that they need to work together. Put aside the infighting and professional differences; reach out and try to understand the other side's views and approaches, and collectively leverage off what each does best.

Crime in our country is rampant. Organised criminals can see where the weaknesses are in the criminal-justice system and are quick to take advantage of them. They know there is tension between agencies. Don't allow them to capitalise on this. Pull together to take the struggle for the complete freedom of our nation forward.

If we fail to curb corruption, counter organised crime and protect public resources against abuse, we will fail our society and our children, and their children will bear the biggest brunt of our failures. By working together, let's find that higher purpose again.

Annexure 1

**Letter written by Belinda Walter to Johann van Loggerenberg,
2 February 2014**

'... I feel compelled to write formally to you to formally offer my sincere apology for an incident where I had an extreme error in judgment and acted in a reprehensible manner. I defamed you out of fear relating to threats against [name removed] and I. At the time however – baseless and idiotic – I felt compelled to say whatever the particular persons wanted to hear to prevent them from doing what I fear the most – hurting [name removed]. I do not wish to compromise the client/persons or you by providing you with more details at this time ...'

Kind Regards
  Belinda Walter

Annexure 2

Letter written by Belinda Walter to attorneys and the advocate for a tobacco company on 2 February 2014

I am writing to you as colleagues to sincerely apologise for, and explain my inexcusable conduct yesterday ...

I had hoped that by exposing myself and explaining about the BAT relationship, it would allay [name of tobacco company's] fears that I have never and would never pose any threat to them and that my son would never be in danger ...

What I said about Johann van Loggerenberg, was untrue and devoid of any truth. Johann conducts himself in such a manner as to always be beyond reproach ... He simply does not and will not cross the lines that [name of tobacco company] so desperately hopes he has. He is not like the industry or its participants, including me. I am deeply ashamed of what I said.

My conduct was reprehensible and inexcusable and I can only offer my apologies and brief explanation as to what had transpired and brought me to your office in the extreme emotional state that I was in.

I am aware that I will need to extend an apology to Johann and I will endeavour to do so without reference to the participants at the meeting or the exact context to ensure that [name of tobacco company] is not compromised in any manner. It is grossly unjustified and I can only hope that you will respect the past I cannot disclose …

Kind Regards
Belinda Walter

Letter written by Belinda Walter to the *Sunday Times* on 3 February 2014 under legal letterhead

I refer to my sms and e-mail correspondence to you on the week-end.

You will recall that on Saturday, I asked twice that you [do] NOT record the meeting and then under [name of tobacco company's] insistence you recorded the meeting and I had no option.

As explained, the statements made regarding various person/s during the interview were false and defamatory. The circumstances which led me to the meeting where I found myself in a state of extreme emotional and mental distress were the fact that I found out that [name of tobacco company] was leveling serious threats against myself and more importantly, my son. I was willing to say or do anything to please them to simply refrain from carrying out the threats that another FITA member had reported to me on Friday, subsequent to the FITA meeting on Thursday. I have incidentally received another telephone call this morning from another FITA member also advising that [name of tobacco company] has leveled a variety of threats against me.

Much of what was said was derived from the usual industry gossip and what had been told to me from the FITA meeting on Thursday. I embellished and added rubbish to pacify them where necessary.

There had also been an incident with [director's name] at the venue where he indicated he had obtained my personal cellphone billing, travel movements etc. and became very aggressive about calls to Dubai and one telephone call to [name removed] in December where I returned a call and simply left a message.

I would therefore ask that you confirm that the recording and/or any copies will be destroyed and that the recording will not be forwarded to any third parties whatsoever.

Kind Regards
Belinda Walter

Letter written by Belinda Walter to the *Sunday Times*, sent on 5 February and again on 7 February 2014 under legal letterhead

Firstly I am an admitted attorney, and understand my responsibilities regarding legal privilege, as well as distinguishing my legal and ethical responsibilities to clients as well as the South African statutory environment. Any suggestion by anybody to the contrary is rejected with the utmost contempt it deserves. The perpetuation of discussing these possibilities and more so publishing in any public media or newspaper, in whatever form, will as a result cast negatively on my reputation.

Both my partner and I are happy to submit to any formal investigation, polygraph etc. in an appropriate forum should the need arise. This is more about common decency and respect than legal arguments and something that I urge you to understand at a basic human level as a father, as a husband, as a son what your reckless actions may result in. Nobody can predict who they will fall in love with. Our situation is no different.

The possibility of a misunderstanding regarding my romantic relationship was discussed at length and thought through with my partner at its inception. Even these original discussions placed the possibility of a relationship under strain and contributed to my personal stress and what later transpired.

We went out of our way to precisely avoid any perceived prejudice to any third party, associated person, employer etc. This should not be construed that we have anything to hide or that we were doing anything wrong. We primarily did so particularly to protect the integrity of the institution for whom my partner works. My partner and I both take our careers very seriously and the responsibilities entrusted to us. Having said that, we also consider our private lives private! These are but some considerations I had to contemplate before pursuing a relationship seriously with my partner. These would be the same considerations I would have needed to consider if, for instance, I pursued a relationship with a journalist at the *Sunday Times*. Even writing this letter to you, I find myself in extreme discomfort having to disclose these private matters to you in confidence because your actions have forced me to.

For the reasons mentioned above, I did a number of things prior to the relationship becoming serious. These included:

I informed a particular client who was involved in litigation with a state department where a possible conflict of interest could be perceived that I was interacting with this person in a social context on text. My client did not express any concerns whatsoever in this regard at that point in time. The discussions are recorded on text messages;

1. the relationship was very young and casual and even though my client was comfortable about this possible romantic relationship, my partner maintained that it would be better for me to consider terminating my mandate with this client to avoid compromising them or the state department in any manner. After giving it some thought, I terminated my mandate and I informed all parties concerned immediately. Once again, this is documented in correspondence. This happened within a space of less than one month from when I first socially interacted with my partner, to

the termination of mandate. I point out that this was at my own financial expense;

2. I never met my partner in his formal capacity or interacted with him in respect of ANY litigation pertaining to this client, or any other client, at any time. In fact, I only ever met with him once which concerned a general discussion about compliance issues in the tobacco industry. At that meeting, I did not represent my client and did not attend in my capacity as an attorney but attended in my capacity as the Chairperson of Fair-Trade Independent Tobacco Association (FITA);

3. our very first social interaction occurred in a group setting arranged by him, after I invited him out. This happened almost 2 months since the abovementioned meeting and with no exchange of communication until the week that we first socially interacted. We agreed up front to not discuss work at all. I had no ulterior motives at all with regard to the social interaction with my partner and the same is true for him;

4. we enjoyed each other's company and agreed to slowly continue social interaction. Bearing in mind that I am a single mother of [a] minor son (who permanently resides with me) and have my own legal practice and the nature of the work hours and responsibility of my partner, we met infrequently. During these meetings we would always take special precautions to keep our interactions strictly private, including to our close family members. That is the extent to which we set the level of privacy to our relationship;

5. we, furthermore, at length discussed and determined boundaries and 'no-go' areas in respect of aspects concerning our professions, and at no stage did I disclose any privileged information or anything else unlawfully to him, and more particularly, nor did he to me. We are both adults and are quite capable of understanding

what that means. Any suggestion otherwise in any form or way is not only false but also slanderous and casts a very negative light on the integrity of both of us. It does not matter if you publish our relationship under the guise of an allegation or attributing it to hearsay or whatever the context you may wish to couch it in, once you have published it and made it known, you will cause us irreparable harm;

6. bearing in mind that this was still in the infancy stages of a new relationship, the other matter of me being the Chairperson of FITA was also raised in discussion. Again, my partner suggested that I consider this carefully in light of the possibility of a long-term relationship that may develop with him. In the immediate future FITA intended to hold its AGM and I believed a new Chairperson would be elected. We therefore agreed to wait the week to let this happen naturally. It turned out that I was re-elected as Chairperson. I then resigned from FITA within the following week formally and notified all parties, including state departments with whom I had interacted on behalf of FITA. Similarly to the above, we never discussed matters concerning FITA as we were focussing on the personal aspects normally associated with romantic relationships as would be the case for any person. Any suggestion otherwise in any form or way is not only false but also slanderous and casts a very negative light on our integrity;

7. I pause to note that I resigned from the particular client, and FITA, within the space of less than two weeks and only then did we agree to pursue the relationship exclusively. What is more, I submitted my practice to an independent audit by an accredited auditor as recommended by the Law Society of the Northern Provinces at the same time. I furthermore, voluntarily, submitted myself to a full tax audit by the South African Revenue Service. In addition to this, even though not required, I also completed a number of statutory

disclosures in this regard as an attorney and which I am not prepared to elaborate on here.

We have always gone out of our way to keep our relationship absolutely private and are desirous to maintain it that way. Not only because of the misconceptions that we contemplated could possibly arise, but also because we are both intensely private people by nature and character. What we do in our private lives we consider to be sacred and wish to keep it so.

With journalists of the *Sunday Times* discussing our private lives simply based on the notion that I may previously have represented 1 taxpayer and a non-profit organisation that happened to fall within the economic sector and scope of the state department my partner works for and is responsible for, is the most gross form of invasion of our privacy possible. You [name of *Sunday Times* journalist] and [name of another journalist] have direct access to both of us and have had since even before I met my partner, you could have just asked us and we would have happily taken you into our confidence and explained the context.

We had nothing, and still have nothing to hide – except to protect our privacy. However, none of you chose to ask either my partner or I at any point. Instead you chose to lend your ears out to so-called 'sources' who spoke about our relationship to you without our permission. I submit that these sources had a hidden agenda as is evident that the level of care we took to keep our relationship private could only have been breached by imposing on our privacy.

As it turns out, and facts have shown this to be the case, the so-called evidence of our relationship is based solely on the word of a company who already stands accused of accessing private data illegally obtained, including that of family members and loved ones of state officials, and having once again illegally accessed my personal cellphone itemised billing data and cross-border movements.

Amazingly it is of no interest to you how exactly the 'sources' obtained information from the respective state department and mobile service provider. For some reason you seem to find those forms of corruption of less public importance.

The level of privacy that we maintained in respect of our relationship was so deep that not the *Sunday Times*, the company nor anybody else would have known about the existence of a relationship but for the illegally obtained cellphone records and movement control. Even that in itself does not prove the existence of a romantic relationship. How we make our relationship public and who we choose to include in our personal and private lives is a private consideration and not some right that the *Sunday Times* or any client can take upon themselves on the supposed argument that it is in the public interest. We are all acutely aware that the company has significant influence over the relevant journalists.

As you know, I have knowledge of certain interactions between the so-called sources and [journalist name] and [journalist name]. I expressed my discomfort to you in this regard previously. You also know that offers of money had been made by this same company for financial benefit in the form of cash, holidays and cocaine to [journalist name] on a number of occasions in exchange for favourable treatment by the *Sunday Times*. He admitted to this in your presence.

You similarly know that [journalist name] received sportswear for her entire team paid for by these 'sources'. This is indeed the same 'source' who has been causing you, [journalist name] and *Sunday Times* to infringe on my rights, by amongst others unlawfully accessing personal data concerning my cellphone billing and my international travel movements. You have been made aware of this on a number of occasions and so has [journalist name]. You know the origin of the original information given to [journalist name] and you also know that there exists an understanding between [journalist name] and the 'sources' that he will not report negatively on them in the media. Furthermore, certain articles penned by [journalist name] and contributed to by [journalist name] originate from these same 'sources' and had the sole intent of unfairly pushing the attention away from their own unlawful activities and onto those of competitors.

Neither [journalist name], nor [journalist name], disclosed any of this to any of their managers at any point in time until they were confronted by you. By then *Sunday Times* had already published a few stories emanating from these 'sources'. This alone brings the *Sunday Times*, you as their Manager and them as journalists, their objectivity, the legality, honesty, fairness, truth, accuracy, context and balance, intent and negligence, independence, potential conflicts of interest, dignity and reputation, and advocacy into serious question ...

There was a particular incident on 1 February 2014 where I, in a state of great emotional distress and fear, conveyed certain information to a limited number of people under legal protection where the assurance was given to me by a Senior Counsel, representing all the parties concerned and present, as well as the assurances given to me by [journalist name] on the same day that that discussion was in confidence, without prejudice and off the record.

I have since, in any event, formally retracted everything that I may have said under duress and in that emotional state that I was in, from all parties concerned and received confirmation from the Senior Counsel, as convenor, that all utterances would be struck. In any event, I also disclosed subsequently that much of what I said that day was influenced by my state of mind and contained a significant amount of fiction, interwoven with few facts. I do not wish to dwell on this incident, save to say, that I view its legal status to be such as if it never happened. It cannot be used by any of the parties in any way or form ...

Given the serious nature of the content of this letter, I would ask that you kindly acknowledge receipt and that you have noted the content and that you will abide by my request.

In the interim, I am forced to reserve my rights fully.

Kind Regards
Belinda Walter

Notes

AUTHORS' NOTE

1 Chapter 6 of the Tax Administration Act 28 of 2011, http://www.gov.za/sites/www.gov.za/files/a28_2011.pdf, accessed 1 August 2016.
2 See http://www.dfa.gov.za/department/accessinfo_act.pdf, accessed 1 August 2016.
3 See http://www.justice.gov.za/legislation/acts/2004-012.pdf, accessed 1 August 2016.
4 See http://www.gov.za/documents/prevention-organised-crime-act, accessed 1 August 2016.
5 See http://www.gov.za/sites/www.gov.za/files/a28_2011.pdf, accessed 1 August 2016.
6 Ibid.

CHAPTER 1

1 SARS Press Release, 5 December 2014, http://www.sars.gov.za/Media/MediaReleases/Pages/5-December-2014---Media-Statement-by-SARS-Commissioner-.aspx, accessed 25 July 2016.
2 Email from attorney who was approached by Niemann addressed to the author, dated 2014. Email states the attorney's willingness to testify to these facts. Email in author's possession.
3 SARS, Resignation of Mr Johann van Loggerenberg, 4 February 2015, http://www.sars.gov.za/Media/MediaReleases/Pages/4-February-2015---Resignation-of-Mr-Johann-van-Loggerenberg.aspx, accessed 26 May 2016.
4 SARS – Johann van Loggerenberg resigns, Eyewitness News, 4 February 2015, http://ewn.co.za/2015/02/04/Sars-Johann-van-Loggerenberg-resigns, accessed 26 May 2016.
5 It was confirmed by a source that 28 employees from Telkom Human Resources joined SARS – reflected in an audit committee report dated December 2013.
6 Natasha Marrian, Exodus at SARS continues as two more senior staff members quit,

Business Day Live, 9 April 2015, http://www.bdlive.co.za/national/2015/04/09/exodus-at-sars-continues-as-two-more-senior-staff-members-quit, accessed 7 May 2016.

7 A source confirmed that in early 2015 Ravele was asked to confirm certain matters that were untrue. He wasn't prepared to do so.

8 Malcolm Rees, Love affair rocks SARS, Times Live, 10 August 2014, http://www.timeslive.co.za/local/2014/08/10/love-affair-rocks-sars1, accessed 23 May 2016.

9 Ibid.

10 Ibid.

11 Piet Rampedi, Mzilikazi wa Afrika, Stephan Hofstatter and Malcolm Rees, SARS bugged Zuma, Times Live, 12 October 2014, http://www.timeslive.co.za/politics/2014/10/12/sars-bugged-zuma1, accessed 23 May 2016.

12 Ibid.

13 Not his real name.

14 Not her real name.

15 Mzilikazi wa Afrika, Piet Rampedi and Stephan Hofstatter, Taxman's rogue unit ran brothel, Times Live, 9 November 2014, http://www.timeslive.co.za/local/2014/11/09/taxman-s-rogue-unit-ran-brothel1, accessed 23 May 2016.

16 Verbal representations made by Piet Rampedi to the Press Ombudsman, 1 December 2015; see also Ivan Pillay and Johann van Loggerenberg, *Sunday Times* SARS reporting driven by malicious intent – Pillay and Van Loggerenberg, Politicsweb, 16 December 2015, http://www.politicsweb.co.za/politics/sunday-times-sars-reporting-driven-by-malicious-in, accessed 25 July 2016.

17 Piet Rampedi, Stephan Hofstatter and Mzilikazi wa Afrika, Pillay faces criminal charges after SARS spies explosive confession, Times Live, 17 May 2015, http://www.timeslive.co.za/sundaytimes/stnews/investigations/2015/05/17/Pillay-faces-criminal-charges-after-SARS-spies-explosive-confession, accessed 4 July 2016.

18 For example, 'On the allegations that the covert unit spied on President Jacob Zuma and ran a brothel, Mr Lebelo said these allegations were included in the terms of reference of the KPMG investigation as well as another one by independent counsel, whose name had yet to be announced.' See Natasha Marrian and Carol Paton, SARS denies bullying, abuse of powers, *Business Day*, 15 May 2015, http://www.bdlive.co.za/national/2015/05/15/sars-denies-bullying-abuse-of-powers, accessed 25 July 2016.

19 Piet Rampedi, Mzilikazi wa Afrika, Stephan Hofstatter and Malcolm Rees, SARS chief acts on 'brothel' claim, Times Live, 16 November 2014, http://www.timeslive.co.za/local/2014/11/16/sars-chief-acts-on-brothel-claim, accessed 4 July 2016.

20 Ibid.

CHAPTER 2

1 Gordhan joined the institution in November 1998 as deputy commissioner. Trevor van Heerden was the first Commissioner of SARS. Gordhan became commissioner on 1 March 1999.

2 O Fjeldstad and M Moore, Revenue authorities and public authority in sub-Saharan Africa, *Journal of Modern African Studies* 47(1): 1–18, March 2009. Cambridge: Cambridge University Press.

3 Trevor Manuel, Remarkable journey began with toasted cheese and tea, letter from Trevor Manuel to Pravin Gordhan, published in *PG*, an in-house SARS publication to celebrate a decade of Gordhan's leadership as commissioner, Pretoria, 2009.

4 Ibid.

5 David Hausman, Reworking the revenue service: Tax collection in South Africa, 1999-2009, Princeton University, Innovations for Successful Societies, 2010, https://successfulsocieties.princeton.edu/publications/reworking-revenue-service-tax-collection-south-africa-1999-2009, accessed 30 May 2016.

6 Louw is also the *ex officio* member of the South African Tax Review Committee, appointed by the Minister of Finance in July 2013.

7 Chantelle Benjamin, SA drags customs into 21st century, *Mail & Guardian*, 6 September 2013, http://mg.co.za/article/2013-09-06-00-sa-drags-customs-into-21st-century, accessed 25 July 2016.

8 Dave Glazier, Barry Hore joins SARS, ITWeb, 4 May 2006, http://www.itweb.co.za/index.php?option=com_content&view=article&id=114481, accessed 25 July 2016.

9 Opening of first dedicated SARS tax practitioner branch in Pretoria, South African Institute of Tax Professionals, 28 June 2011, http://www.thesait.org.za/news/67519/Opening-of-first-dedicated-SARS-Tax-Practitioner-branch-in-Pretoria.htm, accessed 25 July 2016.

10 Stephen Cranston, Mfundo Nkuhlu: New Nedbank COO goes via trade route, *Financial Mail*, 14 August 2014, http://www.financialmail.co.za/fmfox/2014/08/14/mfundo-nkuhlu-new-nedbank-coo-goes-via-trade-route, accessed 25 July 2016.

11 See South African Embassy, Kazakhstan, http://www.dirco.gov.za/astana/gallery.html, accessed 25 July 2016.

12 African Tax Administration Forum gala dinner speech address by the Commissioner of SARS, Mr Oupa Magashula, Uganda, 18 November 2009, http://www.gov.za/african-tax-administration-forum-ataf-gala-dinner-speech-address-commissioner-sars-mr-oupa-magashula, accessed 25 May 2016.

13 SARS boss Oupa Magashula resigns after probe, *Business Day*, 12 July 2013, http://www.bdlive.co.za/economy/2013/07/12/sars-boss-oupa-magashula-resigns-after-probe, accessed 25 July 2016.

14 *V Pillay v Commissioner for SARS*, annexure 'Submission to Sikhakhane panel' – Labour Court Gauteng Division (Johannesburg), December 2014.

15 Parliamentary Monitoring Group, South African Revenue Service (SARS) – Overview of its mandate and work, https://pmg.org.za/committee-meeting/17332/, accessed 25 July 2016.

16 SARS presentation: Portfolio Committee on Trade and Industry, 19 August 2014, https://www.thedti.gov.za/parliament/2014/SARS_Presentation.pdf, accessed 25 July 2016.

17 The powers of SARS include the recoupment of losses through direct payments of penalties or outstanding tax debts (sometimes payment arrangements, financial guarantees and settlements), the preservation of assets, liens, fines, penalties, compound interest and forfeitures. Civil actions may also include obtaining civil debt judgments, executing warrants and selling assets, instituting sequestrations and liquidations (including liquidation enquiries), holding third parties and directors of companies liable in their personal capacity and instituting criminal proceedings.

18 Fikile-Ntsikelelo Moya, Sars: 'The game is up', *Mail & Guardian*, 28 November 2003, http://mg.co.za/article/2003-11-28-sars-the-game-is-up, accessed 25 July 2016.

19 Tax Policy Center, Urban Institute, Brookings Institution and individual authors, *Briefing book: A citizen's guide to the fascinating (though often complex) elements of the federal tax system*, 2016, http://www.taxpolicycenter.org/briefing-book/what-tax-gap, accessed 14 May 2016.

20 Institute for Futures Research, Stellenbosch, 21 October 2011, The Illegal economy: A South African law enforcement perspective, http://www.ifr.sun.ac.za/IFRPresentations/R%20Mastenbroek%20Illegal%20Economy%20Nexus.pdf, accessed 25 July 2016.

21 Ibid.

CHAPTER 3

1 Deep-cover agents were employed by the police, but never known to anyone else. My role was to infiltrate organised-crime syndicates and groups. The role meant remaining undercover for as many years as possible, alongside real criminals, the idea being to surface later as a policeman and testify against major criminal syndicates.

2 A 'coolie' is an outdated and now offensive colonial-era term for an unskilled labourer, mainly in the Indian subcontinent. In South Africa it has always been a racist slur referring to people of Indian descent.

3 SARS, *Annual report 1999*, Commissioner's overview, 29 February 2000, http://www.sars.gov.za/AllDocs/SARSEntDoclib/AnnualReports/SARS-AR-01%20-%20Annual%20Report%201998-1999.pdf, accessed 25 July 2016.

4 SARS presentation: Portfolio Committee on Trade and Industry, 19 August 2014, https://www.thedti.gov.za/parliament/2014/SARS_Presentation.pdf, accessed 25 July 2016.

5 The Tax and Customs Intelligence Unit later changed its name to the Business Intelligence Unit.

6 SARS, *Annual report 2009*, http://www.sars.gov.za/AllDocs/SARSEntDoclib/AnnualReports/SARS-AR-13%20-%20Annual%20Report%202008-2009.pdf, accessed 25 July 2016.

7 Ray Faure, Bridgestone probes tax fraud, Fin24, 3 April 2003, http://www.fin24.com/Companies/Bridgestone-probes-tax-fraud-20030403, accessed 25 July 2016. In 2005 I would return to take over the Tax and Customs Intelligence Unit, reporting

to the general manager, Vuso Shabalala, when the customs and tax parts of it were amalgamated.

8 Marcia Klein, South Africa: Metcash settles with the SARS, *Business Day*, 7 November 2000, http://allafrica.com/stories/200011070317.html, accessed 20 May 2016.

9 Metcash fraudster sentenced, Independent Online, 11 June 2007, http://www.iol.co.za/news/south-africa/metcash-fraudster-sentenced-357046, accessed 25 July 2016.

10 SARS media release, Metcash Constitutional Court judgment, 24 November 2000, http://www.ftomasek.com/archive/m241100a.html, accessed 25 July 2016.

11 David Hausman, Reworking the revenue service: Tax collection in South Africa, 1999-2009, Princeton University, Innovations for Successful Societies, 2010, https://successfulsocieties.princeton.edu/publications/reworking-revenue-service-tax-collection-south-africa-1999-2009, accessed 30 May 2016.

12 Ibid.

13 Ibid.

14 Institute for Futures Research, Stellenbosch, 21 October 2011, The Illegal economy: A South African law enforcement perspective, http://www.ifr.sun.ac.za/IFRPresentations/R%20Mastenbroek%20Illegal%20Economy%20Nexus.pdf, accessed 25 July 2016; see also Parliamentary Monitoring Group, NPA 2005 Overview & Strategy 2020; National Prosecuting Service; Directorate of Special Operations; Asset Forfeiture Unit: brief, https://pmg.org.za/committee-meeting/6847/, accessed 25 July 2016.

15 For example, in *S v Botha and Others*, the accused raised issues of unfairness in the trial on the basis that the investigators and people who collected evidence presented to the court were not police officials. In its judgment, the court acknowledged that law-enforcement agencies would for the foreseeable future not be capable of combating crime meaningfully on their own. The court found that it is constitutional for a person to conduct criminal investigations, even if not a police official, provided certain limitations and rules are abided by.

Further memoranda of understanding soon followed with the NPA, the AFU, the NIA, the SAPS Border Police Unit and Marine Coastal Management.

16 Nedlac, *Final Nedlac report on customs fraud in respect of textile, clothing and footwear*, page 7, paragraph 3.5.7, http://new.nedlac.org.za/wp-content/uploads/2014/10/customs-fraud.pdf, accessed 25 July 2016.

17 In 2012 various organisational changes in the NPA led to a dilution of its dedicated prosecuting capacity and certain units were no longer solely dedicated to SARS matters. As a result, SARS cases now have to compete with other commercial-crime cases.

18 See http://www.ftomasek.com/4745.pdf, accessed 25 July 2016.

19 Bulelwa Makeke, Our sentence agreement with Dave King – NPA, Politicsweb, 29 August 2013, http://www.politicsweb.co.za/party/our-sentence-agreement-with-dave-king--npa, accessed 25 July 2016.

20 Alec Hogg, UNDICTATED: The dogged Mr Chipps who brought Dave King to book, Business Day Live, 2 September 2013, http://www.bdlive.co.za/opinion/

columnists/2013/09/02/undictated-the-dogged-mr-chipps-who-brought-dave-king-to-book, accessed 25 May 2016.

21 Bulelwa Makeke, Our sentence agreement with Dave King – NPA, Politicsweb, 29 August 2013, http://www.politicsweb.co.za/party/our-sentence-agreement-with-dave-king--npa, accessed 25 July 2016.

22 Anil Singh, The taxman pays a visit to Durban businessman, Independent Online, 30 April 2003, http://www.iol.co.za/news/south-africa/the-taxman-pays-a-visit-to-durban-businessman-105674, accessed 25 July 2016.

23 See The Firm, http://www.oocities.org/organizedcrimesyndicates/thefirm.html, accessed 25 July 2016.

CHAPTER 4

1 SARS busts customs scam and nets R67 million, SARS press statement, 7 July 2001, http://www.ftomasek.com/archive/p070701a.html, accessed 9 June 2016.

2 Profurn to pay taxman R26m, 19 January 2001, http://www.fin24.com/Companies/Profurn-to-pay-taxman-R26m-20010119, accessed 24 May 2016.

3 SARS busts customs scam and nets R67 million, SARS press statement, 7 July 2001, http://www.ftomasek.com/archive/p070701a.html, accessed 9 June 2016.

4 Ibid.

5 Ibid.

6 Ibid.

7 Not his real name, composite character.

8 SARS v Tayob family, SARS media release number 9 of 2001, 8 February 2001, http://www.ftomasek.com/archive/m080201a.html, accessed 11 June 2016.

9 Ibid.

10 Ibid.

11 Advocate Muzi Sikhakhane and two other advocates were appointed in September 2014 by then acting SARS commissioner, Ivan Pillay, to investigate allegations made against me in May 2014 by a former romantic partner, after the Kanyane Panel had previously been appointed to look into her allegations.

12 Parliamentarians had been briefed over the years on this and other similar matters in detail by SARS since 2003.

CHAPTER 5

1 In September 2014, at the European Police Chiefs Convention at the Europol head-quarters in The Hague, which SARS attended, this issue was widely canvassed in a country-by-country survey.

2 The new gold, City Press, 24 March 2014, http://www.news24.com/Archives/City-Press/The-new-gold-20150429, accessed 25 July 2016.

3 Not the real location.

4 South African Government, Wage settlement with unions, 16 September 2009, http://www.gov.za/wage-settlement-unions, accessed 25 July 2016.

5 *V Pillay v Commissioner for SARS*, annexure 'Submission to Sikhakhane panel' – Labour Court Gauteng Division (Johannesburg), December 2014.

6 Richer was a member of an underground ANC unit based in Gaborone, together with his wife, Lauren, under the leadership of another ANC and South African Communist Party stalwart Barry Gilder (later the coordinator of Intelligence Services). Richer told me that from the mid-1980s units of the ANC in Botswana came under increasing attack. In 1984 Rogers Nkadimeng was the target of a car bomb. Richer was the target of a raid in 1985 in which 14 people were killed. 'They killed two people in the house across the street but they didn't get to us. We had a news agency, which was a front – they hit that. They basically shot people, and bombed and hand-grenaded the buildings.' Richer and his wife had to flee at night with their two baby daughters. (Authors' interview with Richer, 20 May 2016.)

7 *V Pillay v Commissioner for SARS*, annexure 'Submission to Sikhakhane panel' – Labour Court Gauteng Division (Johannesburg), December 2014.

8 Pillay's proposal was approved by Magashula, head of Corporate Services at the time, on 13 February 2007, see *V Pillay v Commissioner for SARS*, annexure 'Submission to Sikhakhane panel' – Labour Court Gauteng Division (Johannesburg), December 2014.

9 *V Pillay v Commissioner for SARS*, annexure 'Submission to Sikhakhane panel' – Labour Court Gauteng Division (Johannesburg), December 2014.

10 Some names for the unit were bandied about, like the Tiger Team and Special Investigations, but none was formally adopted. The idea of the tiger may have its origin in the fact that law enforcement had a strongly zoological lexicon, with Scorpions, Red Ants, Green Ants and Cobras among its arsenal of capabilities, and someone came up with the idea of a tiger as the logo. But it was nothing more than an idea at that stage.

11 The SANDF members joined SARS in accordance with an agreement that the tax authority would appoint members of the Umkhonto we Sizwe Military Veterans Association, former soldiers of the liberation movements. At the time, many members of this association were deployed in other government departments too, *V Pillay v Commissioner for SARS*, annexure 'Submission to Sikhakhane panel' – Labour Court Gauteng Division (Johannesburg), December 2014.

12 Ibid.

13 *V Pillay v Commissioner for SARS*, annexure 'Submission to Sikhakhane panel' – Labour Court Gauteng Division (Johannesburg), December 2014.

14 Issued as annexure to SARS's line-by-line refutation to the 'Peega dossier' in February 2010.

15 Julian Rademeyer, *Killing for Profit: Exposing the Illegal Rhino Horn Trade*, Penguin Random House, 2012.

16 Section 1 of the National Strategic Intelligence Act 39 of 1994 as amended.

17 *S v Kidson* 1999 (1) SACR 338 (W).

18 Deneesha Pillay, Eskom says security contractor must be able to probe organised crime, *Business Day*, 22 July 2016, http://www.bdlive.co.za/business/energy/2016/07/22/eskom-says-security-contractor-must-be-able-to-probe-organised-crime, accessed 5 August 2016.

19 Sally Scott, Racist resort gets the 3rd Degree, Independent Online, 9 November 2000, http://www.iol.co.za/news/south-africa/racist-resort-gets-the-3rd-degree-52676#.UTN7gaJTCz4, accessed 5 August 2016.

20 See *Carte Blanche*: About, http://carteblanche.dstv.com/about/, accessed 5 August 2016.

21 Irene Kuppan, Two convicted of assaulting TV crew, Independent Online, 5 March 2007, http://www.iol.co.za/news/south-africa/two-convicted-of-assaulting-tv-crew-317637, accessed 5 August 2016.

22 Pierre de Vos, Hawks prosecution mystery, Dispatch Live, 21 May 2016, http://www.dispatchlive.co.za/news/=2016/05/21/=hawks-prosecution-mystery/, accessed 25 May 2016.

23 Not his real name.

24 State of the Nation Address by the President of South Africa, Thabo Mbeki: Joint sitting of Parliament, 9 February 2007, http://www.iol.co.za/news/politics/full-text-of-mbekis-state-of-nation-speech-314525, accessed 25 May 2016.

25 UK Department for International Development, Intelligence in a constitutional democracy – final report to the Minister for Intelligence Services, the Hon. Mr Ronnie Kasrils, MP, 10 September 2008, http://r4d.dfid.gov.uk/Output/178693/, accessed 25 July 2016.

26 Piet Rampedi and Mzilikazi wa Afrika, Tax boss moves to block Finance Minister, *Sunday Times*, 24 January 2016, http://www.timeslive.co.za/sundaytimes/stnews/2016/01/24/Tax-boss-moves-to-block-finance-minister, accessed 3 June 2016.

CHAPTER 6

1 This unit used to be part of the Department of Environmental Affairs. However, in 2010 the MCM was incorporated into the Department of Agriculture and functions as Fisheries. This was as a result of President Zuma's expanding and reconfiguring of Cabinet in 2009.

2 SARS, Authorities seize more than 5 tons of abalone, six arrested in KZN, 11 April 2007, http://www.sars.gov.za/AllDocs/Documents/MediaReleases/2007/SARS-MR-2007-020%20-%20Media%20Release%20on%20Authorities%20seize%20more%20than%205%20tons%20of%20abalone%206%20arrested%20in%20KZN%20-%2011%20April%202007.pdf, accessed 20 May 2016.

3 National Assembly, parliamentary records, Question No. 1595, 12 October 2007, https://www.environment.gov.za/sites/default/files/parliamentary_updates/question1595.pdf, accessed 20 May 2016.

4 Not the real location.

5 Verbal account obtained from sources involved in investigations.

6 Changed description for legal purposes.

7 Changed description for legal purposes.

8 Changed description for legal purposes.

9 Not his real name.

10 Not his real name.

11 Not their real names.

12 SARS, Authorities seize more than 5 tons of abalone, six arrested in KZN, 11 April 2007, http://www.sars.gov.za/AllDocs/Documents/MediaReleases/2007/SARS-MR-2007-020%20-%20Media%20Release%20on%20Authorities%20seize%20more%20than%205%20tons%20of%20abalone%206%20arrested%20in%20KZN%20-%2011%20April%202007.pdf, accessed 20 May 2016.

13 Not the real location.

14 Not the real location.

15 Other early projects included the unit scoping out various premises where it was believed illegally harvested abalone was being stored. They also conducted security assessments at various border posts and harbours, did investigations that led to the seizure of illicit tobacco and foiled a robbery at a SARS state warehouse, which resulted in four suspects being arrested by the police.

16 Trusha Reddy and Andile Sokomani, Corruption and social grants in South Africa, Institute for Security Studies monograph, https://www.issafrica.org/uploads/MONO154FULL.PDF, accessed 25 July 2016.

17 There were also investigations to identify a syndicate believed to be involved in printing fake banknotes, a fraud case involving a pipe manufacturer and attempts to identify distributors of illegal liquor products (drinks mixed with lethal industrial alcohol), but none of them led to anything.

CHAPTER 7

1 This refers to the investigative steps to be followed in an approved project, so that work can be recorded systematically as part of operations management.

2 Not his real name.

3 Not his real name.

4 Not her real name.

5 Michael Peega was identified in 2009 as the author of a publicly distributed document that became known as the 'Peega dossier'. SARS refuted all the allegations in the document, including several annexures. This was distributed to the media in February 2010 and to various other third parties. His name and the facts associated with his dossier are mentioned in this book because they are based on what is now public information.

6 Confirmed in interviews by the author on 4 June 2016 with 'Hector' and 'Johnny', who also recall the incident vividly.

7   Not his real name.

8   South African Government News Agency, SAPS commended for arrest of policemen, court officials, http://www.sanews.gov.za/features/saps-commended-arrest-police-men-court-officials, accessed 20 May 2016.

9   Over the years, the name Mandrax stuck, but new nicknames followed. Illicit manu-facturers often branded their tablets in a particular manner. To manufacture these tablets not only requires the illicit chemical methaqualone, but also experience and skills to press the tablets, as well as a tablet press – something not easily available.

10 Known as quaaludes in other countries, these tablets are typically abused by swallow-ing them in copious numbers and taking them with alcohol. Used in this way, they have the effect of being a 'downer'.

11 SARS, *Annual report 2007–2008*, http://www.gov.za/sites/www.gov.za/files/complete_3.pdf, accessed 20 May 2016.

12 Other projects included the unit looking into pirated DVDs and music CDs. The taxi industry was also investigated but with limited success.

13 Not his real name.

14 The departure of Martin was used as part of the rogue-unit narrative. The *Sunday Times* claimed in 2014 that Martin had blackmailed Pillay and SARS into paying him a 'silence cheque' of over R3 million, so he would keep quiet about how the unit had supposedly broken into the Forest Town home of Jacob Zuma before he became president and planted listening devices there. See Piet Rampedi, Mzilikazi wa Afrika, Stephen Hofstatter and Malcolm Rees, SARS bugged Zuma, Times Live, 12 October 2014, http://www.timeslive.co.za/politics/2014/10/12/sars-bugged-zuma1, accessed 4 July 2016.

15 Solly Maphumulo, Now, Hawks take aim at Gerrie Nel, *The Sunday Independent*, 6 March 2016, http://www.iol.co.za/news/crime-courts/now-hawks-take-aim-at-gerrie-nel-1993942, accessed 13 June 2016.

16 Media statement by the Minister of Finance, http://www.treasury.gov.za/comm_media/press/2016/2016022601%20-%20Ministers%20Statement.pdf, accessed 23 May 2016.

CHAPTER 8

1   Sam Sole, Smokes, sex and the arms deal, *Mail & Guardian*, 28 October 2008, http://mg.co.za/article/2008-10-28-smokes-sex-and-the, accessed 20 May 2016.

2   Not his real name.

3   Sam Sole, Smokes, sex and the arms deal, *Mail & Guardian*, 28 October 2008, http://mg.co.za/article/2008-10-28-smokes-sex-and-the, accessed 20 May 2016.

4   In October 2006 members of the UK Serious Fraud Office (SFO) raided the Berkshire premises of Aviation Consultancy Services (ACS) as part of a broad SFO investigation into possible bribery by British defence giant BAE Systems. At the time, ACS was in a business relationship with BAE Systems and apparently played a key role in lobbying

for BAE to secure the sale of fighter jets and jet trainers as part of South Africa's ill-fated arms deal.

It was revealed that a company associated with ACS, Kayswell Services, registered in the British Virgin Islands, received about £37 million from BAE for its role in the South African deal.

News agency Africa Confidential revealed in 2006 that internal documentation demonstrated how some of the £26 million paid by BAE to Kayswell between June 2003 and September 2005 had been transferred for the benefit of Bredenkamp. The amount was mentioned to be around £10 million (see Sam Sole, Smokes, sex and the arms deal, *Mail & Guardian*, 28 October 2008, http://mg.co.za/article/2008-10-28-smokes-sex-and-the, accessed 20 May 2016).

5 Not his real name.

6 Not the real origin.

7 Not the real location.

8 Not his real name.

9 Chandré Prince, Smoking out Bredenkamp, *The Times*, 5 October 2010, http://www.timeslive.co.za/business/2010/10/05/smoking-out-bredenkamp, accessed 20 May 2016.

10 OECD, *Electronic Sales Suppression: A Threat to Tax Revenues*, http://www.oecd.org/ctp/crime/electronicsalessuppressionathreattotaxrevenues.htm, accessed 26 May 2016.

11 Not his real name.

12 Not the real location.

13 OECD, *Electronic Sales Suppression: A Threat to Tax Revenues*, http://www.oecd.org/ctp/crime/electronicsalessuppressionathreattotaxrevenues.htm, accessed 26 May 2016.

CHAPTER 9

1 Mzilikazi wa Afrika, Piet Rampedi and Stephan Hofstatter, Taxman's rogue unit ran brothel, *Sunday Times*, 9 November 2014, http://www.timeslive.co.za/local/2014/11/09/taxman-s-rogue-unit-ran-brothel1, accessed 23 May 2016.

2 Not his real name.

3 Interview with Johnny and Tony, 21 May 2016.

4 Documents released by SARS in February 2010 included a copy of an affidavit signed by Michael Peega for the police and disciplinary records.

5 Ibid.

6 Ibid.

7 The *Mail & Guardian* reported that Peega did not contest the basic facts of his arrest, but argued that SARS should wait for his criminal case to be completed. See Sam Sole, Mike Peega: The man behind the dossier, *Mail & Guardian*, 26 February 2010, http://mg.co.za/article/2010-02-26-mike-peega-the-man-behind-dossier, accessed 23

May 2016.

8   Sam Sole, Mike Peega: The man behind the dossier, *Mail & Guardian*, 26 February 2010, http://mg.co.za/article/2010-02-26-mike-peega-the-man-behind-dossier, accessed 23 May 2016.

9   Ibid.

10 Mzilikazi wa Afrika, Piet Rampedi, Stephan Hofstatter and Malcolm Rees, Operative's claims not far-fetched now, *Sunday Times*, 12 October 2014, http://www.timeslive.co.za/sundaytimes/2014/10/12/operative-s-claims-not-far-fetched-now, accessed 4 July 2016.

11 Ibid.

12 Pauli van Wyk, *Komplot teen Pravin Gordhan: Leuens moes hom in onguns bring by Jacob Zuma*, *Beeld*, 25 February 2015, http://www.netwerk24.com/Nuus/Politiek/Komplot-teen-Pravin-Gordhan-20150225; see also Plot to discredit Gordhan with Zuma, 25 February 2015, http://www.fin24.com/Economy/Plot-to-discredit-Gordhan-with-Zuma-20150225, accessed 18 June 2016.

13 Amanda Watson, Arrow still aimed at rogue unit, *The Citizen*, 26 January 2016, http://citizen.co.za/963742/arrow-still-aimed-at-rogue-unit/, accessed 23 May 2016.

14 Ibid.

15 Pauli van Wyk, SARS unit an 'open secret', *Beeld*, 9 March 2015, http://www.fin24.com/Economy/Sars-unit-an-open-secret-20150309, accessed 25 July 2016.

16 Kenneth Fitoyi was a SARS Regional Manager who had by 2010 been distributing a series of emails to various media houses, politicians and SARS officials. His emails always had the same narrative: Ivan Pillay and Pravin Gordhan were corrupt and racist, and treated African officials badly, illegally monitored people's communications and spied on taxpayers. I could trace some of these emails back to 2009. Fitoyi resigned from SARS in the face of disciplinary proceedings and criminal charges of fraud against him.

17 Stephen Grootes, Sars also targeted by Malema spy, Eyewitness News, 23 March 2010, http://ewn.co.za/2010/03/23/Sars-also-targeted-by-Malema-spy, accessed 23 May 2016.

18 Nic Dawes and Lynley Donnelly, Can Dave King be linked to Agliotti?, *Mail & Guardian*, 9 November 2008, http://mg.co.za/article/2008-11-09-can-dave-king-be-linked-to-agliotti, accessed 23 May 2016.

19 Piet Rampedi, Mzilikazi wa Afrika, Stephan Hofstatter and Malcolm Rees, SARS bugged Zuma, *Sunday Times*, 12 October 2014, http://www.timeslive.co.za/politics/2014/10/12/sars-bugged-zuma1, accessed 25 July 2016.

CHAPTER 10

1   Lolly Jackson with Vincent Marino, *Stripped: The King of Teaze*, Readme Publishing, 2006.

2   For a detailed account of how the case against Jackson developed, see S Newman, P Piegl and K Maughan, *Lolly Jackson: When Fantasy Becomes Reality*. Johannesburg: Jacana, 2012.

3 S Germaner, SARS might seize Teazers empire, Eyewitness News, 10 May 2013, http://ewn.co.za/2013/05/10/Lolly-Jackson-estate-under-scrutiny, accessed 10 July 2016.

4 Staff reporter, How bodies have piled up around Radovan Krejcir, *Mail & Guardian*, 13 November 2013, http://mg.co.za/article/2013-11-13-fdsfsd, accessed 10 July 2016.

5 Not her real name.

6 Porritt in court over unpaid VAT claim, Legalbrief, http://www.google.co.za/url?sa=t&rct=j&q=&esrc=s&source=web&cd=8&ved=0ahUKEwi9rpWgh4_OAhVDDMAKHYlqAioQFgg8MAc&url=http%3A%2F%2Flegalbrief.co.za%2Fdiary%2Flegalbrief-today%2Fstory%2Fporritt-in-court-over-unpaid-vat-claim%2Fpdf%2F&usg=AFQjCNE-2DWlSrHYzoPT5Vqu8wc4p6wyRA&sig2=yiz4TqDg4tepne-HiAeHfQ, accessed 25 July 2016.

7 The other units under me were the Central Projects Unit (formerly the Significant Case Management Unit), the Evidence Management and Technical Support Unit and the Tactical Intervention Unit.

8 Not his real name.

9 *FATF Report: Illicit Tobacco Trade*, June 2012, http://www.fatf-gafi.org/publications/methodsandtrends/documents/illicittobaccotrade.html, accessed 24 May 2016.

10 Not his real name.

11 Not the real location.

12 Not the real location.

13 S Sole and S Evans, Sars delivers a blow to Krejcir's assets, *Mail & Guardian*, 15 November 2013, http://mg.co.za/article/2013-11-15-sars-krejcirs-assets, accessed 24 May 2016.

14 Mia Lindeque and Mandy Wiener, SA govt gave George Louca an inhumane death, Eyewitness News, 12 May 2015, http://ewn.co.za/2015/05/12/George-Loucas-family-angered-by-manner-in-which-he-died, accessed 11 July 2016.

15 Ibid.

16 Ibid.

17 Update: Krejcir house sold at auction, 28 November 2015, eNews Channel Africa, https://www.enca.com/south-africa/krejcir-house-under-hammer, accessed 11 July 2016.

18 A Serrao, Krejcir's new bid for freedom, *The Star*, 14 January 2014, http://www.iol.co.za/news/crime-courts/krejcirs-new-bid-for-freedom-1628528, accessed 24 May 2016.

19 S Haysom, Sars, Krejcir and the destruction of state capacity, amaBhungane Centre for Investigative Journalism, 1 April 2016, http://amabhungane.co.za/article/2016-04-01-00-sars-krejcir-and-the-destruction-of-state-capacity, accessed 24 May 2016.

CHAPTER 11

1 Ray Maota, Tobacco smuggling up in smoke, Media Club South Africa, 17 January 2013, http://www.mediaclubsouthafrica.com/land-and-people/3215-health176, accessed 26 May 2016.

2 Health Minister Aaron Motsoaledi signed the protocol on 10 January 2013. South Africa was part of the first group of 12 countries to sign the treaty. See Ray Maota, Tobacco smuggling up in smoke, Media Club South Africa, 17 January 2013, http://www.mediaclubsouthafrica.com/land-and-people/3215-health176, accessed 26 May 2016.

3 I have no idea what happened to these investigations after my resignation.

4 C Bailey, SARS to clamp down on tobacco companies, *The Sunday Independent*, 24 November 2013, http://www.iol.co.za/business/companies/sars-to-clamp-down-on-tobacco-companies-1611521, accessed 26 May 2016.

5 According to the centre's website, its primary purpose is to 'assist in the identification of the proceeds of unlawful activities and to combat money laundering activities as well as the financing of terrorism and related activities'. See https://www.fic.gov.za/Pages/FAQ.aspx.

6 S Sole and L Faull, Big tobacco in bed with SA law enforcement agencies, *Mail & Guardian*, 20 March 2014, http://mg.co.za/article/2014-03-20-big-tobacco-in-bed-with-sa-law-enforcement-agencies, accessed 9 July 2016.

7 Ibid.

8 Ibid.

9 Ibid.

10 Malcolm Rees, BAT's smoke and mirrors war on rivals, *Business Day*, 30 March 2014, http://www.bdlive.co.za/business/industrials/2014/03/30/bat-s-smoke-and-mirrors-war-on-rivals, accessed 8 July 2016.

11 Ibid.

12 Ibid.

13 Ibid.

14 Pieter-Louis Myburgh and Angelique Serrao, British American Tobacco 'bribed' police – affidavit, News24, 16 August 2016, http://www.news24.com/SouthAfrica/News/british-american-tobacco-bribed-police-affidavit-20160816, accessed 18 August 2016. Also see Marianne Thamm, SARS wars: Massive data leak alleges British American Tobacco SA's role in bribery and corruption, *Daily Maverick*, 16 August 2016, http://www.dailymaverick.co.za/article/2016-08-16-sars-wars-massive-data-leak-alleges-british-american-tobacco-sas-role-in-bribery-and-corruption/#.V7XJnJh97IV, accessed 18 August 2016.

15 Not the company's real name.

16 Not the real location.

17 Not the real location.

18 Lee Rondganger, Hunt for 'Sars' conman, Independent Online, 17 February 2015, http://www.iol.co.za/news/crime-courts/hunt-for-sars-conman-1819664, accessed 1 August 2016.

19 Audio recordings circa 2013 – in authors' possession.

20 Ibid.

CHAPTER 12

1 The Sikhakhane Panel would later erroneously claim in their report that I was alone at this meeting.

2 The details about the relationship that I set out here have been and still form part of numerous court actions, legal proceedings, criminal complaints and legal correspondence, which have been in the public domain for more than a year now.

3 Legal letter sent by Belinda Walter to the *Sunday Times*, dated 5 and 7 February 2014 – copy in author's possession.

4 The Sikhakhane Panel would later erroneously claim in their report that I did not receive these notifications (on 16 November 2013) – despite the fact that they were annexed to my affidavit submitted to the panel.

5 *Sikhakhane Panel investigation report*, Paragraph 42.3, http://www.sars.gov.za/AllDocs/Documents/Adhoc/Sikhakhane%20Report.pdf, accessed 29 July 2016.

6 Transcript of *Carte Blanche* interview provided by *Carte Blanche* as part of the records for the Broadcasting Complaints Commission hearing (see Chapter 16).

7 The Sikhakhane Panel would later erroneously claim in their report that this was the first time I disclosed the relationship to SARS.

8 Email from the SAPS to JvL dated 1 August 2016.

9 Draft affidavit and annexures, circa April 2015, in author's possession and provided to SAPS.

10 Ibid.

11 Ibid.

12 Ibid.

13 Ibid.

14 In fact, the very act of offering a person 'indefinite immunity' in exchange for that person withholding pertinent facts concerning crimes of money laundering and corruption in itself suggests corruption.

15 Compounding consists of unlawfully and intentionally agreeing, for reward (which doesn't have to be money, but any form of benefit), not to report or prosecute a crime (other than one that is punishable with a fine only – which in this case doesn't apply).

16 Letters by two attorneys dated 16 November 2015 and 16 March 2016 in author's possession.

17 Ibid.

18 Ben Martin, BAT gives law firm 'open door' to probe corruption allegations, *The Telegraph*, 25 February 2016, http://www.telegraph.co.uk/business/2016/02/25/bat-gives-law-firm-open-door-to-probe-corruption-allegations, accessed 8 August 2016.

CHAPTER 13

1 What I set out here in respect of the complaint has formed part of numerous court actions, legal proceedings, criminal complaints and legal correspondence. These details have been in the public domain for more than a year now.

2 Not his real name.

3 In August 2014 tobacco manufacturer Carnilinx brought an interdict application against Walter and British American Tobacco in the North Gauteng High Court. It was vehemently defended by Walter at the time, who went on to state under oath that Carnilinx was conspiring with SARS and me to bring this action against her.

4 After I resigned, I repeatedly asked the Ministry of Finance to provide me with a receipt from SARS that the gun was in safe custody and in the possession of the revenue service. I had the relevant issuance card in my possession and provided a copy of it to the ministry for reference. To date, I have not received a single reply to my request.

5 After I left SARS, I was approached by various lawyers acting for tobacco traders. This happened on three occasions. I always insisted that they record their approaches to me in writing and under legal letterhead, which they did. I always insisted that our interactions should be in the interests of justice and I told them I would never share any confidential SARS information. In one case, I helped a lawyer draft criminal complaints based on evidence he had provided to me, which implicated members of the Illicit-Tobacco Task Team but, to my knowledge, they never registered their complaints with the police. More importantly, I never received a cent from any of them and I always ensured that the authorities were briefed on these approaches during all interactions.

6 Note submitted to SARS, annexed to Ivan Pillay submission to Sikhakhane Panel and Labour Court. Copy of the same note was provided to KPMG by author in mid-2015.

7 Malcolm Rees, Love affair rocks SARS, *Sunday Times*, 10 August 2014, http://www.timeslive.co.za/local/2014/08/10/love-affair-rocks-sars1, accessed 28 May 2016.

8 Legal letters, author's archive, 2-7 February 2014.

9 Jacques Pauw, Sex, Sars and rogue spies, *City Press*, 10 August 2014, http://www.news24.com/Archives/City-Press/Sex-Sars-and-rogue-spies-20150429, accessed 28 May 2016.

10 Ibid.

11 Ibid.

12 Piet Rampedi, Mzilikazi wa Afrika, Stephan Hofstatter and Malcolm Rees, SARS bugged Zuma, *Sunday Times*, 12 October 2014, http://www.timeslive.co.za/politics/2014/10/12/sars-bugged-zuma1, accessed 28 May 2016.

13 Ministry of State Security, Minister of State Security launches a probe following allegations of misconduct, media statement, 13 August 2014, http://www.ssa.gov.za/Portals/0/SSA%20docs/Media%20Releases/2014/Media%20Release%20Minister%20of%20State%20Security%20launches%20a%20probe%20following%20allegations%20of%20misconduct%2013%20August%202014.pdf, accessed 5 August 2016.

14 Gaye Davis, Mahlobo dismisses reports of rogue operatives within SARS, Eyewitness News, 5 May 2015, http://ewn.co.za/2015/05/05/Mahlobo-dismisses-reports-of-rogue-operatives-in-Sars, accessed 30 May 2016.

15 Recorded conversation with Boris, 6 July 2016.

16 We also figured out that the *City Press* got some aspects of their story mixed up. They conflated one unit's activities with an entirely different unit, and various activities were attributed to a single unit. For instance, Walter worked for one particular unit that was involved with the Illicit-Tobacco Task Team, whereas some of the other persons identified by them worked for an entirely different unit. Walter would later use this to deny that she was a spy and underwent a polygraph test, the results of which she made public. See https://www.highbeam.com/doc/1G1-379235999.html, accessed 1 August 2016.

17 Recorded conversation with Boris, 6 July 2016.

CHAPTER 14

1 Stratcom used Winnie to discredit ANC: McPherson, South African Press Association, 28 November 1997, http://www.justice.gov.za/trc/media%5C1997%5C9711/s971128n. htm, accessed 27 May 2016.

2 Mandela United Football Club hearings, day 5, 24 November 1997, http://sabctrc. saha.org.za/documents/special/mandela/56336.htm, accessed 27 May 2016 (author's emphasis).

3 Kanyane report, copy in authors' possession.

4 Ibid.

5 Opposing affidavit by Ms BSG Walter in possession of authors.

6 Stephan Hofstatter, Mzilikazi wa Afrika and Malcolm Rees, SARS sleuth sidelined in aftermath of love affair, *Sunday Times*, 17 August 2014, http://www.timeslive.co.za/local/2014/08/17/sars-sleuth-sidelined-in-aftermath-of-love-affair1, accessed 12 July 2016.

7 Ibid.

8 Ibid.

9 Jacques Pauw, Sex, Sars and rogue spies, *City Press*, 10 August 2014, http://www.news24.com/Archives/City-Press/Sex-Sars-and-rogue-spies-20150429, accessed 28 May 2016.

10 Piet Rampedi, Mzilikazi wa Afrika, Stephan Hofstatter and Malcolm Rees, SARS bugged Zuma, *Sunday Times*, 12 October 2014, http://www.timeslive.co.za/politics/2014/10/12/sars-bugged-zuma1, accessed 27 May 2016.

11 Ibid.

12 Raids on Zuma and Shaik continue, *Mail & Guardian*, 18 August 2005, http://mg.co.za/article/2005-08-18-raids-on-zuma-and-shaik-continue, accessed 27 May 2016.

13 Mzilikazi wa Afrika, Piet Rampedi, Stephan Hofstatter and Malcolm Rees, Operative's claims not far-fetched now, *Sunday Times*, 12 October 2014, http://www.timeslive.co.za/sundaytimes/2014/10/12/operative-s-claims-not-far-fetched-now, accessed 14 July 2016.

14 Ibid.

15 Piet Rampedi, Mzilikazi wa Afrika, Stephan Hofstatter and Malcolm Rees, Pravin's

pal scores on early retirement, *Sunday Times*, 19 October 2014, http://www.timeslive. co.za/sundaytimes/2014/10/19/pravin-s-pal-scores-on-early-retirement, accessed 12 July 2016.

16 Ibid.

17 I can only assume the reference to 'agents' hails from the early days of the unit, when the external appointments were located in the posts that came from the old Customs Border Control Unit, where officials were referred to as Customs Border Control Agents. Except, of the five agent reports, only two related to such staff. The rest hailed from other units within SARS that had totally different job descriptions.

18 Not his real name.

19 Not his real name.

20 Karima Brown, Fired SARS man moonlighted for Mbalula, *Business Day*, 23 March 2010, http://www.bdlive.co.za/articles/2010/03/23/fired-sars-man-moonlighted-for-mbalula, accessed 24 June 2016.

21 Piet Rampedi, Mzilikazi wa Afrika, Stephan Hofstatter and Malcolm Rees, SARS chief acts on 'brothel' claim, *Sunday Times*, 16 November 2014, http://www.timeslive. co.za/local/2014/11/16/sars-chief-acts-on-brothel-claim, accessed 14 July 2016.

22 Ibid.

23 Ibid.

24 Bongani Siqoko, SARS and the *Sunday Times*: our response, *Sunday Times*, 3 April 2016, http://www.timeslive.co.za/sundaytimes/opinion/2016/04/03/SARS-and-the-Sunday-Times-our-response, accessed 14 July 2016.

25 SARS newsflash issued on 13 October 2014.

CHAPTER 15

1 Appointment of an external committee of investigation, SARS media release, 3 September 2014, http://www.sars.gov.za/Media/MediaReleases/Pages/3-September-2014---Appointment-of-an-external-Committee-of-Investigation.aspx, accessed 28 May 2016.

2 Investigation report: Conduct of Mr Johan Hendrikus van Loggerenberg, South African Revenue Service, by Adv. Muzi Sikhakhane, 5 November 2014, http://www. sars.gov.za/AllDocs/Documents/Adhoc/Sikhakhane%20Report.pdf, accessed 17 July 2016.

3 Ibid.

4 Ibid., para. 54.

5 Ibid., para. 89.10.

6 Ibid., paras 93 and 94.

7 Ibid., para. 96.

8 Ibid., para. 42.1.

9 Ibid., para. 14.

10 Submission by Ivan Pillay to SARS Commissioner Tom Moyane, 3 December 2014.

Annexure to court records submitted to Labour Court in December 2014 – *V Pillay v SARS*.

11 Ibid.

12 Investigation report: Conduct of Mr Johan Hendrikus van Loggerenberg, South African Revenue Service, by Adv. Muzi Sikhakhane, 5 November 2014, http://www.sars.gov.za/AllDocs/Documents/Adhoc/Sikhakhane%20Report.pdf, accessed 17 July 2016.

13 Ibid.

14 Ibid.

15 Ibid.

16 Ibid.

17 Submission by Ivan Pillay to SARS Commissioner Tom Moyane, 3 December 2014. Annexure to court records submitted to Labour Court in December 2014 – *V Pillay v SARS*.

18 Ibid.

19 Ibid.

20 Ibid.

21 Investigation report: Conduct of Mr Johan Hendrikus van Loggerenberg, South African Revenue Service, by Adv. Muzi Sikhakhane, 5 November 2014, http://www.sars.gov.za/AllDocs/Documents/Adhoc/Sikhakhane%20Report.pdf, accessed 17 July 2016.

22 Submission by Ivan Pillay to SARS Commissioner Tom Moyane, 3 December 2014. Annexure to court records submitted to Labour Court in December 2014 – *V Pillay v SARS*.

23 Ibid.

24 Investigation report: Conduct of Mr Johan Hendrikus van Loggerenberg, South African Revenue Service, by Adv. Muzi Sikhakhane, 5 November 2014, http://www.sars.gov.za/AllDocs/Documents/Adhoc/Sikhakhane%20Report.pdf, accessed 17 July 2016.

25 Ibid.

26 Ibid.

27 Ibid.

28 SARS, Media statement by SARS Commissioner, 5 December 2014. See http://www.sars.gov.za/Media/MediaReleases/Pages/5-December-2014---Media-Statement-by-SARS-Commissioner-.aspx, accessed 5 August 2016.

29 Ibid.

30 Ibid.

31 Natasha Marrian, SARS official Pillay suspended again, *Business Day*, 23 January 2015, http://www.bdlive.co.za/business/financial/2015/01/23/sars-official-pillay-suspended-again, accessed 17 July 2016.

32 Ibid.

33 Chantelle Benjamin, Sars and Pillay settle dispute, *Mail & Guardian*, 28 January 2015,

http://mg.co.za/article/2015-01-28-sars-and-pillay-settle-dispute, accessed 17 July 2016.

34 Ibid.

35 McBride, Dramat, Pillay claim there is a political conspiracy, *Mail & Guardian*, 17 May 2016, http://mg.co.za/article/2016-05-17-mcbride-dramat-pillay-claim-there-is-a-political-conspiracy, accessed 15 July 2016.

36 Ibid.

37 Kobus Roelofse, A report on the Mdluli investigation, Politicsweb, 17 May 2012, http://www.politicsweb.co.za/documents/a-report-on-the-mdluli-investigation--col-kobus-ro, accessed 12 July 2016.

38 Ibid. (author's emphasis)

39 Ibid.

40 Sent to die: Shocking fate of suspects in alleged rendition deal with Zim cops, *Sunday Times*, 23 October 2011, http://www.timeslive.co.za/local/2011/10/23/sent-to-die-br-shocking-fate-of-suspects-in-alleged-rendition-deal-with-zim-cops, accessed 12 July 2016.

41 Yusuf Abramjee, Did Crime Intelligence bribe journalists?, Politicsweb, 17 May 2012, http://www.politicsweb.co.za/documents/did-crime-intelligence-bribe-journalists--npc, accessed 12 July 2016.

CHAPTER 16

1 Adriaan Basson and Pauli van Wyk, Spat over taxman's new wheels, 24 December 2014, Fin24, http://www.fin24.com/Economy/Spat-over-taxmans-new-wheels-20141224, accessed 17 July 2016.

2 Sars tight-lipped on the resignation of senior officials, *Mail & Guardian*, 15 December 2014, http://mg.co.za/article/2014-12-15-sars-tight-lipped-on-the-regisignation-of-senior-officials, accessed 17 July 2016.

3 Another senior Sars employee resigns, *City Press*, 2 April 2015, http://www.news24.com/Archives/City-Press/Another-senior-Sars-employee-resigns-20150429, accessed 17 July 2016.

4 Transcript of *Carte Blanche* documentary, 23 February 2015.

5 Ibid.

6 Ibid.

7 This Act sets out the provisions for legal authorisation for undercover operations in South Africa.

8 Pauli van Wyk, *SAID het geweet, sê Peega*, *Beeld*, 28 February 2015, http://www.netwerk24.com/Nuus/Politiek/SAID-het-geweet-se-Peega-20150228, accessed 17 July 2016.

9 Candice Baily, Poaching dockets vanish, *The Star*, 22 August 2011, http://www.iol.co.za/news/crime-courts/poaching-dockets-vanish-1122442, accessed 18 June 2016.

10 T Seseane, Faction fight behind purge at South African tax-collection agency, World

Socialist Web Site, 30 December 2014, https://www.wsws.org/en/articles/2014/12/30/sars-d30.html, accessed 17 July 2016.

11 Statement by Minister Nene on SARS's governance arrangements, 25 February 2015, http://www.treasury.gov.za/comm_media/press/2015/2015022501%20-%20Media%20Statement-SARS%20Governance%20Arrangements.pdf, accessed 17 July 2016.

12 Ibid.

13 Ibid.

14 SARS, SARS Advisory Board media release on the Sikhakhane report, 28 April 2015, http://www.sars.gov.za/Media/MediaReleases/Pages/28-April-2015---SARS-Advisory-Board-media-release-on-the-Sikhakhane-Report-.aspx, accessed 30 May 2016.

15 Ibid.

CHAPTER 17

1 John Robbie show, SARS rogue unit: 'Pravin Gordhan was definitely aware of it', 702, 2 February 2015, http://702.co.za/articles/1543/sars-rogue-unit-allegations-pravin-gordhan-was-definitely-aware-of-it, accessed 5 August 2016.

2 Ibid.

3 Pravin Gordhan, SARS unit entirely legal – Pravin Gordhan, Politicsweb, 10 May 2015, http://www.politicsweb.co.za/news-and-analysis/sars-unit-entirely-legal--pravin-gordhan, accessed 18 July 2016.

4 Natasha Marrian, Exodus at SARS continues as two more senior staff members quit, *Business Day*, 9 April 2015, http://www.bdlive.co.za/national/2015/04/09/exodus-at-sars-continues-as-two-more-senior-staff-members-quit, accessed 17 July 2016.

5 A Mashego, SARS saga: Under-fire Pillay and Richer resign, 7 May 2015, http://www.news24.com/SouthAfrica/News/Sars-saga-Under-fire-Pillay-and-Richer-resign-20150507, accessed 17 July 2016.

6 Shanti Aboobaker, Sars' case against Pillay, Independent Online, 15 February 2015, http://www.iol.co.za/business/companies/sars-case-against-pillay-1818321, accessed 16 August 2016.

7 A Mashego, SARS saga: Under-fire Pillay and Richer resign, 7 May 2015, http://www.news24.com/SouthAfrica/News/Sars-saga-Under-fire-Pillay-and-Richer-resign-20150507, accessed 17 July 2016.

8 Piet Rampedi, Stephan Hofstatter and Mzilikazi wa Afrika, Pillay faces criminal charges after SARS spies explosive confession, *Sunday Times*, 17 May 2015, http://www.timeslive.co.za/sundaytimes/stnews/investigations/2015/05/17/Pillay-faces-criminal-charges-after-SARS-spies-explosive-confession, accessed 18 July 2016.

9 A Mashego, Spooks get Gordhan docket, *City Press*, 29 May 2016, http://city-press.news24.com/News/spooks-get-gordhan-docket-20160528, accessed 17 July 2016.

10 Ibid.

11 SARS, SARS Advisory Board media release on the Sikhakhane Report, 28 April

2015, http://www.sars.gov.za/Media/MediaReleases/Pages/28-April-2015---SARS-Advisory-Board-media-release-on-the-Sikhakhane-Report-.aspx, accessed 30 May 2016.

12 Piet Rampedi, Mzilikazi wa Afrika and Stephan Hofstatter, Call to probe Pravin over SARS spy saga, *Sunday Times*, 4 October 2015, http://www.timeslive.co.za/sunday-times/stnews/2015/10/04/Call-to-probe-Pravin-over-SARS-spy-saga, accessed 30 May 2016.

13 Ibid.

14 Stephan Hofstatter, Piet Rampedi and Mzilikazi wa Afrika, Taxmen's braai with prostitutes – 'not a brothel', *Sunday Times*, 4 October 2015, http://www.timeslive.co.za/sundaytimes/stnews/investigations/2015/10/04/Taxmens-braai-with-prostitutes-not-a-brothel, accessed 18 July 2016.

15 Editorial: Keep shady doings in SARS out in the open, *Sunday Times*, 4 October 2015, http://www.timeslive.co.za/sundaytimes/opinion/2015/10/04/Editorial-Keep-shady-doings-in-SARS-out-in-the-open, accessed 31 May 2016.

16 Pravin Gordhan vs. *Sunday Times*, ruling of the Press Ombudsman, 15 December 2015, http://www.presscouncil.org.za/Ruling/View/pravin-gordhan-vs-sunday-times-2873, accessed 24 June 2016.

17 Affidavit by Pearlie Joubert as submitted to the Press Ombudsman by Ivan Pillay. The affidavit refers to a letter to the then Finance Minister, Nhlanhla Nene, the Deputy Minister of Finance and the Kroon Advisory Board, which was attached to the affidavit as an annexure. Copies of both of these documents are in the author's possession.

18 Ivan Pillay vs. *Sunday Times*, ruling by the Press Ombudsman and a panel of adjudicators, 16 December 2015, http://www.presscouncil.org.za/Ruling/View/ivan-pillay-vs-sunday-times-2875, accessed 24 June 2016.

19 A Lees, Minister Nene must table full KPMG report on 'rogue unit' before Parliament, Democratic Alliance press release, 25 August 2015, http://www.politicsweb.co.za/politics/kpmg-has-submitted-report-on-sars-spy-unit-to-nene, accessed 18 July 2016.

20 Marianne Thamm, SARS wars, season two: How can we trust the KPMG report?, *Daily Maverick*, 26 January 2016, http://www.dailymaverick.co.za/article/2016-01-24-sars-wars-season-two-how-can-we-trust-the-kpmg-report/#.V6RFIrh97IU, accessed 5 August 2016.

21 Marianne Thamm, SARS wars: KPMG, SARS, and Mashiane Moodley and Monama – who's telling the truth?, *Daily Maverick*, 26 January 2016, http://www.dailymaverick.co.za/article/2016-01-26-sars-wars-kpmg-sars-and-mashiane-moodley-and-monama-whos-telling-the-truth/#.V4zrRfl97IV, accessed 18 July 2016, Accessed on 30 May 2016.

22 Sunday Times stories on rogue unit are backed by three probes, *Sunday Times*, 6 December 2015, http://www.timeslive.co.za/sundaytimes/stnews/2015/12/06/Sunday-Times-stories-on-rogue-SARS-unit-are-backed-by-three-probes, accessed 31 May 2016.

23 KPMG: SARS report – KPMG press release, Politicsweb, 25 January 2015, http://www.polity.org.za/article/kpmg-sars-report---kpmg-press-statement-2016-01-25, accessed

31 May 2016.

24 Ibid.

25 Ibid. (author's emphasis).

26 KPMG, *Executive report on allegations of misconduct and irregularities*, 3 September 2015. See http://cdn.bdlive.co.za/images/pdf/KPMGreport.pdf, accessed 5 August 2016.

CHAPTER 18

1 Alec Hogg, Calculating Zuma's R500bn #Nenegate blunder – rand depreciation excluded, Fin24, 7 March 2016, http://www.fin24.com/BizNews/calculating-zumas-r500bn-nenegate-blunder-rand-depreciation-excluded-20160307, accessed 20 July 2016.

2 Media statement by the Minister of Finance, http://www.treasury.gov.za/comm_media/press/2016/2016022601%20-%20Ministers%20Statement.pdf, accessed 23 May 2016.

3 The 27 questions the Hawks sent to Gordhan, *Finweek*, 28 February 2015, http://www.fin24.com/Economy/the-27-questions-the-hawks-sent-to-gordhan-20160228, accessed 30 May 2016.

4 Ibid.

5 Ibid.

6 Sam Sole, Pravin Gordhan's 27 SARS questions answered, *Mail & Guardian*, 4 March 2016, http://mg.co.za/article/2016-03-04-00-pravin-gordhans-27-sars-questions-answered, accessed 20 July 2016.

7 Matthew le Cordeur and Carin Smith, Gordhan asks Hawks to clarify Sars 'rogue unit' probe, *Mail & Guardian*, 2 March 2016, http://mg.co.za/article/2016-03-02-gordhan-asks-hawks-to-clarify-sars-rogue-unit-probe, accessed 20 July 2016.

8 Ibid.

9 Pierre de Vos, Is there any basis for investigating Minister Pravin Gordhan? Constitutionally Speaking, 17 May 2016, http://constitutionallyspeaking.co.za/is-there-any-legal-basis-for-investigating-minister-pravin-gordhan/, accessed 21 July 2016.

10 Ibid.

11 Marianne Thamm, 27 Hawks' questions to Gordhan – the complete list: All about the 'Covert Unit', *Daily Maverick*, 28 February 2016, http://www.dailymaverick.co.za/article/2016-02-28-27-hawks-questions-to-gordhan-the-complete-list-all-about-covert-unit-all-facts-out-there-already-so-why-are-hawks-targeting-gordhan, accessed 5 August 2016.

12 Marianne Thamm, SARS wars: Season two – how can we trust the KPMG report?, *Daily Maverick*, 24 January 2016, http://www.dailymaverick.co.za/article/2016-01-24-sars-wars-season-two-how-can-we-trust-the-kpmg-report/#.V4ztTPl97IU, accessed 18 July 2016.

13 Natasha Marrian, SARS fires salvo in Moyane-Gordhan row, *Business Day*, 2 March

2016, http://www.bdlive.co.za/national/2016/03/02/sars-fires-salvo-in-moyane-gordhan-row, accessed 20 July 2016.

14 L Ensor, Gordhan halts SARS revamp, *Business Day*, 7 January 2016, http://www.bdlive.co.za/national/2016/01/07/gordhan-halts-sars-revamp, accessed 20 July 2016.

15 Natasha Marrian, I'm not at war with Gordhan says Zuma, *Business Day*, 1 March 2016, http://www.bdlive.co.za/national/2016/03/01/im-not-at-war-with-gordhan-says-zuma, accessed 20 July 2016.

16 Most interestingly, Moyane gave the correct date for the first media reports about the 'rogue unit' (October 2014) in a media statement of 5 December 2014. See http://www.sars.gov.za/Media/MediaReleases/Pages/5-December-2014---Media-Statement-by-SARS-Commissioner-.aspx, accessed 5 August 2016.

17 South African Government, Minister Nkosinathi Nhleko: Presentation on investigation into Sars unit, 2 March 2016, http://www.gov.za/speeches/ministers-presentation-investigation-so-called-rouge-unit-2-mar-2016-0000, accessed 20 July 2016.

18 Matthew le Cordeur, Gordhan answers Hawks over Sars 'rogue' unit, Fin24, 30 March 2016, http://www.fin24.com/Economy/breaking-gordhan-responds-to-hawks-questions-20160330, accessed 20 July 2016.

19 Full statement: Gordhan responds to Hawks, Fin24, 30 March 2016, http://www.fin24.com/Economy/full-statement-gordhan-responds-to-hawks-20160330, accessed 20 July 2016.

20 Ibid.

21 Ibid.

22 Bongani Siqoko, SARS and the *Sunday Times*: Our response, Finally we agreed to lay to rest the controversies surrounding SARS and the *Sunday Times, Sunday Times*, 3 April 2016, http://www.timeslive.co.za/sundaytimes/opinion/2016/04/03/SARS-and-the-Sunday-Times-our-response, accessed 20 July 2016.

23 Genevieve Quintal, I didn't want to be part of 'unethical and immoral' practices – ex-Sunday Times journalist, Fin24, 1 December 2015, http://www.news24.com/SouthAfrica/News/i-didnt-want-to-be-part-of-unethical-and-immoral-practices-ex-sunday-times-journalist-20151201, accessed 21 July 2016.

24 Karl Gernetzky, Songezo Zibi resigns as editor of *Business Day*, 21 January 2016, http://www.bdlive.co.za/national/media/2016/01/21/songezo-zibi-resigns-as-editor-of-business-day, accessed 21 July 2016.

25 Zibi's departure from *Business Day* disturbing – Harber, 702, 22 January 2016, http://www.702.co.za/articles/11029/zibi-s-departure-from-business-day-disturbing-harber, accessed 21 July 2016.

26 Times Media appoints three new editors, *Sunday Times*, 1 February 2016, http://www.timeslive.co.za/sundaytimes/businesstimes/2016/02/01/Times-Media-appoints-three-new-editors, accessed 21 July 2016.

27 Ibid.

28 This is according to Adrian Lackay's records. There was a heated email exchange,

lawyers were involved and management had to intervene.

29 Sars collected over R1 trillion during 2015/2016 tax year, *Eyewitness News*, 1 April 2016, http://ewn.co.za/2016/04/01/Sars-collected-over-R1-trillion-during-20152016-fiscal-year, accessed 30 May 2016.

30 Lionel Faull, Court rules Tigon duo must face charges, *Business Day*, 28 April, 2016, http://www.bdlive.co.za/business/financial/2016/04/28/court-rules-tigon-duo-must-face-charges, accessed 21 July 2016.

31 Ibid.

32 Nathi Olifant, Qaanitah Hunter and Thanduxolo Jika, Pravin Gordhan faces imminent arrest, *Sunday Times*, 15 May 2016, http://www.timeslive.co.za/sundaytimes/stnews/2016/05/15/Pravin-Gordhan-faces-imminent-arrest, accessed 27 June 2016.

33 Mpho Raborife, You are putting Gordhan in a dangerous position, Mantashe tells media, News24, 31 May 2016, http://www.news24.com/SouthAfrica/News/you-are-putting-gordhan-in-a-dangerous-postion-mantashe-tells-media-20160531, accessed 1 June 2016.

34 Natasha Marrian, Hawks home in on 'rogue unit' staff, *Business Day*, 30 May 2016, http://www.bdlive.co.za/national/2016/05/30/hawks-home-in-on-rogue-unit-staff, accessed 1 June 2016.

35 A Mashego, Spooks get Gordhan docket, *City Press*, 29 May 2016, http://city-press.news24.com/News/spooks-get-gordhan-docket-20160528, accessed 17 July 2016.

EPILOGUE

1 Although SARS and I filed exceptions and cause to remove action, and although Walter filed notices to amend her particulars of claim in 2014, she never saw the process through to its conclusion. At some stage in 2015, Walter offered to withdraw her civil suit against SARS on the basis that all parties accept costs incurred. SARS never bothered to reply. In early 2016 Walter's attorney informed my attorney that she intended amending her original claim. I intend to have the matter prosecuted before court as soon as possible and simultaneously institute a counter-suit against her. I hope that this court case will provide me with a means to expose much of what I have been unable to say openly and in public at the same time.

2 One of the early allegations made against me was that my laptop contained evidence of illegal interceptions. I wanted to prove this was not the case.

Index

Acknowledgements

Thank you to Annie Olivier of Jonathan Ball Publishers, who initially approached us, had faith in our story and believed that it had to be told. Thank you for putting up with our late edits and changes, and for guiding us through the process. Many thanks to Jeremy Boraine and his team at Jonathan Ball, and the editor, Mark Ronan. Their editorial wisdom helped us to weave many complex threads together into what is hopefully a meaningful chronicle of our experiences.

We appreciate the patience and support of our families, who put up with the long hours needed to allow us to complete this work.

We also want to acknowledge the tremendous support of former and current SARS colleagues, even though we cannot mention them by name. At the time of writing, the Hawks were still interviewing some of them. Whether they are regarded as witnesses or suspects is still unknown.

We remain grateful to many of our former SARS colleagues who were adversely affected by the events recorded in this book, in particular Ivan and Pete, and their families.

A special word of thanks to the human-rights and political activists, the businesspeople and legal practitioners who have stood by us – in particular, Karien Norval and her team at Cheadle Thompson & Haysom for their advice and guidance, and advocate Wim Trengrove SC, who provided his considered opinion and expert legal views.

Judge Johann Kriegler has every right to enjoy a well-deserved retirement after many decades on the bench as one of this country's leading jurists. His work in advancing human rights and working towards establishing electoral systems in support of democracy in some of the world's most troubled countries is recognised globally. Yet he and his wife, Betty Welz, have not remained passive observers of the plight that has befallen public institutions and their leading officials since 2014. Theirs is a sincere concern for the future of our constitutional democracy. Their assistance to us, and to many other civil servants who share a fate similar to ours, has been emphatic. Judge Kriegler's foreword attests to this.

We would also like to acknowledge the willingness of *Sunday Times* editor, Bongani Siqoko, and his colleagues at the Times Media Group, who were ultimately prepared to hear us out and attempt to set the record straight.

Johann van Loggerenberg wishes to thank Toby and Mr K for helping him dispel the 'rogue-unit' narrative among senior government officials when needed, and to Mr M for his support throughout. Sorry I couldn't give you the opportunity to have sight of the manuscript, but I've acknowledged you, as you have said you wanted to be.

We would also like to thank Warren Goldblatt, Paul Simpson and Muhammad Seedat, who afforded us the time to complete this book.

Lastly, many thanks to the countless South Africans who didn't believe the 'rogue-unit' narrative, and the many journalists and law-enforcement officials who continue to do their work independently and in pursuit of the truth.

CPSIA information can be obtained
at www.ICGtesting.com
Printed in the USA
BVHW041146170919
558659BV00012B/96/P